The
Lone Piper

The Story of Bill Millin,
Lord Lovat's D-Day Piper

Ian Moran

Double Scotch Publishing
330 Gate Street,
Niagara-on-the-Lake, Ontario
Canada

First Edition (A01011905)
First published – 2019
© John and Lorraine Moran, 2019
Typeset in Niagara-on-the-Lake

Library Cataloguing in Publication Data
Moran, Ian
   The Lone Piper
   1. World War
   2. Normandy campaign
   3. Biographies

DDC 940.53

ISBN 978-1-1706961-25-3

*For **all** the brave men who fought in World War Two.*
To you, we owe our lives.

Contents

Sword Beach to Bénouville (Pegasus) and Ranville (Horsa) bridges

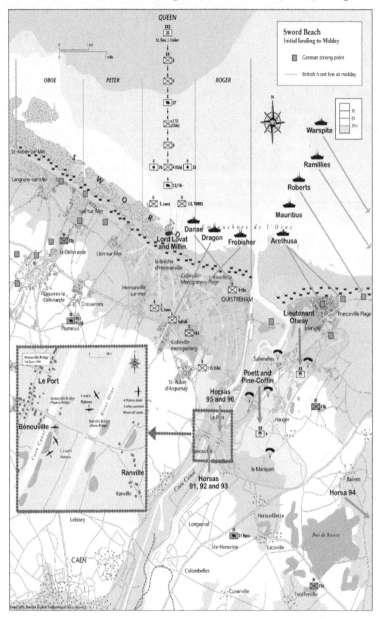

1. Frasers & Millins

Better lo'ed ye canna be
Will ye no' come back again?[1]

Success for the invasion would require men, machines, artillery, supplies, and although it was never written down, a level of courage on a monumental scale. Codenamed Operation Overlord, the proposal for the Normandy Invasion was conceived in early 1943, then presented to and approved by the Allied leadership in December of that year. The master plan, as approved by Joseph Stalin, Franklin D. Roosevelt, and Winston Churchill, certainly did not call for or anticipate one man landing on the beaches of Normandy wearing a kilt. Nonetheless, each brigade was charged with executing their individual mission and for the commandos of the 1st Special Service Brigade this would include a kilted catalyst to incite its men to bravery.

The 1st Special Service Brigade was commanded by Brigadier Lord Lovat, a proud Scottish Lord who planned to utilize his 'personal piper' in the Normandy invasion. Lovat, a Highlander, was going to follow tradition and have a piper lead his men into battle. He would use 21-year old Piper Bill Millin as the stimulus to inspire the fifth and most abstract element of the D-Day invasion. Lovat knew that landing on

---

[1] Bonnie Charlie – Traditional / Carolina Oliphant

the beaches of Normandy would require an uncommon motivation for his men to charge forward, where death could be waiting in the French sands. Over one million troops would land on the beaches in the first month of the invasion, but only Millin would be wearing the traditional dress of a Scottish Highlander. He would wade ashore carrying his bagpipes instead of his rifle. To understand why Lovat and Millin would take such a risk, is to understand the history of the bagpipes and the Highland Clans.

Brigadier Lovat was a Fraser. He was Lord Lovat, the Chief of Clan Fraser, a clan with a long and proud military history. Lovat's ancestral roots stretch back across the history of the Scottish Highlands to the time of the Norman kings and the arrival of the bagpipes. The Allied landing on the beaches of Normandy was particularly well suited for the Clan Fraser. In the twelfth century, a majestic French knight, Frézeau de la Frézelière, came from Normandy and settled in Scotland. Over the following centuries, his name would be anglicized to 'Fraser' and his descendants would become one of the fiercest, most powerful clans in Scotland. Lord Lovat's landing on the beaches of Normandy was a military homecoming almost a millennium in the making.

William the Conqueror was the first Norman King of England. Arriving in Britain from continental Europe, William brought with him imposing French knights. With a promise of land grants, the Norman knights were enticed to travel north to Scotland. The grants were offered to the French nobles in return for 'policing' the wild, uncontrolled land to the north. With much of Scotland still occupied by Vikings, the Norman kings needed a way to maintain control. The noble knights also brought with them a strange wind instrument. The bagpipes, which are so closely associated with Scotland, were originally brought to the Highlands from France.

The French knights established 'clans' (Gaelic for 'offspring') and the families of the Norman nobles grew in terms of size and power. The deeded land that came with clan settlement in Scotland provided great resources for survival in a harsh environment. The Highland clans enjoyed deer and salmon, as well as vast tracts of grazing lands suitable for raising sheep. Protecting the herds came easily to the descendants of the French knights and Vikings. The clans of the Highlands developed scattered combat styles and unique fighting skills that would prove deadly for anyone trying to steal from their herds.

These same skills soon presented similar challenges for the armies that dared to fight against the Highlanders.

For thousands of years, wars had been archaic, organized slaughters. Battles were fought by armies that arrived at battlefields, sometimes at preordained times, where both sides would charge at each other wielding weapons. Campaigns were usually won based on manpower, provisions, skill level and an element of bravery. As warfare developed, the addition of tactics such as out flanking, charging manoeuvres and pincer movements, provided the early British Army a way to increase their success in battle. The advancement in warfare strategies came with the development of professional soldiers; gentlemen who served to reinforce the battlefield etiquette.

Highlanders, like the Frasers of Inverness-shire and the Millins of Argyllshire, employed a fighting style more comparable to Guerrilla warfare. Using ambushes, skirmishes and surprise attacks, they would fight their enemies in swamps, rivers and hillsides. They didn't meet at preordained times and locations. Highlanders were led into battle by a piper and a heavily armed warrior that commanded a tight formation wielding a battle axe or claymore[2]. The claymore was the weapon of choice for the Clan Millin, adorning their coat of arms.

The Fraser Highlanders built their ancestral home in Inverness-shire, near the river Beauly[3], known for its stark and unbridled beauty. The Clan Fraser accumulated a long history of military victories. Their fighting spirit and use of the Highland tactics, helped the Frasers to grow their influence, territory and powerbase. Frasers fought in the Scottish Wars of Independence alongside William Wallace and Robert the Bruce, defeating the English at the Battle of Roslin. Sir Simon Fraser was awarded three crowns for saving King Robert's life and thus three crowns adorn the Lovat Coat of Arms. The Frasers also fought at the Battle of Bannockburn, where Highlanders were marched into battle by a bagpiper. The cry of the 'war pipes' was said to instill fear in the English army.

Over the centuries, Clan Fraser has been led by illustrious Clan Chiefs, many of whom were noble in stature, while others were notorious. Both the noble and the notorious alike were sentenced to death by English courts. Sir Simon Fraser was captured[4] by the

---

[2] A large two-sided sword.
[3] When Mary Queen of Scots arrived at this Highland village, she said "what a beautiful place" or "C'est un beau lieu" in her native French.

government forces, then shipped to London where he was hung, drawn and quartered (where the body is pulled apart by the arms and legs, then the four pieces of the remains are taken to the four corners of the country so it can't be reassembled by its spirit). His head was kept in London, where it was displayed, along with William Wallace's, impaled on a spike on the London Bridge.

Much of the clan warfare was against other clans, usually in disputes over land. The Frasers were continually in clashes with Clan Donald. Hugh Fraser of Lovat led his clan to a victory over the Macdonalds at the Battle of Mamsha[5]. The Frasers now controlled the land to the west and the south of Inverness. When the Scottish peerage of Lovat was created, Hugh Fraser became the first Lord Lovat[6].

The clans had their share of military failures as well. Highlanders didn't fare as well whenever they fought in more conventional combat formations. At the age of 18-years old, Thomas Fraser, the Chief of Clan Fraser and also the 10th Lord Lovat, led 1,000 Fraser men in support of the deposed Stuarts in a battle against Oliver Cromwell's army[7]. The Highlanders joined the 16,000-man army of Charles II. Unfamiliar with the battle formations and outmanned by an army of twice the size, the Highlanders found themselves on the losing side of the battle. As a result, Lord Lovat was jailed in Inverness. Almost a century later, his son would make the same mistake.

One of Brigadier Lovat's more infamous ancestors was Simon 'the Fox', the 10th Lord Lovat's son. He earned his name because of how he became clan chief. Although his father was Lord Lovat, Simon was the youngest son and according to the rules of peerage, another branch of the family had a stronger claim to the chiefdom. In order to strengthen his claim as chief, Simon proposed to the widow of his cousin the 9th Lord Lovat. When he was rebuffed, Simon kidnapped, raped and forcibly married her, using the bagpipes to drown out any objections. Simon Fraser eventually became the 11th Lord Lovat and Clan Chief of the Frasers.

When 'Bonnie Prince Charlie' arrived in Scotland from France[8], he lay claim to the Scottish throne. Despite being born in Rome, the

---

[4] In 1306.
[5] In 1429.
[6] In 1464.
[7] In 1650.
[8] In 1745.

Prince was the grandson of the King of England James II and a Stuart, the Scottish line of royalty. The resulting war pitted clan against clan. Some clans, such as the Clan Fraser, came down from the Highlands to fight for the Prince's instatement, while other clans, such as the Campbells, fought on the side of the English king.

French troops battled alongside clans in Prince Charlie's Jacobite Army. Dubbed 'Charles the Pretender (to the throne)' by the English, his army did not fight using Highland tactics. Charlie had been trained in warfare in France, so he refused to attack before the enemy had positioned their armies. He allowed time for the government forces to ready their men and artillery, the way a gentleman fights a war. In two major battles, first at Falkirk and a year later at Culloden, his army was thoroughly defeated. The Jacobite Highlanders once again found themselves part of an army that did not take advantage of their fighting style. In the bogs of Culloden, in less than an hour, Charlie's army was defeated, and most of the Highlanders were slaughtered.

Just like his father, Simon was arrested and convicted of treason against the crown. He was also sentenced to be hung, drawn and quartered. There was a public demand to witness his death, so to provide greater access, the government announced that he would be beheaded instead. His execution turned into a 'standing room only' spectacle at the Tower of London.

Beheading was a tradition that was introduced to England by the Norman knights of William the Conqueror. Commoners would be hung, but death by beheading was reserved for offenders of a high rank. It was considered to be an honour and sometimes the equivalent of being killed in battle. The last person to receive this honour on Tower Hill in London, was Simon the Fox.

"You're going to have your head cut off, you ugly old Scotch dog!" a woman called out from the crowd.

The now rotund and extremely heavy Simon came to a pause and looked down from the execution platform. He locked eyes with the woman that had called out to him.

"I believe I shall," replied Simon the Fox, and then calmly added, "you ugly old English bitch."

Simon was so widely despised in London, that there was an overcrowding of spectators at his execution. This caused one of the audience scaffolds at the Ship Alehouse to collapse, killing nine English onlookers and badly injuring many others. The scene served to amuse the 11th Lord Lovat and throughout the resulting commotion he broke into fits of laughter.

"Stop laughing, immediately." demanded the executioner.

"Or else?" asked Simon, still laughing and now amused by his executioner's meaningless threat.

"Sentenced men are to use their time before death to make peace with God," the executioner ordered, not wanting to behead a man who was not praying.

The absurdity of his head not being severed because he was laughing, resulted in an even bigger outburst of laughter from Simon the Fox. He then asked if he could examine the axe and the executioner presented it to him. Simon ran his fingers down the length of the blade.

"I believe this will do," he mocked and proceeded to laugh again.

The audience that had come to jeer the reviled Scotsman, were not getting what they expected to see. Frustrated, one of the city Sheriffs ordered the executioner to proceed. Simon was still laughing when the executioner beheaded him and thus the phrase 'to laugh your head off' was born.

"Dulce et decorum est pro patria mori," were Lord Lovat's last words ('How sweet and proper it is to die for one's country').

This is not the end of the story for this Simon Fraser however. The axe and block used for the beheading are still on display at the Tower of London. Then, 250 years later, the novel *Dragonfly in Amber*, part of Diana Gabaldon's *Outlander* series, would feature the 11th Lord Lovat, Simon Fraser. His fictional grandson Jamie Fraser is the main male protagonist in Gabaldon's stories. Gabaldon doesn't alter Simon Fraser's sorted history, except for adding a fictitious branch to his family tree. She figured, given Lovat's reputation, this would not be considered character assassination. The Lord Lovat character would also be included in the television series, with the character of Simon Fraser played by Clive Russell.

Simon had been tried after the Battle of Culloden, where it had been clan versus clan; one side fighting for the Scottish Prince and the other side fighting for the English King. Both sides were led into battle by bagpipers. James Reid was one of the pipers on the side of Bonnie Prince Charlie. After the battle, he was one of hundreds of Highlanders to be captured and taken to England for trial. The captives were not prisoners of war. Worse, they were accused of the crime of high treason against the English crown. If found guilty, the punishment for treason was death.

James stood trial for his role in the battle. His defense was that he did not carry a sword or a musket. He was just a musician. The judges however did not share this opinion. The court cited that a Highland army never marched to war without a piper to lead it. Therefore, in the eyes of English law, the bagpipe was 'an instrument of war'. Reid was found guilty and he was the first piper to receive the statutory penalty of being hung, drawn and quartered.

Over the next 250 years, whenever the British Army performed an inventory of military supplies, the weapon count would include rifles, swords and munitions. The bagpipes were also included on this list of weapons, whereas the bugle and drums were listed as musical instruments. The bagpipes remained an instrument of war, according to English law, until a Scotsman was charged with playing the pipes in public. In London, there was a bylaw prohibiting any loud musical instrument being played at night. In his defense, the Scotsman cited the common law precedent case of James Reid and the court's finding that bagpipes were not a musical instrument. This time, the court found that the pipes were first and primarily a musical instrument. The year was 1996 and the bagpipes had finally been returned to their rightful place in music.

Simon the Fox was too old and obese to have actually fought in the Battle of Culloden. Thus, he was not on the battlefield the day that bagpipes were deemed to be used an instrument of war, but his son was. Simon sent his son to lead the Clan Fraser into battle at Culloden. While Simon was executed for his actions, the court showed mercy on his young his son and only sentence him to prison. The English government was now determined to destroy the clan system, and they set out to quash the Highland culture. Playing the bagpipes, speaking Gaelic or wearing a kilt, were all forbidden and deemed punishable by hanging. Clan lands were stripped away from the lairds.

Simon the Fox's son was Simon Fraser of Lovat. He was imprisoned for taking his father's place in battle and the Scottish peerage was not passed on to him. After the young Fraser was released from prison, he went on to study law. Simon qualified as a lawyer and went to work in Edinburgh. He prosecuted a significant case on behalf of the government and in doing so, Clan Fraser had effectively switched to the side that he fought against at Culloden. The English government eventually made peace with the clans and the Highlands became a recruiting ground for the British Army.

With an expanding empire and ongoing wars in Europe, the British forces needed more manpower. The British government realized that the kilted clansmen's ancient attacking tactics could be put to good use in battle. The introduction of muskets and cannons into warfare had made the previous British formations less effective and left their troops vulnerable. Highlanders were added as shock troops to create a tactical advantage. The introduction of the 'Highland charge' combined the best of the British Army campaigns with the Highlander fighting approach. In this manoeuvre, the Highlanders charged up the middle of the formation, through the enemy line, to split the enemy's forces. The call to the troops to move into formation for the Highland charge was not a trumpet, it was the bagpipes.

Simon Fraser of Lovat joined the British Army and raised a regime of 500 men in a few days, consisting largely of Frasers. Simon used the Highland charge stratagem to defeat the French in Canada and again in battle during the American Revolution. Military fortunes would return power back to the clans as they served for the same army that had tried to destroy their culture. Ordinary servicemen in Clan Fraser were eventually acquiring tenure and they were granted estates in Scotland and in the New World.

In one generation, the Frasers had been stripped of their wealth for fighting against the King and then regained their wealth fighting for the King. Simon Fraser of Lovat retired as a Major-General in the British Army and he lived on Downing Street in London as a friend to William Pitt, the British Prime Minister. He had amassed a fortune large enough to buy back his ancestral lands in Scotland. Simon's descendants would continue to raise regiments to fight for King and country by recruiting men from the Highlands. This Simon Fraser also made it into Diana Gabaldon's *Outlander* series when the protagonist Jamie Fraser is at his bedside as Simon dies.

The Clan Millin[9] did not have such infamous characters in their heritage. The Millins lived their lives as Highlanders, largely settling on the west coast of Scotland, including the Hebrides. Millins became attached to other larger clans including the Camerons. In 1793. Sir

---

[9] It would not be uncommon for clansmen to be born with one spelling, marry under another, then have another variation appear on his headstone. Millin derivations include MacMillin, Millan, Millen, Mullan, Mullen, McMullen, MacGhille and Mholain.

Alan Cameron of Erracht formed the Queen's Own Cameron Highlanders in Fort William, a British Army regiment in which Millins and Frasers would fight.

Brigadier Lovat's father, also a Simon Fraser, was the 14th Lord Lovat. He was a distinguished soldier commissioned into the Queen's Own Cameron Highlanders in 1890, where he fought for Queen Victoria. In 1900, he formed the Lovat Scouts, a British Army unit that fought in the Boer War. The war in South Africa had been a challenge for the British because the natives fought with guerilla warfare tactics using ambushes, sabotage and raids. Being a Highland regiment, the Scouts were particularly qualified for this type of combat and were successful in their South African campaigns.

In 1911, at Beaufort Castle in Inverness, Scotland, the 15th Lord Lovat was born to the 14th Lord Lovat. The succession would continue a line of peerage that dated back more than 500 years. Born Simon Christopher Joseph Fraser, Master Lovat would become the 15th Lord when his father passed away. Nicknamed Shimi[10], young Simon Fraser grew to become the archetypical Scottish Laird, with a long, proud, Highland heritage. Along with his two sisters Magdalen and Veronica, and his brother Hugh, Simon travelled across Scotland by train, where his mother Laura would teach the children the names of all the Scottish villages. Onboard, she would also read Scottish tales and legends to the children. At train stations across the Highlands, the stop would always include listening to a town piper.

For 500 years, Scottish fighters had been led into battle by the skirl of the pipes. World War I would put an end to this practice. At the start of the Great War, Scottish regiments always had a piper in their ranks. The piper played to the troops in the trenches, boosting morale at the most opportune times. The pipes also acted as a demoralizer for the German army by signalling a failure in an attack. If the Germans mounted an assault by running across no-man's land, then retreated to their own trenches, the piper would play to let the Germans know that they had failed to break the line.

In 1915, the King's Own Scottish Borderers was a regiment positioned on the front line in France. By this point in the war, mustard gas was being used and the regiment had just suffered a severe gas

---

[10] Shimi is the anglicised version of Simon in the Scottish Gaelic language. In the Clan Fraser, they refer to Lord Lovat as MacShimidh, his Gaelic patronym, meaning Son of Simon.

attack. The gas was dispersed onto the battlefield by the Allies, but the wind blew it back into their own trenches. The commanding officer, Lieutenant Young, had a challenge to get his ailing troops to find the will to make a charge against the enemy. He ordered Private Laidlaw to start playing his bagpipes and to lead an attack out of the trenches. Laidlaw rose from the trenches, started playing *All the Blue Bonnets are Over the Border* and the men followed him to the German line. Wounded by shrapnel in the left ankle and leg, he hobbled on and changed the tune to *The Standard on the Braes of Mar*. Armed only with his pipes and a revolver (some pipers tied their revolvers to their wrists for quick access), he was shot as he reached the German trenches and in recognition of his bravery, Laidlaw was awarded the Victoria Cross by Great Britain and the Criox de Guerre by France.

The effectiveness of the pipes to encourage men resulted in the common use of the piper to lead the troops 'over the top' of the trench parapet to attack enemy trenches. Whenever the German troops heard the bellow of the pipes, they knew an attack was coming, thus the pipers were labeled 'ladies from hell'. Perceiving the confidence boost that was being provided by the bagpipes, the German troops started to tactically aim at the unarmed, easy-to-spot pipers. Soon the enemy was achieving a negative morale impact by the slaughtering every piper they saw. Over a thousand pipers listed as casualties in the Great War. This led the British War Office to issue a ban on the pipers' involvement in leading attacks. The new British Army regulation specifically forbade the playing of pipes on the front line of combat.

Even with the new restriction, some pipers still believed their contribution outweighed the risk. In 1916, Private Richardson was a piper in the Canadian Army. He asked his commanding officer for permission to participate in an attack. When the Manitoba regiment charged, they encountered heavy fire and sustained heavy casualties. They had reached a line of barbed wire. Richardson marched up and down along the wire, playing his pipes, displaying great courage, which inspired the troops to push through the obstacle and overcome the enemy's position.

In a subsequent battle, Richardson was accompanying a wounded soldier to the rear of the regiment. He realized that he left his pipes and he ran back to get them. Richardson was never seen again and was presumed to have been killed. Richardson was awarded the Victoria Cross posthumously. A Scottish Chaplain found the blood-stained, mud-soaked pipes a year later and took them back to the school where he worked in Perthshire. In 2006, the pipes were identified and returned to Canada where they were put on public display in the British Columbia Legislature.

The Lovat Scouts were skilled riflemen thanks to their highland hunting. Shimi's father continued to lead the Scouts during World War I, where they were deployed in France as snipers (called 'sharpshooters' at the time). The 14th Lord Lovat, was made a Brigadier-General and was appointed to command the Highland Mounted Brigade. After the First World War, he turned to politics, taking a position as the Chairman of the Forestry Commission, followed by an appointment as the Under-Secretary of State for Dominion Affairs. The descendants of the Lord Lovat that supported the Great Pretender against the King of England, were now playing an integral part in British politics.

Lovat's future piper, William Haskill Millin, was born on the Canadian prairies where the tallest building in a 500-mile radius was a mere two-storeys high. Billy's father, John Millin, a working-class Scotsman, had also fought in World War I as part of the Queen's Own Cameron Highlanders. The Cameron kilts worn by the regiment were a sett that is distinctly Scottish, with a green and dark blue background crossed with red and yellow lines. Wearing his regimental kilt, Billy's father fought alongside the Highlanders in some of the Great War's bloodiest battles, including the battle at Flanders Fields.

After the war, John Millin wanted to distance himself from the memories of the European conflict. At the age of 33, he married Elizabeth O'Rourke and the newlyweds left Glasgow for the promise of a new life in Canada. As a war veteran, John qualified for a position of peace officer, so he took a post with the Royal Canadian Mounted Police in the heart of the Canadian prairies, where the average winter temperature was -20°F. Elizabeth gave birth to the couple's first little 'Canadian', in 1921. Billy's sister Olive was born in Wawota, Saskatchewan. A year later, Billy was born in Regina. He wouldn't be there long enough to have any memories of his prairie life.

When Billy was just under three-years old, his parents decided to give up on the Canadian experiment. Just after the start of the new year in 1924, the family boarded a train to start their journey home to Scotland. Even with their large iron snowplows, the trains had a challenge making their way east through the heavy snows of January.

After five days of stop-and-go trekking, the family made their way to the east coast of Canada. From New Brunswick, they boarded the Canadian Pacific steamship *Marburn* and headed back to Glasgow. Young Billy, whose heart and mind would always belong to Scotland, was going to be raised as a Scot.

With his Canadian experience, John was able to secure a position as a policeman back in Glasgow. The family settled in Shettleston on Maukinfauld Road. Shettleston was a village that had been consumed as the City of Glasgow expanded east. To this day, it is the only place in the United Kingdom where life expectancy is still falling. Poor living conditions, poor diet and poor health (brought on by heavy smoking and drinking), was the norm in Shettleston. Life there was arduous, and a policeman's son had to become streetwise at a very young age. Billy received his education in Glasgow, finishing up at Uddingston Grammar School.

In contrast, Master Lovat was educated by Benedictine monks in Yorkshire, then he attended Oxford where he studied History. He had a particular interest in the history of the Highlands, but also studied the battle tactics of the First World War. Before assuming the title of Lord, Simon Fraser found his calling in the British Army. He joined the Scots Guards at the seasoned age of 21 but had to retire one year later when his father suddenly passed away. At a very young age, Simon took his father's place, inheriting the Fraser estate and becoming the 25th Chief of Clan Fraser. The estate was 200,000 acres of Highland terrain, including Beaufort Castle overlooking the river Beauly. The 15th Lord Lovat maintained his military connection, retaining a commission in the Army Reserves as part of the Lovat Scouts.

Shimi and Billy grew up experiencing two different Scotlands. One raised in the majestic Highlands, the other in the industrial Lowlands. However, both developed a deep appreciation for bagpipe music and history. In Billy's world, the Scottish image of a piper playing at sunset in the Highlands was not a vision that would be commonly invoked in Shettleston. A Dickens-like neighbourhood, with families working long hours in smoke-stacked Glaswegian factories, would be a much more familiar image to the people who lived on Maukinfauld Road. Fortunately for Billy, many of the families from the police force lived close to each other. His next-door neighbour, Charlie Moir, played in the Glasgow police pipe band and Billy grew up listening to the police piper. At the age of 12, Billy started to learn the bagpipes in the Boys' Brigade where Mr. Moir tutored. As both his pipe tutor and his next-door neighbour, Moir kept the young piper disciplined in his study of the pipes and made sure he was practicing regularly.

The bagpipes are one of the oldest instruments, dating back to their use by the Egyptians and making their way across Europe to France. However, the pipes and Scotland are inextricably linked. Upon hearing the call of the pipes, one can't help but conjure up an image of the mist flowing through the valleys and mountains of the Scottish Highlands. Unlike other wind instruments, the sound is not produced by blowing directly into the instrument. Blowing into the blowpipe puts air in a bag, and the sound is only produced when the piper's arm squeezes the air out of the bag and through the reeded drones. There should be very little sound when the piper is filling the bag, but a novice piper will often allow some air to be accidentally pushed through drones, thus creating the chiff and noisy bellow that is associated with the beginning of a pipe tune.

"Pity the man wha hears the 'pipes and wisnae born in Scotland."[11]

Once the air is flowing, different notes are produced by altering fingering on the chanter that hangs down in front of the bag. The drones are lengthened to adjust the 'tuning' of the pipes. An untuned set of pipes can be one of the worst sounds known to man. The drones produce a long continuous tone underneath the changing notes of the chanter, in a bellow effect similar to an organ. Because the sound is constantly being squeezed out of the bag during a song, the piper is constantly refilling the bag. However, there is no relationship between the timing of blowing to fill the bag and the timing of the changing notes in a tune. This also means that pipe music is constant. Once a piece starts, there are no musical rests or silences until the end of the song.

Billy became a fine piper. When he was 15-years old, as the storm clouds of war were gathering over Europe, Billy left school and volunteered to play pipes for the 7th Battalion of the Highland Light Infantry. Later that year, Billy's family moved to Fort William; the Scottish opposite of Shettleston. With a population of under 10,000 people, Fort William is still one of the largest towns in the Scottish Highlands. The Fort is close to Glencoe, a national tourist attraction. Each year people came to the area for the scenic beauty of Ben Nevis

---

[11] From the 1953 Allan Ladd film *Paratrooper*.

and to visit the location of the Massacre of Glencoe (where the Clan Macgregor betrayed the Jacobite Clan McDonald who were subsequently massacred by the English).

The historical significance and inherent majesty of the area around Fort William is such an idyllic version of Scotland that it has been used to portray the Highlands in numerous movies and television series. The area was featured in major Hollywood films including *Harry Potter*, *Braveheart*, *Highlander* and *Rob Roy*. Living in the personification of the Scottish Highlands, Billy Millin joined the regular army in his father's old regiment, the Cameron Highlanders in Fort George. The piping skills that Charlie Moir instilled in Billy, helped him get into the pipe band of the regular army. When his mother heard that he had joined the regular army, she said Billy "was always a good fighter".

With the outbreak of war, the Scottish regiments did not have the luxury of maintaining pipe bands. Each battalion would only retain five pipers, one per company. Like many pipers, Millin was part of the Royal Army Medical Corps section in the 'Ack Ack' gun group. The Ack Acks was the nickname for the unit that drove trucks with a Lewis gun mounted on the back. The light machinegun was used to defend the medical regiment when it was on manoeuvres. When it was time for a parade, the Ack Ack men would form a pipe band.

On October 10, 1938, eleven months before the start of World War II, Lord Lovat married Rosamond Broughton. The Lord and Lady lived where Simon Fraser was born, in Beaufort Castle. While still majestic, many of the great works of art and books in Beaufort were destroyed by a catastrophic fire that gutted the picture gallery and the library. Eight months after the wedding, Simon Fraser resigned from his position in the Army Reserves. However, after only a one-month respite, the mounting fears of a European conflict convinced Lord Lovat to rejoin the Army Reserves. He assumed his role as a Captain in the Lovat Scouts, the British Army unit formed by his father.

The Scouts had fought in World War I and had remained as a reserve unit during peace time. When World War II finally broke out, the Lovat Scouts were deployed to the Faroe Islands where they patrolled, on watch for a German invasion.

2. Dynamo, Claymore, Abercrombie, Archery & Jubilee

Tell me o' my kilted Clan,
Gin they fought, or gin they ran[12]

While not often highlighted in history texts, tens of thousands of Allied lives would be saved in World War II, thanks to unused planes, secret codes, birthday parties, Highland fighting tactics and of course, beach music. In an almost farcical series of events, this random set of unrelated circumstances, would all play their part in contributing to the Nazi downfall.

At the start of the war, Germany was undoubtedly poised to win, and win decidedly. They had a superior army, navy and air force, which were using superior artillery, ships and planes. On land, the Germans held a substantial advantage having better machineguns (the Spandau), better tanks (both Panzer and Tiger) and better anti-tank weapons (the Panzerfaust). In the air, the German investment in research and technology would result in the first use of jet engines and rockets in warfare. On the seas, Britain had continued to build large battleships, but Germany invested considerably in U-boats. While not

---

[12] Hieland Laddie – Traditional / Beethoven Op. 108 no.7

necessarily the strongest weapon in military battles, the U-boats were particularly strong in economic warfare. Attacking merchant vessels, the German submarines would be successful in isolating Great Britain's supply chain, limiting provisions that were being shipped from Canada and elsewhere.

Germany had also established strong alliances with Russia and Italy, providing protection on its Southern and Eastern borders. Germany's strengths contrasted sharply with the Allies' lack of readiness. Only Britain and France declared war against Germany after they launched Blitzkrieg on Poland. The rest of the beleaguered European nations were content to wait until Germany invaded their soil, before they would declare war.

By the time the Normandy Invasion was launched, Germany had lost its strategic advantage. Failure to maintain only one front, necessitated splitting its forces in a brutal clash against Russia, thus dividing its resources. The Nazis also lost the chance to deliver a crushing blow to Britain when their panzers stopped advancing at Dieppe, allowing the British troops to escape. After that, Great Britain displayed great fortitude by persevering until the United States entered the war. Once Germany launched a second front to the east, they had abandoned the idea of invading Great Britain.

Poised to win at the start of the war, the Nazis invaded Poland on September 1, 1939. Employing Blitzkrieg, or lightening war, they used extremely mobile warfare tactics to attack and advance quickly. Two days later, after an ultimatum for Germany to retreat from Poland was ignored, France and Great Britain declared war. The attack patterns of the new German Army were vastly different than the static trench warfare of the previous war. The defense against extremely mobile troops, would require a tactic that had not yet been adopted by either France or Britain.

When World War I began, the combat started quickly. Troops boarded ships in Britain and headed for Europe with the unfulfilled promise to be 'home for Christmas'. In contrast, at the start of World War II, war was declared by France and Great Britain, but very little fighting followed. Other European countries such as Belgium, Holland and Luxembourg, were on high alert, but were hesitant to enter the war. During the first year of 'war', very little had changed and there was little evidence of a conflict. The period after the start of the Second World War is often referred to as the 'Phoney War' because of the limited engagements and confrontations. There was only one attack on Germany by France, followed by a few minor German counterattacks. The relative inaction created a false sense of calmness, Germany continued to develop its war machine in the shadows.

Willy Messerschmitt believed in combining load bearing parts to create lightweight aircraft construction components. This made the German manufactured Messerschmitt a vastly superior plane to the Spitfire, however Germany limited its use. German Junkers (with an unfortunate English connotation to their name) were largely used in the Battle of Britain. The new Messerschmitt was employed sparingly because the German Luftwaffe was waiting for the production of a jet engine version. Messerschmitt had designed the first jet-powered fighter plane[13] as well as the first rocket-powered interceptor plane[14]. Both planes were developed in 1941 but not put into use until 1944.

Before the outbreak of the war, British Prime Minister Chamberlain had returned home with an agreement that would provide 'Peace for Our Time'[15]. Thus, it would hypocritical for Britain to chide other countries for believing they could negotiate a peaceful resolution to the mounting conflicts. During late 1939 and early 1940, the lack of combat during the Phoney War led many to believe that a diplomatic solution could still be found. Surely Germany's cessation of expansion was an indication that they were willing to negotiate. In reality, after capturing Poland to the West, the Nazis had fully planned to quickly launch another invasion to the east. This came to an end however, when one Messerschmitt got lost and crashed in Belgium.

Shortly after Britain declared war, German aviator Major Hoenmanns enjoyed a drink in the mess with Major Reinburger in Loddenheide, Germany. Reinburger told Hoenmanns that he was taking a train in the morning to Cologne. The pilot was not a big fan of the train and he convinced his comrade to fly in the new Messerschmitt instead. The next day they headed south but low fogbanks caused Hoenmanns to lose his way. In the snow-covered countryside, the pilot had trouble finding the Rhine. Suddenly the plane's engine sputtered, then cut out (the pilot may have accidently switched off the fuel supply). The pilot was able to make an emergency landing, crashing down in a nearby field. Before he could bring the plane to a stop,

---

[13] The Me 262
[14] The Me 163
[15] Not 'Peace in Our Time' as is often misquoted

Hoenmanns tried to squeeze between two Canadian poplar trees, which resulted in tearing off both wings of the new plane.

Both the pilot and his passenger survived the crash with only bumps and bruises. The plane wreck sat in the field and the two men headed toward to a farmhand for help. As soon as the farmworker spoke, the two German officers realized that they were no longer in Germany. Lost in the fog, they had crossed through the Netherlands and crashed in a field in Belgium. A panicked look came over Reinburger's face. He pulled the pilot aside and informed him that he was carrying secret plans for the invasion of Belgium, Luxembourg and the Netherlands. Reinburger ran back to the plane to retrieve his briefcase, leaving Hoenmanns to answer any questions. Reinburger decided he would try to destroy the plans.

Hoenmanns distracted a growing number onlookers as Reinburger tried to burn the papers with the plane's cigarette lighter. The papers were too thick to ignite, so he ran back, papers in hand, to the farmhand. He told the Belgian that he was desperate for a cigarette to calm his nerves, and he headed off to the bushes once he had received a single match. In the shrubbery, he attempted to burn the papers, just as two helpful border guards arrived on bicycles. Seeing the fire, they assumed that Reinburger was trying to put it out, so they helped. They were now holding the charred papers of the invasion plan. As they tried to read the German documents, Reinburger tried to run away but surrendered when the guards fired a warning shot. The two German officers probably could have taken a small reprimand for landing in a neutral country with an explanation of the plane malfunction in the bad weather conditions, but their attempt to destroy the papers only served to highlight a more clandestine mission.

The German officers were taken to a guardhouse and questioned as the scorched plans lay on the table. Again, they tried to destroy the evidence. Hoenmanns distracted the Belgian guards by asking to go the toilet so that Reinburger could throw the papers in a burning stove. This plan also failed as the pilot screamed in pain when he tried to lift the lid on the hot stove. Now they had highlighted the value of the toasted documents. Reinburger realized that he would be executed when he returned to Germany, so he tried to grab one of the guard's guns to attempt suicide.

When Belgian intelligence arrived that afternoon, they were able to understand the German documents. They were in a Lowland country holding the German plans to invade the Lowland countries. The documents were dated and signed, decreed by Hitler with the invasion date of January 17, 1940. Belgian Intelligence was unsure if this was a real document or a stunt to make Belgium move forces to the wrong location. They decided to trick Reinburger by questioning him in such a way as to make him believe that the plan had been burned enough to make it undecipherable. Before releasing him, they allowed him to meet with German Army attachées in a room that was secretly mic'ed. As Reinburger relayed the information that the plan had been rendered unreadable, the relief by the Army representatives confirmed that the plan must be real. The German Army had been tricked into believing that the invasion plans had not been revealed.

Belgium informed the other Lowland countries about the German plans. Over the next week, Belgium recalled 80,000 soldiers on leave and ordered barriers to be moved aside on the southern border with France (this would allow the Allied forces to advance through Belgium quicker). January 17th came and went with no invasion. Some believed that the documents were fake and had been allowed to fall into Belgian hands to see how they might react. However, it was Belgium's military actions that had betrayed their successful deceit and allowed Germany to realize that the plans had in fact been uncovered.

It finally became clear that Belgium held real plans for a German invasion when Hitler fired two of his Generals; the one that Hoenmanns reported to and the one that Reinburger reported to. The German Army also put new procedures in place, including the use of the new Enigma machine, an electro-mechanical encryption device that would limit the usefulness of any further captured communications.

The Phoney War continued with only a few skirmishes. Still, there were those that stated that the plans retrieved by Belgium were not based on a real invasion intent. Countries settled back into a nervous calmness again, with no significant warfare being waged. This dangerous complacency came to an end in May 1940. With a new set of invasion plans, the German war machine mobilized and overran the Lowland countries quickly. On May 10th Germany invaded Luxembourg, Netherlands and Belgium. Luxembourg fell on the first day, Netherlands surrendered on May 15th, and Belgium held out until May 28th. Germany continued west and most of France was under German control in just six weeks. The photographs of German flags flying in Paris shocked the world. As the Western Front collapsed, the

Allies retreated and found themselves backed to the sea at Dunkirk. Facing the loss of hundreds of thousands of now surrounded Belgian, French and British troops, Operation Dynamo was implemented to evacuate the soldiers using civilian vessels. The operation successfully saved over 300,000 men but after the fall of mainland Europe, it became clear that for the German forces the next stop would be Great Britain. It was during this darkest period of Great Britain's war that the commando units were set up. These units were the first in Great Britain to adapt a mobile attack strategy, mirroring the Highland raiding tactics.

"We shall not be content with a defensive war," Winston Churchill declared. "We should immediately set to work to organize self-contained, thoroughly equipped raiding units."

The first commando units consisted of highly trained infantry assault teams. Almost immediately the commandos performed small-scale stealth raids and generally harassed the German Army. Training was a challenge as much of the artillery and equipment had been left behind in Dunkirk. The commando training would include wilderness survival, close combat, navigation, weapons, demolition and amphibious assault techniques. In addition, for each assignment, there would be mission specific training.

In 1940, Millin performed at his first public piping event in support of the war effort, to raise money for the construction of the Spitfire. That same year, the new elite commando unit was formed with some of the toughest men from the British Army and the British Marines. Based in Achnacarry, Scotland, the new commando unit began recruiting volunteers to put through the rigorous training to become commandos. Looking for more excitement, Millin volunteered to try out for the unit. The 18-year old piper was soon accepted into the squad as a permanent member of the demonstration troop.

Achnacarry is a small hamlet that sits 12 miles away from Fort William. Achnacarry Castle was originally built by the Chief of Clan Cameron (of Lochiel), Sir Ewen Cameron in 1655. The original castle was destroyed in battle and then rebuilt in 1802. The 'new' castle, decorated in Cameron plaid, was used as the home base for the British Army Commando Training Depot for World War II and became known as Commando Castle. Achnacarry, deep in the heather-painted Highlands covered by craggy marshes, was 'beautiful to the eye but unpleasant to the skin'. The wild, severely undulating terrain is punctuated by lochs that would allow commando trainees to practice water landings in secure surroundings.

The unforgiving hills surrounding Achnacarry would more accurately be called mountains, particularly Ben Nevis, the highest point in Great Britain. Climbing these hills would require mountaineering, rockface ascents and ice climbing. The topology surrounding Achnacarry was daunting, especially to troops who came from the cities. They would arrive at a land of epic grandeur and enduring legend. The Highland castle was surrounded by rugged glens that were home to ancient battles, deep eerie lakes that held claim to medieval monsters, and soaring peaks shrouded in mist and mystery.

After a few short weeks, the locals knew there was something going on at the castle and they knew to stay away from the training fields. The lush, manicured lawn surrounding Sir Donald's castle was replaced by drill square asphalt and surrounded by bell tents or austere Nissens. The wild gusts of wind around the hills of Loch Ness, were now consumed with machinegun fire and mortar explosions.

On his first day at Achnacarry, the rosy-cheeked Millin met the stern moustached Lieutenant Colonel Vaughan, the officer in charge of the training facility. Young Millin, dressed in the military khaki shirt and trousers of a Private, stood at attention, hands by his side and eyes faced forward. Dressed in his green beret, shirt, tie, and a military jacket wielding his medals, Vaughan greeted the new recruits with his well-rehearse day-one speech.

"You see these 'ere hills?" Vaughan asked in his cockney accent. "You will climb every one of them."

The military training could have been entitled 'How to be a Highlander'. The new commando mobile warfare approach paralleled the Highland tactics used 400 years earlier. Deep in the Scottish Highlands, the commandos learned how to stalk deer, a skill that they would use as snipers in Normandy. With a Highland deer, you had to approach from the side because of its acute sight and sense of smell. If you let the deer smell your approach, it would dart away. The commandos would shoot to kill. The deer would then be skinned, and the meat was taken to local hospitals.

Captain Lovat had a disagreement with his commanding officer in the Lovat Scouts. Wanting to make a more meaningful contribution to the war effort, he decided to volunteer to join the new commando unit. Joining the regular army, he is registered as:

Service Number:	44718
First Name:	The Lord
Last Name:	Lovat

When 'The Lord' left the Scouts, he took some of his best Highland men along with him to the commandos. The commando training included a mobile combat style, stealth attack methods and enduring reconnaissance missions. The Highlanders had always been particularly suited for this style of warfare. The commando battle techniques closely aligned to both how the Highlanders fought and how they lived. At home in the Highlands, they already knew how to quietly stalk deer and how to patiently fish for salmon, skills that would prove useful to commandos.

There were two commando units, No. 3 and No. 4 (No. 1 and No. 2 were reserved for commando paratroopers, but these units were never created). In February 1941, Lovat was attached to No. 4 Commando unit as an observer, joining the troops when they set out for Operation Claymore. Key to the covert nature of the commando operations, the objectives of each mission were shrouded in secrecy. For Claymore, the commandos believed they were going offshore in Northern Scotland for training. Instead, once onboard their transport ship, the real objective of the exercise was revealed. Claymore was the first of twelve raids that the commandos would make on Norway. This time, the mission was to raid the Lofoten Islands and destroy fish oil plants. The Lofoten Islands are an archipelago in northern Norway with distinctive mountainous terrain and sheltered bays. The fish oil manufactured on the islands was being shipped to Germany where it was used in the manufacture of explosives.

When the commandos reached Scapa Flow, nestled in among the Orkney Islands, consistent with the commando model, they commenced detailed training specifically aimed at accomplishing the operational requirements of the mission. Scapa Flow was the location of the main British Naval Base. Off the northern shore of Scotland, the distance from German airfields provided a logistical challenge for the Luftwaffe and thus a natural protection during the First World War.

The Royal Navy saw no need to move its main base, even after the Japanese attack on Pearl Harbor.

The commandos attended training lectures and rehearsed the various components of the mission including disembarking, attacking and even escaping capture. The plan was to avoid skirmishes with German infantry, but the exercises included combat training as a contingency. Non-commissioned officers were given pants with fly buttons that disassembled and reassembled into a compass. Small silk maps of Norway were sewn into their clothes to assist in escaping the country if need be. This was an ideal operation for Lovat to see the level of preparedness that the commandos used to execute their missions.

Operation Claymore was successfully launched the next month. The commandos destroyed 11 fish oil factories, sank 10 ships, recruited 315 Norwegian freedom fighters and took 225 German prisoners and Quisling regime[16] collaborators. More than 18,000 tons of German naval vessels were sunk using a combination of explosives set by Royal Engineers and coordinated Royal Navy gunfire. When the unit came across an armed German trawler[17], the tactic of using commandos instead of Naval firepower reaped massive dividends. Rather than sink the trawler, the commandos captured it and discovered one of the key components that would lead to the defeat of Germany. The commandos found a keycode book and rotor wheels for an Enigma machine, the device that was used to encode German military orders. The rotors are the heart of the encrypting device and their capture allowed the team at Bletchley Park, using techniques developed by Polish mathematicians, to crack German communications. The successful decryption of German messages allowed the British fleet to avoid U-boat attacks and was a major factor in the Allied success.

The triumph of the commandos was not turned into a propaganda campaign. The stealth nature of the mission meant that the acquired assets remained a secret after the completion of each mission. Martin Linge, the former Norwegian actor who became the commander of the Norwegian freedom fighters, was critical of the value of the raid on Lofoten Islands. He would have preferred a more direct attack to help free his country. However, he was never told about the capture of the Enigma rotors. The success of the commandos reached Winston Churchill who wrote an internal memo to congratulate the team "on a

---

[16] The Norwegian fascist collaborationist government
[17] The *Krebs*

very satisfactory operation". The reputation of the commandos continued to be confirmed within the military and Captain Lovat knew this was where he was meant to be.

Once selected for commando training, the troops were shipped to Achnacarry. They took a 24-hour train ride in a blacked-out train with no food and only rainwater from the carriage roofs. They arrived at Spean Bridge railway station, but the train stopped away from the platforms. The commando trainees had to jump down, where they would find out that there were also no transport trucks. The training officers that were waiting on the platform were extremely fit. The recruits had to hike, with all their kit, seven miles to the castle. This would be the first of many hikes. They knew that this would be very different training well before they reached 'heartbreak hill', a steep incline on the way to the castle that marked only three miles left to hike.

One mile away from the camp, the trainees would hear Millin and the other commando pipers, playing their welcome music at military march pace. While disheartening as the commandos had to pick up their pace to match the march tempo of the bagpipe tune, the music was somehow welcoming.

"The kilted pipers, standing at the entrance, greeted us with one of their traditional Highland tunes. It did wonders for morale. No matter how tired the soldiers were, the bagpipe music set adrenaline flowing. With pride we marched into camp in step, heads high," said Sergeant Slaughter.

As recruits entered the castle for training, the first thing they passed were graves. Mock graves were made informing the new commandos that: 'this man advanced over cover, instead of going around the side', 'this man put a bomb down a three-inch mortar the wrong way', 'this man failed to examine his climbing rope' and 'these three fired a mortar under a tree'.

It was at this point that the new commandos were informed that 'here, we train with live ammo'. With live gun fire, you didn't zigzag when you were asked to run a straight line. With real bombs exploding in a river below you, you didn't dare let go of your zipline.

Almost every second day, the commandos would participate in a seven-mile race to Spean Bridge and back again. They were dressed in full kit, carrying their rucksacks. There was strong competition across the different trainee units as to which unit would do the best. 'We'll beat you next time', etc. They also often made the twenty-mile march over the mountains. The terrain around Fort Williams was so hilly, that many intakes would complain that most hills went up. When they moved to the mountains, it became a real metric for a soldier's endurance level.

"Of course, these 20-mile marches over mountains turned out to feel like 50 miles, because you are not just marching 20 miles down the road, you're marching over mountains and that was brilliant. I used to enjoy that … 'ard work, but it's better than walking along the road," Private Treacher of the Royal Marines remembered.

The training at Commando Castle was gruelling. There were speed marches, unarmed combat, cliff climbing, boat drills and weapons training. Things that appeared simple, like how to enter a house, came along with techniques such as entering through the roof by removing a few shingles.

Everything that was studied during the day, also had to be repeated at night. Managing night operations soon became second nature. They learned tricks such as acclimatizing your eyes by closing one eye when coming out of a lighted place. They ran night patrols, practiced night firing, night house clearing and night exercises that paralleled the day exercises. For several weeks, reveille was at 8 p.m. and the commandos worked only at night. They learned how to move without making a sound, how to open doors or walk on floors silently, and when to move (you move when a plane flies overhead).

"The dark is your friend," explained Captain Bryan Hilton-Jones. "In daylight the enemy can see you better, so they can shoot you more easily. If you keep still at night and blend with the background, you are totally invisible. The defender has an obvious advantage over the attacker, or the reconnoitering intruder. The defender can sit still while the protagonist has to move. Therefore, you have to learn how to move as quietly and as invisibly as humanly possible. Patience is essential."

One of the first tests for new recruits was when they were taken and dropped off, at night, in the rain-drenched Scottish moors with only a compass and a map to navigate back to Commando Castle. Recruits were graded by umpires who observed the intake's performance.

Colonel Vaughan, who was affectionately called either 'Rommel of the North' or 'Laird of Achnacarry' by the troops, had created an asceticism machine that would deliver 25,000 high caliber troops before the end of the war.

"It is hard to exaggerate the importance of what was achieved at Achnacarry. To the instructors, commissioned and non-commissioned alike, who worked there so tirelessly and with such controlled enthusiasm, the Commandos in particular, and the country in general, owe a very great debt, and to no one more than to Vaughan," stated Lieutenant Saunders.

As part of the permanent demonstration troop, Millin had completed all the commando training and was now helping train the new recruits. One day he might be disembarking from a landing craft to demonstrate the proper method, the next day he could be firing live mortar rounds at the recruits as they attempted their landing. The intakes didn't realize it, but they were training for D-Day. The demonstration troop also had to perform in the pipe band. Despite being English, it was Vaughan's idea to give the demonstration troops double duty and even though many of the men had never played the pipes before, they were soon learning the basics. The bagpipes would be played at various times during the day, including the 6 a.m. reveille.

Millin was the troop's best piper at the castle and would often lead the rest of the troop in chanter practice. He also enjoyed many of the other tasks assigned to him in the demonstrations. His favorite was at fieldcraft lectures where he would be assigned to demonstrate how to fire mortars. There were lots of lectures, training and practice on all types of artillery. The commando was expected to be an expert in all areas so that if need be, he could take the place of a fallen comrade and complete the mission. Before entering Achnacarry, explosives were just explosives. Soon the intake was experimenting with different kinds of explosives, including shattering, lifting, and concussion. They set the charges with different techniques including fuses, primers and detonators.

For many, blowing things up became the fun part of the day. One exercise involved a 2x4 with a hunk of explosive. The intakes approached the door of a house where they needed to gain entry, leaned the lumber against the door, set the charge and walked for cover (walked, never ran, if you ran you could trip). The explosion went off and the commandos dove through the hole. Millin was always amused when the intake failed to create a large enough hole and the want-to-be commandos would bang their heads diving through the smoke only to discover there was no hole.

This exercise was practised by some commandos in a bombed-out house in Wales. The next-door neighbour to the flattened house, was a particularly bitter old lady.

"This noise will simply have to stop," she called from the second floor of her house that had remarkably been spared by the bombing.

"There's a war on, madam," one of the intakes replied.

"I shall call Mr. Churchill, and we'll see about that," she yelled back as she slammed her window closed.

One of the stranger jobs, which gave Millin plenty of time to himself, was standing as a lookout at ropes that hung from the Bunarkaig bridge. The task was to man the bridge over the River Arkaig and watch for any new intakes being carried away down the river. Commando Castle had an obstacle course known as the Tarzan course. The course included a five-mile climb up a hill, a ten-foot wall to scale, steep ravines, rope swings and rope bridges over the river. Life-sized targets would pop-up and the intakes would have to decide if they were going to use their rifle or bayonet. If an umpire deemed that a candidate was wounded in the exercise, then his platoon would have to carry that man, to complete their mission.

The course would have been challenging enough for the intakes, but when they made their way across the river on a rope bridge, someone would detonate live explosives in the water below them. This would sometimes knock some men off the ropes and into the fast-flowing river. Before Millin had joined the team, five men were knocked off into the river and carried away to a nearby loch, where they drowned. The solution to ensuring that this never happened again was to hang ropes from a bridge downstream. If the intakes were blasted off the rope bridge, they would have to grab the hanging ropes at the stone bridge and climb out. Millin's task would be to man the bridge and watch to make sure the recruits managed to save themselves. Failure to complete the Tarzan course on time meant the entire squad had to run repeat the exercise on Sunday. Training continued every Sunday, but at least if you didn't have to repeat the course, you would have enough time to wash your clothes.

Commando training was much more rigorous than regular infantry training. You never stood with your hands in your pockets. You never walked anywhere, it was either a march or a run. The men would soon be at their peak physical form. The unit expanded when the 1er Bataillon de Fusilliers Marins of France became the first foreign volunteers to sign up for the merciless British Commando training. The unit was made up of French nationals who had left France to join General Charles de Gaulle in Britain. Led by Capitaine de Corvette Kieffer, the men in the French unit had escaped from Vichy France or evacuated at Dunkirk four years earlier. One French volunteer had even made his way from Monaco, arriving in a rowboat. For the French trainees, they would not only have to endure the training, but also the Scottish porridge.

"We could not leave the barracks without listening to a British instructor, who yelled at us 'Quick March'," explained French commando Lance Corporal Meudal, who had just turned 20 when he entered Achnacarry. "We had to run all the time. If we left, we had to run. That was also a part of the game. We had to be always under pressure and finally it became a habit! You no longer wanted to walk; you ran."

A veteran of World War I, Colonel Vaughan set the standard for the camp and he strongly believed that severe training would save lives. He often commented that Hitler didn't stop the war because it was Sunday, so training at Commando Castle went on seven days a week without a break. There was no time to head into town for a beer at the pub, and the men would have been too exhausted even if there was time. Hitler also didn't stop the war when it was raining or snowing. It rained at Achnacarry, 'twice every five minutes'. The men would spend time in the rain, in the mud, during the day and at night, all the time performing exhausting exercises or taking never-ending marches with their rucksacks. Eventually, they would reach their peak physical conditioning.

Sergeant-Major Dunning described Vaughan as someone who "accepted nothing but the best, whether it be in fitness, training, weaponry and musketry, fieldcraft and tactics, drill and turnout, or even in the more apparently mundane matters of administration which included feeding and hygiene."

After several weeks, the selection began to determine who from the trainees would become a green beret. The recruits had to march an eliminatory march of seven miles with a 65-pound rucksack. The march had to be finished in an hour. The first failure meant a repeat trip. The second failure was followed up with an order to RTU (return to unit).

"It meant you would never get a green beret. It's over for you. Green beret, farewell," French commando Corporal Gautier said summing up the unforgiving nature of the training tests.

On the last day of training, the recruits who passed all the tests, received their green beret. The beret was a distinctive symbol of the elite forces. It was the commando's reward for proving that he was up to the task. The commandos learned how to shrink and shape their berets in boiling water, then they were desperate to be seen wearing their berets in town. With every successive mission, the reputation of the green beret commandos was growing, such that the berets would be saluted to, by equal or even higher ranked officers.

After seven weeks of training, the troops that were not RTU'd were assigned to a commando unit and once posted the new commando would report to where the unit was installed. For example, the No. 4 unit was based out of Troon in Ayrshire, Scotland, where there were no barracks. By not being in barracks, it was more difficult for the Germans to track troop movements and operation preparation. Instead, the troops were assigned to landladies and lived in civilian digs.

"We paid them a weekly sum of money and they gave us two meals a day," said Private Spearman, "and we were there for five years, or something. We were there for a long time anyway."

For new intakes at Commando Castle, everyone slept in the same corrugated iron shelters called Nissens, not in the castle like the recruiting brochures hinted. At Achnacarry, there were no ranks. Officers and infantry alike were put through the same training. The only people observing the advancement were the few training officers and Demonstration Troop. In February 1942, Captain Lovat was supernumerary when the 'lead training officer' position became open. Lovat accepted the position to head up No. 4 unit and lead the training for the full commando brigade. The commando unit now fell under the unusual combination of Vaughan, a traditional military man and a Cockney who worked his way up the ranks, plus Lovat, an Oxford graduate and a Highlander Clan Chief who joined the military through the Army unit his father started. Despite their differences, the two men held the shared ideal: train hard, fight easy. They both believed that the commando literally had to be able to do his job in the dark.

"I had been brought up to believe that I could not operate a machine more complex than a pair of scissors. Suddenly, I found myself, while blindfolded, stripping and reassembling Bren guns, tommy guns, and

Colt .45 pistols," recalled Corporal Masters. "I shall never forget a little black crow-shaped part in an aperture of the Colt, into which a steel locking pin had to be fitted in no more than two minutes. It was hard enough to do when you could see. Blindfolded it was murder."

Lovat scheduled relentless rounds of training. There was a full troop exercise on mountain climbing on the Isle of Skye and in Glencoe. The troops were also taken to the Outer Hebrides for mock attacks with live ammunition. A variety of water-based landings were also rehearsed, including beach and rocky shores. In addition, the standard training routines, such as cross-country marches and rifle range practice, were stepped up.

Achnacarry Castle hosted and trained commandos from around the world including French, Dutch, Belgian, Polish, Norwegian, Czechoslovakian, Canadian and of course British. In addition to the 100 men from the No. 4 Commando unit, Lovat also commanded 50 men from Canada and some Royal Engineers.

As an acting Major, Lovat's first major non-training assignment, Operation Abercrombie, was a reconnaissance raid on the French coastal village of Hardelot. A small farming village about eight miles south of Boulogne, Hardelot had been easily occupied when the German army crossed into France. The objective of the commandos was to capture prisoners and destroy equipment, including aircraft searchlights. Again, mission specific training was used, this time near Southampton. The *HMS Prins Albert*, a pre-war Belgian cross-Channel ferry, would be used as the landing ship. This ship would be put to good use a number of times by the commandos, both for training and for actual missions.

In July 1942, for Abercrombie, motor gun boats transported the commandos and for the first time, landing craft (LCIs[18]) assault boats were used to go ashore. The LCIs were manufactured for the commandos 'below the radar' at various small boatyards and furniture manufacturers across Britain. While the mission did not go without its challenges (one of the LCIs took on water), they were successful in the destruction of several German watercrafts.

"The interesting feature of this operation was the very small opposition encountered throughout. It seems probable that the enemy

---

[18] Landing Craft – Infantry

was confused from the onset by the naval engagement which took place some 15 minutes after the landing," reported Lovat.

For the success of the raid, Major Lovat was awarded the Military Cross and he assumed the position of acting Lieutenant Colonel. The town of Hardelot was not so lucky. Before fleeing, the Germans would loot the village, then much of the town was destroyed when the Allies blew it up.

The next major mission was Operation Archery, which used No. 3 Commando unit and parts of No. 4. Archery was another raid on German installations in Norway, this time with the additional support of the Royal Air Force who attacked the German airbase and provided air-based cover. The operations were becoming larger and more complex as the naval support consisted of a cruiser, four destroyers and two landing ships. Again, the mission was a success with 150 Germans killed compared to 19 British forces. As a consequence, Germany reinforced their troops using men that could have been more valuable at the front.

As part of Operation Archery, acting Lieutenant Colonel Lovat witnessed the exploits of Major Churchill (Mad Jack), second in command with the No. 3 Command unit. Mad Jack had already become known as the only British soldier to have killed an enemy soldier using a longbow. As the landing craft arrived in Norway and dropped their ramps, Mad Jack started up his bagpipes and jumped ashore playing *March of the Cameron Men*, then he threw a grenade to start the attack on the beach. For his bravery (and insanity), he received the Military Cross and Bar.

In August of 1942, acting Lieutenant Colonel Lovat was appointed commanding officer of No. 4 Commando. Lovat was no ordinary soldier. Quite the opposite, Lovat had proven to be an eccentric but brilliant military commander. He was a Highlander that was training his unit how to fight using Highlander raiding techniques. Lovat believed the unit was only as strong as its weakest link and he was completely intolerable of any commando that wasn't up to his own personal standards.

"Hey you, you're my staff captain," Lovat told Captain Harper-Gow after he recruited him, "but I can tell you this, if you're no bloody good you'll be out on your arse before you even know you've started."

'The Lord Lovat' was a natural born leader, able to attract a unit of dedicated commandos and guide them with a unique intensity that was well suited for commando operations. He believed in overtraining and he measured the success for each of the training efforts. Lovat was demanding and he did not shy away from sending soldiers back to their home regiments if they failed in training exercises, even though they had volunteered for the deadly missions of the commando unit. Winston Churchill described Lovat as 'the mildest-mannered man that ever scuttled a ship or cut a throat'.

"He was completely intolerant of inefficiency. And ruthless when he had to be. He had me, so to speak, on my toes from the word go. It was like that with everyone. But, withal there was a debonair, almost romantic air about him, which intrigued and brought the best out of one," said Harper-Gow, the Scottish financial giant that served under Lovat in No. 4 Commando unit.

As the training intensified, there were some tragedies. While rehearsing beach landings, a landing craft stopped short of the beach and two men, Lance Corporal Orchin and Private Hellyer, were pulled under in the waters off the Isle of Arran. The other commandos assumed that the men had made it ashore and got subsequently lost somewhere on the island. Tragically, the bodies washed up two days later in Brodick Bay. Earlier that year, Orchin had married a young girl from Troon, a young girl who was now a young army widow, even though her husband had never seen combat.

On a training exercise under the leadership of Captain Porteous, there was a mock raid on the cliffs near St. Ives in Cornwall. The exercise involved coming ashore using landing vehicles, unloading the craft, storing the craft, then climbing up the cliffs (up the chimney) known as The Brandys. The weather was dreadful, but this did not deter the commandos as 'war was not only waged on sunny days'. In the stormy seas, Lance Sergeant Chitty and Lance Corporal Hoodless were thrown out of the landing vehicle and the two men drowned at sea. The accident happened in 1943 … June 6th. The exercise was postponed for one day, and the commandos completed their training the next day.

The commandos had been trained to keep going if a man went down, even if there was a tragedy, however any loss was deeply felt. The rest of the commandos returned to Castle Commando and continued with their training. Deep in the Scottish Highlands, the castle was surrounded by inhospitable terrain well-suited for the tough endurance challenges that the green berets had to undergo. The commandos were becoming an unrivalled fighting force that was building a reputation for being fearless. Their involvement in the British Army's key campaigns, was critical in the success of the operations and the Allied victory.

The next operation that used No. 4 Commando unit's full force was also a success but unfortunately it was part of an overall mission that was a miserable failure. Lovat's first operation as the commanding officer was codenamed Cauldron and was part of Operation Jubilee, the raid on the German-occupied port of Dieppe. The raid on Dieppe was designed to capture and hold the French territory for a short period of time. It was a preparatory exercise for the eventual D-Day. The objective was to test the feasibility of a landing invasion and to learn from the German defense strategy. While they were there, the Allies were to also destroy coastal defenses, ports and strategic locations. Brigadier Laycock came to personally discuss Dieppe with Lovat, who, at the time, was participating in field firing exercises with the commandos at the Dundonald Castle ruins in Ayrshire. As Laycock described the objectives, Lovat became excited about a plan that could help in the overall success of the raid, but also show the full abilities of the green berets. Lovat was able to subsequently ensure that the commandos would land before daybreak and the commandos could plan and fight independently, with no outside interference.

Success would boost overall morale and show Britain's commitment to establishing a front in Europe. However, the troops landed and were trapped by the defense obstacles designed to stop motorized advancement on the beach. The Canadian troops had never seen action before, and their tanks had problems negotiating the stone beaches. The German firepower also caught the Allies off guard as they far outweighed the Allied forces. Over 4,000 men died in the raid, most of whom were Canadians, and the Nazi propaganda machine stacked the failure at Dieppe on top of the 1940 retreat at Dunkirk and the fall of France, to purport the military superiority of the Third Reich. Instead of being boosted, Allied morale became deflated.

Amid the death and destruction on the beaches of Dieppe, the No. 4 Commando unit was charged with attacking and destroying the Varengeville battery, a battery of six 150mm guns set on concrete emplacements and aimed to protect the beach. If the guns were not taken out, even more lives would have been lost during the landing attempt. Lovat's deft battle plan was masterful, and it exploited most of the skills that the commandos had been rehearsing in their training. The basis for the plan was a 'fire and movement' attack, again much like the infamous Highlander's technique.

Under cover of night, the commandos crossed to Dieppe onboard the *HMS Prins Albert*. By design, the size of the squad was limited to 255 men, which included a few French commandos, 50 United States Army Rangers, three Canadian signallers, medics and intelligence specialists. The commandos were divided into two groups. Group one was the 'fire' team under the command of Colonel Mills-Roberts and was the first to go ashore just before daybreak on August 19, 1942. Group two was the 'movement' team, which Lovat would command himself.

To identify themselves, everyone received the password 'monkey' and the response 'nuts'. Group one headed out in a flotilla of landing vehicles at 3:40 a.m. The combat engineers in group one used two Bangalore torpedoes[19] to blow a hole in the barbed wire fence protecting cliffs from a shore approach. To maintain a stealth advantage, the detonation of the torpedo was timed to explode as a handful of RAF bombers passed overhead.

Group one then used their newly acquired mountaineering skills to scale the cliffs. They were in position 30 minutes faster than planned. First objective accomplished. The commandos immediately opened fire on the German battery with sniper rifles, machineguns and mortars. One of the mortars landed in the German ammunition stores and exploded the battery.

"There was an explosion – louder and longer than anything we had heard that morning. It made us crouch immediately. It seemed to be the mother of all explosions," reported A.B. Austen, a war correspondent who landed with the commandos.

Group one had successfully put the German battery out of commission and started firing at the main German defense positions.

Meanwhile, group two landed on the beach further west and were faced with an onslaught of machinegun fire from two German pillboxes that were defending the area. The commandos took their first casualties as men were shot getting off the landing craft. Once ashore, a small section stayed to shoot at the pillbox, while Lovat and the rest of the group ran just under two miles to approach the rear of the assault.

---

[19] A Bangalore torpedo is an explosive charge that is placed in a series of tubes and is used to blow a hole in wire when a direct approach could not be used

They ambushed a surprised German patrol and took out an anti-aircraft tower. On the way, they stumbled across a machinegun post moving through orchards and into the town. They came under fire a few times as they raced to position. Cutting through Dieppe, some of lead commandos were killed by enemy fire. As the sun came over the horizon, acting Lieutenant Colonel Lovat fired a flare to commence the attack on the battery. Group one ceased fire and group two charged the main battery with fixed bayonets.

Close contact combat always takes its toll. If the enemy doesn't immediately surrender, then they are faced with the 'kill or be killed' response. Major Porteous took a bullet in his hand rendering his right arm useless. He had to act quick to fire back at his opponent, killing the man with a left-handed shot. Porteous then ran against open fire to take charge of his troops and he was the first to reach the battery guns. He took a second bullet in his thigh, but the troops managed to defeat the Germans. Once the battery was overrun, demolition experts rigged explosives and took out the battery.

No. 4 Commando unit's mission in Dieppe was successfully executed, with most men returning home safely. Even though he lost enough blood to pass out, Porteous made it home. When the combat was finished, a squadron of Messerschmitt swept in low overhead, fortunately, since there was no fighting, they mistook the Commandos for Germans and continued on their way.

"In the Dieppe raid, his plan for the capture of the Varengeville battery was masterly. And proved brilliantly successful. Yet he had to fight the orthodox planning from above tenaciously to get his way. His was the choice of the landing beaches. And the successful scaling of the formidable cliffs and the fierce bloody attack and hand-to-hand fighting to take the battery were a model of what a commando raid from the sea could be. Every gun was silenced. And although the main attack on the harbour was a disaster, it could have been much worse if the guns had not been so successfully silenced," said Captain Harper-Gow.

While considered a very successful mission, it should be noted that 70 men were killed or missing in action, others were wounded, and several were taken prisoner. Lance Corporal Joe Pasquale and his brother Private Domenic Pasquale, were part of the Royal Army Medical Corps, assigned as medics to No. 4 Commando unit. The brothers fearlessly ran back and forth to patch up the wounded and get them back to the landing craft.

A group of commandos had ambushed some surprised Germans, but in the combat Sergeant Major Williams and a few others were badly injured. While Joe was carrying Williams back to the boat, Domenic stayed with the other wounded. When another Nazi patrol approached, Domenic had to decide if he was going to scurry back to the boat or stay with the injured. Unselfishly, Domenic Pasquale remained with the wounded and was captured by the German infantry.

The mission was completed just as the orders came in for everyone to withdraw. Lovat knew that some of the men had been killed in the fighting. He told the commandos that Scots never leave their dead behind and ordered them to gather their fallen comrades. Since bringing the fallen men down the cliff would be too dangerous, Lovat had gasoline poured over them and burned the bodies before following the orders to retreat.

Major General Laycock relayed a message from King George VI, praising the Commando units' performance. This was almost never done. There was considerable praise for the success of the commando operation, but there was also a growing awareness about how unique Lovat was as a soldier, a leader and a trainer. He had trained and rehearsed his commandos for the Dieppe raid and had successfully used that operation as a rehearsal for D-Day.

"His coolness seemed to be imperturbable … there he was in corduroy slacks with his rifle, stripped down to the essentials … he clearly had the air of absolute confidence," said Corporal Lilley.

It was noted by the British Army that acting Lieutenant Colonel Lovat did not simply plan the raid, he directed its success by being on the ground and participated in the raid. Major Porteous received a Victoria Cross and Lovat was awarded the Distinguished Service Order. On seeing the accolades, Adolf Hitler put a £30,000 reward for The Lord Lovat's death or capture.

Later that year, the German High Command would issue 'The Commando Order' requiring that all captured commandos were to be killed immediately, without trial. Any commandos that were discovered by other means were to be immediately handed over to the Sicherheitsdienst (the Intelligence Service of the SS), which would also result in death. The order was that any commando taken in for interrogation, should not 'survive for more than twenty-four hours'.

The Messerschmitt accident that delayed the advancement of the Nazi war machine, had also compelled Germany's mandatory use of the Enigma encryption machine. A British commando unit used Highland raiding tactics to obtain the tools to crack the encryption code, a key component in planning D-Day. That same commando unit had rehearsed their D-Day tactics at Dieppe and would march ashore to the skirl of the bagpipes at Normandy on June 6, 1944.

3.   Bodyguard, Titanic & Glimmer

Oh, the far Coolins are puttin' love on me.
As step I wi' my cromack to the Isles.[20]

By November 1943, Hitler was very concerned about the possibility of an invasion on France's northern coast. Despite war on the Eastern front with Russia and battles in Africa and Italy, he dedicated resources to be used in France. The Führer assigned Field Marshal Rommel to be in charge of the defense operations. Without knowing the exact location for the invasion, Rommel started building the 'Atlantic Wall', a fortification of shore obstacles, bunkers, landmines, artillery and troops that would stretch across 2,400 miles. The plan was to defend every part of the coast and to have mobile reinforcements quickly deploy to the actual invasion location. The task of cracking the wall was daunting.

Lovat described the Atlantic Wall:

> *The immediate defenses were laid out with German thoroughness: they were not ... a continuous row of gross butts, but rather a system of ingeniously interlocked defense works equipped with every weapon, from underwater*

---

[20] Road to the Isles – McLeod

> *obstacles and devices to set the sea on fire, to wire and minefields at the water's edge, ranging back through strongpoints laced with machineguns and anti-tank guns, to distant artillery and self-propelled half-track cannon – all bearing on the beach. Beyond lay German infantry dug into weapon pits – again with interlocking fields of fire. The tanks and armour were held some distance to the rear. It was a question of how long they would stay there!*

The Commando unit continued to refine its training. Lovat introduced a new mandatory, cross-country run on Friday afternoons. At the end of the run, the troops could collect their pay. If a commando was too slow on the run, the pay office would be closed, and the soldier would have to wait until Saturday to collect his pay. As a member of the demonstration troop, Millin was constantly on the move, so he stayed fit. When he wasn't demonstrating, he was playing the bagpipes, a real workout for the lungs. Fortunately, at least Millin didn't have to do the run on payday.

Field trips were organized to various locations to rehearse for both sea landings and land fighting. On one field trip, Commando unit No. 4 went to Woolston (the neighbourhood where the Spitfire had been developed). This area of Southampton had been bombed severely during the Battle of Britain. Walking through streets with bombed houses surrounding them, as live fire came down upon them, the commandos were training for the march through French villages, although they had not been informed of the plans for D-Day. As the commandos trained in the destroyed neighbourhoods where many civilians had died, the silver lining was that Germany had provided the ideal training ground for the liberation of France.

Operation Bodyguard was the codename for the mendacity aimed at deceiving the German defenses and it consisted of several parallel operations. The main objective was to convince the Germans that they had valid information about an invasion, and they would hopefully adjust their defenses accordingly. To mislead the German high command, the key elements of an invasion, including the date, time and location, were all leaked. The German troops stationed on the occupied coast were likely to remain in place. However, the ruse was designed to delay the deployment of German reinforcements from arriving at the real landing areas.

The most logical place to invade France was at Pas-de-Calais. This is the narrowest point between Britain and France, and also the shortest route to launch a march to Berlin. Plans were drawn up for an invasion at that location and the information was disseminated such that it would fall into the hands of known German spies. Another set of plans had Norway as the entry point and this was also leaked to Germany. With the decryption of the Enigma machine, the Allied forces were now able to monitor German communications and ensure that their deception had been successful.

With two sets of invasion plans, Germany would have to decide which one was real. The deception continued with the movement of fake equipment and more false information distributed to spies. To back it up all up, intelligence was also dispersed through misleading radio transmissions and double agents.

Juan Pujol García was an anti-fascist Spaniard who offered his assistance to the Allies as a spy. They turned him down, so instead he decided to spy for the Axis, in order to gain their trust. From his home in Spain, he pretended to be in Great Britain, gathering information. The intelligence he passed on was details he picked up from train schedules, travel brochures and magazine advertisements. He soon gained the trust of the Nazis who believed that he was an asset living in England. He approached the Allies again, now offering his connections to the German intelligence gathering operations. The Allies gave García a test by supplying him with information to relay to the Nazis. The British forces were impressed when García's contacts resulted in the Germans trying to hunt down a non-existent sea convoy. García and his family were quickly moved to England so he could pass on the particulars of the Bodyguard invasion. A lot of detailed information about the planned assault that would never happen, was passed over to the German side.

The Allies now needed to have a reasonable amount of military activity to convince the Nazis that the García information was valid. If the Germans believed the intelligence in terms of size, methods and organization, then they would also believe the location and timing. For the Allies to really convince the Nazis that their espionage had returned valid information, there would need to be military manoeuvres to support the pretend invasion. Phantom armies were created for both the fake Norway invasion and the fake Pas-de-Calais invasion. Because Rommel was a fan of U.S. General Patton, the phantom army for the French invasion was put under the command of Patton. The First United States Army Group (FUSAG) was created with only a few administrative positions and it was stationed across the Channel from Pas-de-Calais. The fictitious army had to be real enough that when the Germans received word of the invasion in Normandy, they would believe that this was the ploy that Britain was using to distract their army from 'the real invasion' at Pas-de-Calais.

The more the Germans believed that the FUSAG existed, the longer they would believe that Normandy was a diversionary attack, and the longer they would delay sending reinforcements. Full sized bases were established for the non-existent forces. Orders were transmitted, manoeuvres were set up and supplies scheduled to be shipped. The administrative effort to support the skeleton army was as much as a full-forced army.

Once the camp was set up and securely fenced off, the people from the town were organized to trample across fields on a daily basis. The fabricated invasion would also require fabricated air and naval support. Fake aircraft, inflatable tanks and 255 landing craft were built out of canvas and wood. The landing craft were moved around so they looked like they were being used for exercises and were left in different positions.

A nonexistent army would not be complete without a nonexistent source of fuel. Technicians from Shepperton Film Studios built a fake oil storage depot. To add to its authenticity, King George VI visited the facility. The newspapers unwittingly supported the hoax with coverage as they published the King's visit and his approval of the operations. The approval was sincere, as he was actually very impressed by the efforts behind the creation of a non-existent army.

Tracking the Luftwaffe, the British anti-aircraft guns were instructed not to shoot down the German air reconnaissance mission that flew over Dover. Both the British and the Germans were pleased that the mission to take photographs of the south coast of England was a success. When the reconnaissance planes returned on another mission, they would take more pictures, this time revealing that the soldiers' tracks in the grass fields had changed and the equipment had shifted. The Germans were convinced that they knew exactly were the invasion force was stationed.

Field Marshall Montgomery headed to Scotland to plan the real invasion. In order to send a signal that the invasion was not imminent, a soldier and ex-actor, Meyrick Clifton-James, was hired to impersonate Monty. He headed to Gibraltar, then Algiers, then ended up in a hotel in Cairo. The German High Command was convinced that Montgomery would not be in North Africa if the invasion was planned for France. The risk in being a double for the leader of the British Army is that you might get assassinated and you don't have the same level of security as the real general. The real Montgomery insisted that Clifton-James received the same protection and a full general's pay while he wore the uniform.

Operation Titanic was a series of fictitious operations that were aimed at convincing the Germans that the Allied invasion had started and that the tactics depended on deep infiltration inland. The night before the actual invasion, the Royal Air Force and the Special Air Service would fly to various locations (not Normandy) and drop 500 dummy parachutists. The objective was to have the Germans shift their defenses inland and to confirm that the invasion had begun in Pas-de-Calais. Just to add confusion, dummies were also dropped in Norway.

Operation Glimmer was a series of fictitious naval fleet movements. Thanks again to the cracking of the Enigma codes, the Allies had concluded that they could fool the resolution of the German radar, by using aluminum foil chaff to have the Nazis believe there was a fleet approaching. On the eve of the real invasion, a false fleet of smaller boats trolling chaff would be launched toward Pas-de-Calais.

Since Hitler expected an invasion and the creation of a western front, it was the location and the date that was secret, not the event. The south of England got ready. Camps to hold incoming troops were set up all along the southern coast. Hospital beds were emptied. Firemen were moved to the south. Tanks, jeeps and truck loads of troops were spilling over onto town streets. Employers had to lengthen lunch breaks as it was considerably harder to cross the road just to eat. The jeeps and tanks also reeked havoc in small village roads as they knocked down fence posts and street signs.

In addition to deception, the successful launch of the Normandy Invasion depended on intelligence, planning, preparation and training. The British Army was reorganized to support this plan. The commando units were assembled under one command to form the 1st Special Service Brigade. Lovat was appointed Brigadier and the commander of the newly formed Brigade.

"Gentlemen, your flashes that you have on which are silk-screened, will not be worn anymore," Lord Lovat announced to his troops. "You will be wearing embroidered flashes. Also, you will not dubbin your boots, you will polish your boots. And you will receive new suits. You are now in the first SS brigade."

Although they didn't realize it, the next series of training exercises for the commandos was aimed at preparing for Operation Overlord, the Normandy Invasion. The harsh training began in June of 1943 without revealing any specifics of the plan to the troops. For No. 4 Commando units, that training included mountain warfare training at the Commando Snow and Mountain Warfare Training Centre in the Scottish Highlands. The live ammunition training was so severe that several more commandos died during the exercises. The commandos learned to fight and survive in the mountains and then they were relocated to Sussex for the next phase in their training.

In England's south coast, the commando unit was split up and they concentrated heavily on their landing exercises. When they reunited, they worked together on large scale landings, using both day and night drills. Then then worked on more live fire exercises, where they had to avoid being shot as they landed en masse. In February 1944, some of No. 4 were sent to qualify as parachutists. Two months later, the 1st Special Service Brigade had an influx of new trainees. No. 4 Commando unit grew in force dramatically with the addition of two French troops. This was followed by the arrival of equipment and artillery, including new Lee-Enfield rifles and Vickers K machineguns. The commandos went back to the range to learn how to use the new ordnance, then back to the landing exercises to practice carrying the new equipment ashore. The commandos were taken to bombed areas of London to practice street fighting, then back to north-west Scotland to stalk more deer, then back to the seaside for more landing training.

As the heavy rains of April lashed down, Millin practiced carrying his Lee-Enfield through the cold waters of the English Channel from a landing craft to the rocky shores. Soldiers and civilians alike, all knew that an invasion was in the works, but the date and the location were carefully guarded.

All across the south of England, British, Canadian and American troops were arriving. Training exercises were planned, using the southern coast of England as a reflection of the beaches in France to the south. There was considerable security to the beach landing rehearsals, but most of the troops couldn't divulge anything because they hadn't been told anything. One such training exercise wasn't uncovered until the 1970s. Ken Small was walking on the beaches near Slapton Sands, in south Devon, when he found some U.S. unspent ammunition. On another day, he found U.S. money from the 1940s, then a U.S. flag from the war, then personal effects from U.S. service men. He began to research the individuals involved and after a run-in with the British and American authorities, he uncovered Exercise Tiger which took place on April 28, 1944. What Small discovered was 946 U.S. troops were killed in a training drill and the survivors were sworn to secrecy to protect the D-Day veil of mystery.

What had transpired was a series of tragic events that resulted in both deaths by friendly fire and deaths by enemy attack. The U.S. Navy was supposed to provide 'the sounds and smell' of a naval bombardment and instead, due to a communication error, launched a bombing assault that landed on the rehearsal troops. In addition, a German U-boat was not defended against by the British Navy. It slipped through to find the unprotected landing vehicles, so it fired torpedoes and hit four landing vehicles.

As a result of the disaster, radio frequencies were standardized, better life vest training was enacted and plans for 'how to pick up floating survivors' were developed. Ken Small bought the rights for a tank that had been submerged off the coast. In 1984, he raised the tank and brought it ashore as a monument to the forgotten soldiers.

On May 26th, the commandos were relocated to the Marshalling Area in Southampton. Before heading down south, Millin was able to make a quick trip home to visit his parents in Glasgow. When he left them, they assumed that he was on his way back to Fort George, and he didn't correct them. Many of the troops arriving in the south of England, arrived by train. The windows of the carriages had been blacked-out, both so the troops didn't know exactly where they were headed and so no one else would know that the commandos were on the move. Millin arrived at the camp in Woolsten to find it secured, covered under canvas and surrounded by barbed wire. The camp had been sealed off such that the soldiers were restricted from contact with the rest of the world. The people living in the south of England were also clamped down as mail was stopped and travel was restricted. For the few marches that allowed the men out of the camp, the soldiers would be accompanied by the military police who limited any contact with civilians. The piper managed to sneak in a visit to his sister Olive who was living in the area. Then the briefings began for Operation Overlord and access to the camp was completely shutdown. The American guards were ordered to shoot anyone coming or going to the camp.

"It was like being in the nick," commented Private Ives of No. 4 Commando unit. Ives would be shot in Normandy the next day, then returned to England where he passed away on June 8, 1944.

"The weather was quite unpleasant, which was just as well as we were under canvas," said Private Bidmead of No. 4 Commando unit.

There was no more training. The troops were as prepared as they were going to be.

"It was pretty grim," explained Lord Lovat, "… your preparations are complete and you're in the hands of the Navy after that. We had a pretty good team with us, as a flotilla of landing craft. We practiced for over a year with them. That is essential, I think, to know your sailor if you are a combined operations man."

The men were informed that the invasion was scheduled but they were not informed where they were going to land. They were given small pieces of paper with the layout of a section of beach, with exit roads, houses and known artillery. In addition to the maps, they viewed air reconnaissance and even holiday photographs of beachfront. The men in Capitaine Kieffer's French commando unit were able to recognize the beaches and immediately knew they were headed to the beaches near Ouistreham (Oyster village). One of the French commandos had worked on the lock gates at the Caen canal, one of the targets of the mission.

"I'm going to invade my own country on D-Day," joked the Frenchman Corporal Gautier. Before the war, he lived in Ouistreham about 400 yards from the beach. He was one of the men that immediately recognized the landing site.

The small maps that were distributed to the men had no names of the towns. When Brigadier Lovat learned that the French commandos knew the names of the objectives, he met with Kieffer to stress that his men were not to release the information to the British troops. Kieffer confined his men to their barracks until it was time to board. The Allies had been feeding information to German spies, so they were quite aware that the spies existed. If the information reached Germany on the timing of the invasion, this would coincide with Operations

Titanic and Glimmer. However, if the departure point was discovered, it might be clear that the destination was not Pas-de-Calais. Even as the troops were boarding their landing craft, they had not been informed of their final destination or the nature of their mission.

With D-Day impending, Brigadier Lovat came to the commando camp on June 4th. He gave a speech to all the soldiers of the 1st Special Services Brigade. Most of his speech was in English with a touch of Scottish brogue, then a sentence in French at the conclusion.

"I wish you all the best of luck in what lies ahead," Lovat started. "This will be the greatest military venture of all time, and the Commando brigade has an important role to play ... A hundred years from now your children's children will say 'They must have been giants in those days'."

Lovat saved the last line for the benefit of Kieffer's countrymen, the French commandos.

"Messieurs les François, demain les Boches on les aura!"[21] Lovat concluded.

General Eisenhower had originally selected Monday, May 8th as the invasion date and this was communicated to Stalin. However, there would not be enough landing craft ready on time and in order to arrive with the right tides, the date had to be pushed out. Thus, Monday, June 5, 1944 was selected to be D-Day.

"General Marcks, who was the corps commander, at that time, and he knew the British very well," recounted German Major von Luck, "and he said the day before, as far as I know the British, they will go to church on Sunday and land ... on Monday."

This time however, poor weather conditions would push the date out. Meteorologist Captain Stagg predicted that a weather front would produce strong winds, thick low-lying clouds and constant rain, which would preclude both airborne and amphibious operations. It was the worst weather conditions for June in more than 20 years. Ships would be okay to cross the Channel in rough waters, but the flat-bottomed landing craft would not fare as well.

"There seemed on our weather charts to be nothing but a series of great depressions, with almost winter-like intensity," Stagg recalled.

---

[21] French gentleman, tomorrow we will have the Krauts

The allies had studied tides, beach landing suitability, in-country support, distances from bases, reach of the aircraft, naval accessibility, foreign port abilities, reconnaissance intelligence and German defenses. However, after all the detailed planning, the invasion launch was now dependent on the predictions from a weatherman.

Eisenhower, Field Marshal Montgomery and the Allied commanders were literally sitting listening to a weather report to decide when they would call for the invasion. That day, the Germans weren't the enemy, the weather and the tides were. Standing in the Map room of Southwick House in Scotland, Stagg, a lanky 43-year old Scottish meteorologist, nervously delivered his prediction that the storm should lessen in time for an invasion 24 hours later. This was better than his pessimistic prediction from the day before, so D-Day was reset. The invasion would be on June 6th. What Stagg didn't take account for in his weather prediction was the strong cross-current that would push many landing craft 200-yards further east than the plan called for.

With a slightly better atmospheric outlook, Operation Overlord was moved 24 hours later. The day would still be bleak, which would reduce the German anticipation of an attack, but Stagg's longer-range forecast looked better for the march inland. Moving the invasion by one day provided some serendipitous opportunities. June 5th was Rommel's wife Lucie's 50th birthday. Although the Allies didn't know it, the creator of the Atlantic Wall left his headquarters in Paris that day and flew home to Herrlingen in south-west Germany. He gave his wife a pair of grey suede shoes that one of his aides purchased in Paris, however he had chosen the wrong size. It would be 24 hours before Rommel understood that the shoes were not his biggest mistake that day. He was also going to ask Hitler for five extra Panzer divisions to be brought to the Normandy coast but delayed asking through communications and scheduled an in-person meeting instead.

"You are about to embark upon the Great Crusade, toward which we have striven these many months. The eyes of the world are upon you," Eisenhower addressed the troops.

The American troops related to Lieutenant General Patton's candid, guileless speech. His words to his men, before the launch of the D-Day offensive, was one of his most blunt, yet powerfully motivating speeches. The men of the 3rd Army sat and listened in complete silence:

I don't want to get any messages saying, 'I am holding my position'. We are not holding a goddamned thing. Let the Germans do that. We are advancing constantly, and we are not interested in holding onto anything, except the enemy's balls. We are going to twist his balls and kick the living shit out of him all of the time. Our basic plan of operation is to advance and to keep on advancing regardless of whether we have to go over, under, or through the enemy. We are going to go through him like crap through a goose...

There is one great thing that you men will all be able to say after this war is over and you are home once again. You may be thankful that 20 years from now when you are sitting by the fireplace with your grandson on your knee and he asks you what you did in the great World War II, you won't have to cough, shift him to the other knee and say, 'Well, your Granddaddy shovelled shit in Louisiana'. No, sir, you can look him straight in the eye and say, 'Son, your Granddaddy rode with the Great 3rd Army and a son-of-a-goddamned bitch named Georgie Patton!'

An abbreviated and less profane version of the speech would appear in the movie *Patton* in 1970. The soldiers of 3rd Army were ready for battle.

The success of the invasion would rest with the first troops to land on the beaches and would have to perilously try to push inland. The commandos had been given that honour. Field Marshal Montgomery visited the commandos and addressed them standing on top of his jeep. Montgomery had never lost a battle against Rommel. It was a Montgomery that successfully led William the Conqueror's troops nine centuries earlier. The Field Marshal stressed the importance of the mission and the role that his 'Corps D'Elite' would play.

The magnitude of the endeavor and the sheer numbers for the invasion are staggering. On June 5, 1944, Lovat and Millin were two of the 9,000 Scottish soldiers that arrived in Normandy, and the newly formed 1st Special Service Brigade was part of 160,000 initial troops that landed on the beaches. This was the largest seaborne force that had ever been readied for battle. The landing forces would be supported by 11,000 aircraft. The organizational effort to transport the troops to their appropriate locations was a monumental set of planning that relied on 5,000 ships and landing craft to transport men, machines and supplies. Each brigade had different objectives that had to be coordinated across various divisions. Brigadier Lovat had his orders and he knew how he was going to deliver.

Piper Millin was eating in the mess tent when the announcement came over the speaker 'All personnel to report to your unit immediately.'

Lovat's success and his rapid rise as a leader, meant that the piper had been playing for a man of greater and greater stature. In training, Millin had been selected as the personal piper for a Captain who became a Major. Then, he was the piper for a Lieutenant Colonel who became a commanding officer. Finally, Millin became a Brigadier's personal piper, all the while remaining a Private.

Lovat's troops were transported to just outside of Southampton by the Hamble River and they waited to embark. Looking out to the river, the outlet bay was filled with various sized ships, most of which were landing craft and transporters. Flat front-loading doors had their ramps lowered and armoured vehicles were being loaded. With the magnitude of the invasion, the loading order was part of the organized chaos.

On the payday before the invasion, each man had been given 200 French francs, a tin of Taverner and Rutledge quality boiled sweets and two condoms. The condoms were used to protect rifle barrels from the sand and seawater, or to keep watches and other valuables waterproofed during the landing.

Before embarking, the commandos were asked to splice their identity discs to hang them around their necks, to make out their wills and to list the name of the person that should be 'warned in case of disappearance'. The plan at the Allied Headquarter was to be prepared for a loss of 50 percent of the troops and even more for those brave enough to land early. Under one scenario, as many as 10,000 men could be lost on the first day alone. As Millin filled out his contact information, he reflected on his decision not to tell his family that he was going to be deployed abroad. This would be the first time that he had been on a seafaring boat since his family had sailed home from Canada to Scotland.

With such a large force boarding, it might be assumed that the locals knew that the invasion was imminent. However, boarding at port towns and landing on small British islands, was being rehearsed every other day. To the townsfolk, there was nothing unusual regarding the troop activities on June 5th. However, this time the embarkment was taking place in every town across the southern coast of England. Even some of the soldiers hadn't caught on that this was not a drill. As some of the infantry were boarding the landing craft, they discussed where they were heading.

"We're in a bloody hurry today, aren't we?' Where are we going this time – Hayling Island?" one of the crew says to Sergeant Bellows on an landing craft sailing from Southampton.

"No, France," replies Bellows.

"Don't mess about, mate. Where are we going?" the crew member asks again.

"France!" Bellows responds again, this time pulling out the French Francs that they had been given.

It was time to board. Millin was also readying himself for the fight. He told Brigadier Lovat that he was prepared to arm himself, but Lovat said no. He asked Millin to only bring his pipes with him to the boarding.

"A Scotsman is going the lead the invasion and a Scots piper is going the lead those two million men into Hitler's Europe," Lovat said describing his role and how Millin would help.

"There was no way in hell that he, Lord Lovat, the twenty-fourth chieftain of Clan Fraser, was going to wade ashore without the whining skirl of bagpipes. They were essential to men's morale, as impactful as any weapon Millin might otherwise carry," described Alex Kershaw.

Millin came to the boarding call, dressed in the traditional uniform of a piper, including his father's 100-year old kilt with the Cameron of Erracht tartan, which was worn in Flanders fields during World War I. At Lovat's request, Millin played to the troops who were waiting to board the landing craft. Everyone now had the sense that this was bigger than they had imagined. The troops were heading to the world's largest military assault. They waited to board and the thought of what lay ahead, became stressful. Lovat knew that the pipes would help to take the troops' minds off the impending battle and the inevitable bloodshed.

The order to go ahead reached the officers. Lovat had his piper play to signal it was time to board.

"No return ticket please," joked one of the French commandos as he boarded his landing craft to head home.

Almost 2,000 commandos would land on the beaches of Normandy on the first morning. Commander Curtis was in charge of Convoy S9, a flotilla of 24 LCIs, including Brigadier Lovat's LCI 519, which Curtis captained. He was hand-picked to pilot Brigadier Lovat's 105-foot landing craft and he would lead the commando boats out to sea. Millin piped and the commandos boarded their landing craft, showing their boarding ticket as they got on the boat. When he was finished, Millin put his pipes back in the box and Lovat came over to him.

"You better get them out of the box again because once we set sail by nine thirty or nine o'clock, you can play us out of the Solent. We will be in line astern. You will be in the leading craft with me," Brigadier Lovat told his piper.

Millin boarded the small craft along with 21 other commandos and he squeezed into the small troop space below deck. Lovat hadn't given Millin any more specific instructions for the trip. He realized that his piper would know exactly what to do on the crossing. Millin also knew that when they arrived in Normandy, he would have to pipe the men ashore to the beaches of France. The commandos headed down the Hamble in convoy S9, to the Solent and out to the English Channel.

Millin came back to the deck with his pipes and played *The Road to the Isles* several times. He stood in the bowsprit. Curtis had one of the sailors open the microphone in front of Millin and the pipes were soon blaring over the loudhailer. The sound of the pipes, which were loud enough on their own, bellowed through the boat's speaker system and carried across the water for miles. The piper started playing *Skye Boat Song*, a slow, powerful lament. Just off the Isle of Wight (codenamed 'Piccadilly Circus'), thousand of transports with tens of thousands of soldiers gathered for the invasion and they heard the pipes telling stories to lead the men into battle. Someone watching from a battleship tossed their hat in the air. Soon thousands threw their hats in the air and started cheering. Millin could hear the cheering above the sounds of the sea, the ships and the blare from his pipes.

"We embarked in a grotesque gala atmosphere more like a regatta than a page of history, with gay music from the ship's loudhailers and a more-than-usual quota of jocular farewells bandied between friends … At 21.00 we set out to war with Lord Lovat's piper playing in the bows.

It was exhilarating, glorious and heartbreaking when the crews and troops began to cheer, and the cheers came faintly across the water gradually taken up by ship after ship. I never loved England so truly as at that moment," remembered Captain Smith of the No. 4 Commando unit.

"As we was going down the Solent, you've never seen a sight like it …" recounted Private Treacher. "We was going through all these ships, there was ships everywhere, loaded with guns, loaded with tanks, loaded with lorries and troops and things like that, but our little craft sailed out of Warsash, and as we was going out of Warsash our piper, Bill Millin, was piping us out onboard of another boat. And you should hear the pipes, oh the pipes as sounding beautiful like, and everyone was cheering like, you know."

"It was a great moment, because I had a piper playing in the bows," Lovat remembered, "… and pipes sound well across the water. And the big ships that were waiting to come out after us, all the soldiers were on deck and cheered us to the echoes as we passed down between about seven miles of shipping."

"As we pulled out, with Bill Millin playing his silly bagpipes, all the boats started tooting their hooters … whoo, whoo, whoo … and all the men on the decks were cheering. It reminded us of footballers playing for England against Germany, coming out of the tunnel onto the pitch, where all the crowd all cheered as they came out. It was just like that … we were all standing on the deck, and I'd seen some very tough lads there, the tears were running down their face due to the emotion that was being stirred up," said commando Private Cadman.

"It was an amazing, amazing sight" described Corporal Nield-Siddall. "Everywhere you looked, there were ships of all shapes and sizes and the sky always seemed to be full of OUR planes, with the black and white stripes on them ... and it was a lovely feeling, because they were all OURS. Everything was OURS."

A large Scott class Admiral type flotilla destroyer, launched in 1919, approached Millin's landing craft and the troops lined up on one side, cheered loudly, then the destroyer swerved away again. The Scott class destroyers were all named after famous figures in Scottish history. This one, was the HMS Montrose. Brigadier Lovat look round, smiled and waved. The Lovat family had been linked historically with the Montrose line (the Marquess of Montrose had fought with the 10th Lord Lovat in support of Charles I, for which he was sentenced to death).

The men on the boats were flush with confidence. Crossing the Channel, they had no apprehension about their task ahead. The commandos were excited to be finally heading off to fight, but at the same time, they were ignorant to the thought of their mortality. Adrenaline was snapping in their systems and they were finally going to put all that training to use. Each man could picture the man beside him getting shot and possibly killed, but when they considered enemy fire coming their way, they pictured themselves getting wounded at worst.

Back in England, instead of hearing the noise of an invading Luftwaffe squadron, the skies were echoing with the sound of the RAF bombers. The sound of outward-bound aircraft was a welcome change, but after an hour of constant noise keeping people awake, the south coast began to conclude that something big was happening. There was an increase in excitement and pride as people opened their bedroom windows and stared up at the skies. Perhaps this was it. There would be some confusion in the morning when people opened their newspapers only to find the headline was still on the fall of Rome. Since the Allies didn't announce the invasion, the civilians were left to ponder what the commotion was on the night before.

Starting out to the Channel, the troops on the landing craft could hear the comforting rumble of the RAF passing overhead. The planes were setting off on a mixture of bombing missions, six glider landings and flights that would deliver paratroopers to Normandy. Many of the bombers would miss their targets, the six gliders would all crash land and most of the paratroopers would land in the wrong locations. That night, 23,400 American and British paratroopers were dropped all-across Normandy. The drops were far from successful and many of the paratroopers' missions would not be completed.

To drop the paratroopers, the planes needed to slow down to 100 miles per hour. The Nazi anti-aircraft guns started firing into the skies when they heard the planes and some of the aircraft were getting hit. Some pilots had never delivered paratroops before and many had never encountered anti-aircraft fire. This resulted in planes flying too low or too fast for successful drops. Many pilots hit the green light to signal the jump, at the wrong location. Jumping at too high of a speed, meant that equipment would be torn away from the paratroopers' kit. Many paratroopers were being scattered, behind the lines, with limited weapons and miles away from their rendezvous points.

Paratrooper Lance Corporal Stan Eckert, and his closest friend, Private George White, of the 9th (Eastern and Home Counties) Parachute Battalion, landed somewhere in Normandy on June 6th. The platoon was never able to locate the two men, so both were reported missing on D-Day. In June 1944, Robert and May Eckert, received a telegram notification that their son Stan was missing in action. The telegram still gave them some hope. In August, they received another telegram informing them that their other son Cyril, also a paratrooper, had been killed in action. Cyril had been wounded in Pont l'Evéque and had eventually succumbed to his injuries. Later that month, a commando found Stan and George's bodies. Stan's parents received a third telegram, this time confirming that he had been killed in action as well. Cyril was 20 years old and Stan was 19.

The 9th (Eastern and Home Counties) Parachute Battalion had a dog as a mascot, ironically a German Shepherd. 'Glen' was a well-trained explosives sniffer dog, able to track people and could carry messages. He was also a trained paradog who was fitted with his own parachute and to participate in parachuting exercises. On June 6th, 1944, Glen jumped along side his 19-year old keeper Private Corteil.

Unfortunately, both Glen and Corteil were killed by friendly fire after they landed.

The paratroopers were asked to write letters to home. Private Verrier wrote:

June 6, 1944.

Dear Mum & Dad,

Well folks at last I can write a few lines after a very long morning. As you can guess I'm off, on the long awaited "Second Front". HMM! It's a real do. No Billy Beano.

Tell that Dad of mine, I can tell him something soon. HA! HA! He hasn't said much about what happened to him, but I will soon, very soon, realize what did happen to him. I can remember his motto last time, "What is to be will be!", and I guess that it will be my motto. From father to son, through the ages!

Now then Mum, if you don't worry, I won't be worrying, so keep your chin up, and get the house ready for another "big nuisance". I may be home again soon, when this war is over.

All this business is very fascinating, marvellous organisations, etc!

There's only one thing I wish, that is to have Dad on one side and Uncle Jack on the other side of me, to tell me when I go wrong. Still I have plenty of confidence, so all should go well.

Remember me to all relations folks, I love 'em all. So, folks being another quick letter I must now close!

Wishing you tons of good luck and the very best of health, and boy oh boy will I be pleased when we get those B____ on the run.

Bye for Now,
Your Loving Son, Sid

Private Verrier survived the jump, survived D-Day and survived the war. He would make it home to see his family again.

"My chute developed normally, and as my body swung into the vertical, I looked around … To my front, but some distance away numbers of red and orange balls were shooting up into the sky. This display I reasoned was the ack-ack defence of Caen. I stared at them

---

far too long, because when I finally looked down, much to my horror it seemed I was destined to land in one of the orchards bordering the eastern side of the DZ ... I prepared myself for a tree landing. I had never made such a landing, but I remembered what to do; head down on the chest, arms crossed in front of it, and knees raised to protect my marriage prospects," said Lieutenant Dean.

"Down I came, crashing through branches and foliage, without so much as a scratch or bruise, but when I stopped falling and opened my eyes, I was completely surrounded by greenery. I felt around for a branch to get my feet on, but found none, So I turned the quick release on the parachute harness, gave it a bang, the straps flew apart, and my Sten which was broken into three parts, and threaded under them, fell to the ground. I slid out of the harness, keeping a tight grip on it, lowered myself to the end of the leg straps, and I hadn't reached the ground and was still enclosed in the foliage. I let go of the webbing harness and dropped all of twelve inches to the soil of Normandy," mused Dean.

Private Johns, a paratrooper with the 13th (Lancashire) Parachute Battalion, landed in Normandy on June 6th. Only 60 percent of his battalion were able to reach the rendezvous point. Despite the shortage of men, they headed out to complete their mission. In one swift battle, they liberated and secured the village of Ranville. Johns fought in several other battles over the next six weeks, until he was shot on July 23, 1944. He eventually died of his wounds. When the Army informed William and Daisy Johns of Portsmouth, that their son had been killed in action, there were upset, surprised and confused. They were not aware that their son was part of the invasion. They thought he was assisting in the Home Guard. Private Johns had lied about his age and signed up for the army when he was only 14-years old.

Sainte-Mère-Église would be the first village liberated by the U.S. Army. The plan was for the paratroopers to land in waves to the west of the town, rendezvous, then commence an attack on the Germans in the village. However, paratroopers were delivered right in the centre of the town and the German soldiers stationed there, started firing into the night. Paratroopers were being shot out of the sky. Private Steele was injured, and he dropped right in the middle of the town's main square, on the side where the main Catholic church sits. His chute got caught in one of the towers of the Notre-Dame-de-l'Assomption church, leaving him an easy target for the Germans that were now on patrol in the town.

Wounded and bleeding, Steele played possum, hanging limp from the twelfth century church pinnacle. Believing he was already dead; the Germans did not shoot him. However, after two hours they went to cut down his body, only to find that he was alive. Steele was taken prisoner of war, but fortunately four days later he managed to escape, rejoined his division and continued to fight.

"We were fired at by small arms fire ..." recalled Lieutenant Colonel Otway. "There were incendiary bullets coming up at me and actually going through my chute, which was disturbing, in fact I was bloody angry about it...! It had never occurred to me that my chute might catch on fire while I was in it, but I thought of it then going down - but it didn't. We were widely dispersed due to all this small arms fire coming up, and due to various factors, we were scattered."

"A lot of men missed the dropping zone, including me, and that is why I had so few," continued Otway. "Plus the fact that Rommel had ordered all the flat area there to be flooded. We waded through, at times, chest high water to get there and we saw a lot of our men drowned, there was nothing we could do about it. They had all their equipment and they also had a heavy kit bag, which should have been released and in some cases wasn't, but anyway the result of this was, we couldn't get them out of the water, they couldn't get out."

Corporal Wilson was Lieutenant Colonel Otway's batman. Wilson jumped at 1 a.m. and landed very close to a small French farmhouse. The house was occupied by German soldiers. Wilson crashed through the glass ceiling of a jardin d'hiver causing a tremendous shattering noise. The Germans came to the window and started to fire. Wilson, short on munitions, picked up a brick and threw it through one of the farmhouse windows. The Germans hit the ground assuming that the

brick was a grenade. When they stood back up, Wilson had
disappeared into the darkness.

Wilson made it to the rendezvous only to find 50 out of 750 made it
there by the 1:30 arrival time. Even Lieutenant Otway wasn't there yet.

The night before the invasion, the 6th Airborne Division would
arrive inland, in a daring glider-based and paratrooper assault, to seize
bridges and neutralize artillery. The Merville battery was built to
protect the beach where the commandos planned to land. Immobilizing
this battery was key to the success of the beach landing and could mean
life or death for thousands of men approaching in landing craft. The
battery was believed to have four 150mm guns contained in bomb-
proof bunkers. For defenses, the battery sat surrounded by two
minefields and 15-foot entanglement of barbed-wire. British
Intelligence had concluded that there were 200 men guarding the
battery, with cannons and machineguns. Before the 6th Airborne
jumped, 100 RAF Lancasters would bomb the battery, then gliders
would deliver jeeps and flame-throwers, then the paratroopers would
arrive to hold the position at the battery. The plan even called for two
paratroopers to be fluent in German to call out misleading commands.

The man behind the plan was Lieutenant Colonel Otway. Before
leaving, Otway explained the plan to the 750 men that were rehearsing
for the mission. He then arranged for 30 members of the Women's
Auxiliary Air Force to dress in civilian clothes and visit the pubs next
to where the paratroopers were training. Their assignment was 'to woo
the men' and try to get information on the Merville battery attack. To
Otway's pleasant surprise, none of the men gave up the information.

Before the paratroopers arrived, the RAF Lancasters dropped 382
bombs on the Merville battery. Every bomb missed the target. The
paratroopers' attack on the battery had already been considered one of
the riskiest missions but would now be even more challenging and
dangerous. Then the gliders with the heavy equipment were either shot
down or landed miles away from the battery. The paratroopers
themselves were spread all over the area, most without a lot of
firepower. Otway jumped and was pleased to see the countryside
looked just like his scale model but was taken aback by bullets that
screeched passed him.

Otway had to avoid marshes and Germans on his landing, but he made his way to the rendezvous point as fast as he could and even he was late. The paratroopers used a bird call signal or snapped clickers for identification. 750 paratroopers had made the jump but only 150 men turned up to the rendezvous. Not enough men or equipment arrived to mount the attack on two hundred well-protected, heavily armed German soldiers.

Among the paratroopers that didn't make it to the rendezvous, were the engineers that were supposed to blow up the battery. There were also no medical staff there. Otway had two radio men, neither of which made it to the pre-set location, so there were no working radio sets. Corporal Wilson, Otway's batman, was a 200-pound boxer and he was one of the few men that had made it to the rendezvous on time.

"What the hell am I going to do?" asked Otway.

"Only one thing to do, sir," Wilson answered. "No need to ask me."

"Yes, I know," Otway said as he chuckled. "Get the officers and NCOs. We'll move in five minutes."

Wilson's confidence had given Otway the answer. He quickly reconstituted a new plan and four assault groups were created. The troops headed towards the battery. On the way, they found where the RAF had bombed, as they were forced to crawl in and out of bomb holes that were up to ten feet deep. Once they arrived at the battery, they were immediately fired on by German machineguns. After a bloody battle, the small contingent of paratroopers were able to take the battery in three hours of close-up combat. Most of the 200 Germans troops were killed, but 23 were taken prisoner. Of the 150-paratrooper force, 75 of Otway's men were dead or wounded. If the battery had not been removed from action on time for the invasion, thousands more men could have died on the beaches. Otway had successfully saved some lives of Lovat's landing force, now he had to wait for Lovat's commandos to land, fight their way inland and provide relief. Once the battery had been captured, the plan was to radio the Royal Navy, otherwise they planned to bombard the battery at 6 a.m. Without a radio, Otway launched flares which were spotted by the *HMS Arethusa*, and Otway was relieved to see the battleship send up flares in return.

In Normandy, Guillaume Mercader, listened to the BBC, just like he did every night. 'It is hot in the Suez. It is hot in the Suez'. Meaningless, just like the last three months. Then the announcer said 'The dice are on the table. The dice are on the table'. That was it. D-

Day was tomorrow. The BBC had been sending out messages every day, and while most were meaningless, this one was meant for Mercader, the French Resistance chief near the Normandy beaches. He would now record the anti-aircraft guns' positions and rush the information to the Resistance headquarters in Caen. Within the hour, he had observed guns without writing anything down and was cycling on his way to Caen. Once the task was completed, he went down to the seaside and anxiously watched the horizon to see if his beach had been selected for the invasion.

As LCI 519 rounded Piccadilly Circus, the sea began to become choppy, so Millin put his pipes back in the box. The troops were now headed across the English Channel to Normandy. Once the flotilla left British waters, the men were given the name of the town they were headed to. Millin had never heard of Ouistreham before.

For the French commandos onboard LCI 528, the landing at the Normandy beaches took on greater meaning. For Corporal Chauvet, the name of the town made the mission seem 'even more real'. He had heard a rumour that they were actually going to Africa, so this was a relief. Sergeant de Montlaur was happy that the German stronghold was the casino in Ouistreham. De Montlaur had lost a few fortunes at that casino and would be happy to throw a couple of grenades at the building. The French commandos were headed through the wet, cold night to 'liberate' their homeland.

"The wind howled, and it rained in vicious scuds. The skipper had said in his talk, 'The Allied High Command must be heavily counting on surprise, for the Germans must surely think that not even Englishmen could be fools enough to start an invasion on a night like this'," thought Captain Patterson, an RAMC medical officer and one of the many fighting Scots in the No. 4 Commando unit.

"Going across the Channel, of course, the enormity of everything began to become apparent," said Private Spearman, "because no matter which way you looked, you found ships of all shapes and sizes. Warships and Merchant ships like we were on, in every direction as far as the eye could see. On an ordinary raid, you just wouldn't see this sort of thing. You'd be chugging along knowing, there was nothing else chugging except yourselves, but here everything was chugging."

A mix of sea spray and lashing rain made the boat ride even more unpleasant. While the mission had been called off the day before because of weather, they had set sail on a night that was only moderately better. An officer onboard LCI 519 pulled out a bottle of gin and passed it around. Soon, the men battened down the hatches and headed downstairs, and the boat suddenly became very small. Lovat remained aboveboard with the sailors for awhile, then he joined the men below. One of the commandos found a book in a sailor's bunk. Fuelled by the gin, the men were laughing as they read the paperback, *Dr. Marie Stopes' Marital Advice Bureau for Young Couples*. On deck, Curtis could hear Lovat's men laughing. He found the juxtaposition of their mirth and their mission, to be a sign of great confidence.

"There was no doubt in their mind about the outcome," Curtis recalled.

Some of the men played cards and others read to take their mind off the journey. One young soldier was reading a western book with a picture of a cowboy on the front. Millin, who was only 21-years old, thought the lad looked perfectly in place reading cowboy books, but too young to be heading out to war. Soon, it seemed like everyone was smoking and the cramped quarters, together with the choppiness of the Channel waters, started to make some men sick. Millin was one of them. The flat-bottomed landing craft were known to heave, pitch and roll with each wave. One landing vehicle pilot described the boat as like 'driving a bulldozer in the water'.

An announcement came over the loudhailer asking men to have something to eat. Their kits contained tins of self-heating soup with a fuse down the middle. The fuse would be lit with a match and the can would start to cook the soup. With its lights off, the boat steered in circles several times on the voyage across the Channel. The men began to relax as they took off their boots, loosened their battledress and tried to sleep. Eventually, Millin was able to sleep, even if it was fitfully.

Brigadier Lovat remained awake, contemplating the importance of tomorrow's mission. The entire eastern flank of the Normandy Invasion rested on an overnight glider raid to capture two bridges. Lovat's men were tasked with linking up with the glider force to provide relief. In just under five hours, the commandos would have to land, fight their way ashore, then march eight miles inland fully burdened. Failure to provide timely relief could mean a breach in the eastern flank, which could result in the death of thousands of soldiers and possibly another Dieppe.

4.   **Firsts**

From this day to the ending of the World,
... we in it shall be remembered
... we band of brothers.[22]

The *first* action of the Normandy Invasion does not take place on the beaches. The fighting on French soil begins when six gliders crash land behind enemy lines shortly after midnight. For weeks prior to the landings, glider pilots and paratroopers gathered in RAF Tarrant Rushton in Dorset to train for the secret mission. A few days before D-Day, the mission details are revealed to the airman. The mission, Operation Tonga[23], is to 'take control of areas north of Caen and east of Sword beach, protecting the eastern flank of the landing zone on D-Day'.

Major Howard's orders are brief: '*Seize two bridges. Under cover by night, take by surprise and capture intact by your raiders. At night, without benefit of ground support, you will assault the garrison overwhelm it and hold until relieved*'.

Hold until relieved, that will be the real challenge.

---

[22] Henry V – William Shakespeare
[23] Part of Operation Deadstick

Major Howard is confident that his men will be able to seize control of the bridges but holding the position will be a challenge. His lightly armed men will be little match for the nearby German Panzer division. Howard is a demanding but inspirational leader, and a shrewd tactician. His men are tasked with taking control of two bridges in German occupied France. The first bridge, coming in from the west with access to the beach, is the Bénouville bridge which spans over the Caen Canal. Two hundred-yards further east is the Ranville bridge[24], which crosses the Orne River. This is to be the eastern flank of the invasion. Control of the bridges will stop the German Panzers from reaching the invasion troops at the beaches. Holding the bridges will also open-up a supply line from the beach, to assist in the battle to take Caen and the rest of France. The fall of Caen, the capital of Normandy, is the optimistic *first* day objective of the British Army.

The plan to take the two bridges requires a small stealth fighting force. If the attack involved paratroopers, it would leave men open to enemy fire, and require a rendezvous after the landing, before launching an attack. This option would give the Germans enough time prepare to for combat and maybe blow up the bridges. Rather than parachute in, Howard's men will use gliders. The benefit of the gliders is the silent approach, but they are only one-way vehicles and there are no fields long enough for a proper landing near the targets. Just to add complexity, the men are also to perform the stealth operation without the benefit of light, landing in the middle of the night.

"The idea of landing at night by a glider had never been contemplated before," recalls Lieutenant Smith, "but one of the advantages we had was the operation would be a surprise, that we had the best sky pilots available and that they could land us exactly where we wanted to … and of course, our ignorance of the hazards of the whole operation."

The planners of the operation have no delusion that the mission will be free of casualties. Nor do they rely on the men being able to take and hold the bridges. The planners include contingencies and refer to Howard's mission as 'the forlorn hope'. The primary concern of the operation is to ensure that the soldiers stop the Germans from blowing the bridges up on D-Day. If the bridges are destroyed, the armoury from the beach landings will have to march over ten miles inland to

---

[24] The construction of the bridge is attributed to the young engineer Gustave Eiffel.

Caen, before they find a bridge strong enough to support a Sherman or Churchill tank.

Even on paper the plan looks faulty. The western flank of the entire Normandy invasion rested in a scheme to crash six planes with less than 200 men, who will then have to take a German Division by surprise and then hold off counterattacks for the following thirteen hours. The success or failure of this operation could gravely affect the success or failure of the entire invasion. It is a risky strategy, which will require intense preparation if it is to have any chance of succeeding.

The training for the mission runs all through May, using the strongest six flyers that the Glider Pilot Regiment can provide. These men are infantry that have been trained for the mission, not men assigned from the Air Force that are also pilots outside of the war. With so few men, the glider pilots are expected to land the aircraft and then take part in the fighting. They are soldiers that have volunteered for glider training. The volunteers are first trained by the Air Force, then they move to the Army Air Corps to be trained on light gliders. Finally, they work their way up to Hamilcar or Horsa gliders, capable of carrying thirty men. Owing to the war shortage of steel, Airspeed Limited designed the Horsa glider to be largely constructed out of wood, with most parts manufactured by furniture companies. The wooden Horsa manufacturing process was the aviation antithesis of the sleek sophistication of the German Messerschmitt production line.

Preparing for the mission, the glider pilots practice landing on fields during the day, then at night, then with blacked-out goggles to simulate landing in poor weather conditions at night. The gliders are pulled down the runway by bombers ('tugs'), which take them to a predetermined height and location, then release the gliders. To time direction changes, the glider pilots use stopwatches, not their instrument panel. During the day, the gliders are released above a yellow cross painted onto a field next to the aerodrome. The pilots circle the field to get their bearings and then attempt to land on the spot.

Howard's main planner is Second Lieutenant Tillett. During one training exercise, Tillett takes off from Harwell in a glider being pulled out to sea by a bomber tug. The glider is loaded with men and equipment to test a fully weighted flight, but the impact of this additional payload has not been fully factored into the drill. Before the tug can turn around to return for a practice landing, the tow rope snaps.

The glider is several miles out to sea, so the pilot immediately turns back towards the coast. The aircraft didn't make it back to land and shatters as it hits the bitter waters of the Channel near Bournemouth.

Inside the sinking glider, Tillett is being squashed up against the bulkhead by a jeep. Stuck there with water pouring in, he looks behind the jeep. It is pulling a trailer full of live ammunition. The glider shifts as it starts to sink. Tillett watches as another passenger onboard drowns. He knows he needs to do something at that moment. In great pain, he pushes with all his might and manages to work himself free. He escapes through a gap in the glider walls and spots a motorcycle tire. Grabbing on to the tire, Tillett is able to stay afloat in the cold Channel waters until he is rescued. In the hospital, he discovers that the pain he was feeling when the jeep pressed him into the fuselage, was caused by a broken a neck bone. Tillett, who is planning most of the mission, is relying on gliders to transport Howard's troops and he realizes that there is so much more work to be done.

During another training exercise, a Whitley bomber is towing a glider when it has an engine failure. The glider is released a few hundred feet above the ground, nowhere near the landing target. Lance Corporal Gregory is in the glider as it heads towards a nearby village and crashes into a church. He receives a severe leg injury but has no self-pity for his injuries when he learns that five other people were killed in the accident, including both pilots. Gregory is with the field ambulance unit, so he feels like a celebrity when a jeep shows up to pick him up as he walks out of the hospital. The feeling doesn't last long as the jeep drives him straight to the airfield. Howard's next assignment for Gregory is to immediately go back up in a glider to 'face his fears'.

Once the daytime landings are mastered, the pilots learn how to land at night. The same spot is marked this time with paraffin candles and the gliders are released again. At night, without the use of visual aids, the planes are unable to land close to their target. In one exercise, Pilot Barkway lands a half mile away from the target and crashes down into a country lane. He then gets out and walks to a phone box to call in for a ride. On that particular landing, in order to avoid a crash with another plane, the glider had been released too soon. The bomber pilots are very aware of the risks that the long tow ropes pose.

With the kinks supposedly all worked out, the next challenge is to land at night with multiple gliders. For three days and nights, they move the training to the Countess Wear River and Canal swing bridges, near Exeter. Here, they have two bridges over two parallel bodies of water, similar to what they will be looking at in France. The pilots can rehearse multi-plane landings, using the stretches of water as the marker, first during the day and then at night.

"You will be towed at one-minute intervals to 4,000 feet, which will take about one hour," says Colonel Chatterton, the Pilot Glider Regiment Commander, in the pilot briefing. "You will then release three miles away at a point decided by your tug, from where you will be able to see these triangles. Numbers 1, 2 and 3 will land in this one, making a right-hand circuit, and 4, 5 and 6 on t'other from a left-hand circuit. Now hop off for lunch. All gliders are ready and assembled on the towpath. Take off 1300 hours."

Since three gliders are to land on each side of the main bridge, the gliders were numbered 1, 2 and 3; and 4, 5 and 6. If a pilot arrives at the landing field to discover the glider in front of them isn't there, then the instruction is to swap positions. Pilot Barkway is flying glider 2. As he lands, neither he nor his co-pilot Staff Sergeant Boyle, can see glider 1. They assume they are the first to land, so they head for the number 1 landing position. As they speed across the field in a near perfect landing, suddenly, through the dark, they see the tail of glider 1, which has already landed. Barkway and Boyle come to a crashing stop as they shatter through the rear of glider 1 and the plywood structure of the two planes rips apart.

Across the bridge, glider 4 lands smoothly. Glider 5, lands close to 4 but doesn't hit it. However, glider 6 crashes right in the centre of gliders 4 and 5, demolishing all three planes. Glider 3 lands on the wrong field, and it is the only glider that isn't smashed up. No one is injured, but once again, there is clearly more work to be done. Modifications are made to the gliders with improvements specifically for the operation. Perspex is added below the pilot so he can try to get a better fix on the land at night. The position of the pilot and co-pilot is swapped as the landing in France will require two right turns. The pilots also realize that they need more time to adjust their plane, so they increase the release height for the practice runs. As the gliders rehearse from a higher altitude, it becomes clear that a more powerful tug is also required. They start using Halifax bombers and climb to 6,000 feet before being released. The pilots run a total of 43 practice landings and walk away from dozens of crash landings.

The infantry that will board the gliders are Major Howard's D Company of the 2nd Battalion Oxfordshire and Buckinghamshire Light Infantry, known generally as the Ox and Bucks. For this operation they are referred to as 'The Coup de Main' Force. Howard's men are very well regarded within the British Army, and thus it is no surprise that they have been selected for this mission. While getting ready for the mission, one trainer watches men hurl themselves onto barbed wire so that other men could cross using their bodies as stepping-stones.

The trainer shakes his head and says, "I pity the bloody Germans; these buggers are mad!"

Once the Ox and Bucks are in camp, under canvas and surrounded by barbed wire, the details of the plan are explained to them. The plan sounds insane, but the men have confidence in Major Howard as he explains that the pilots are all trained and ready. The Ox and Bucks are now assigned to a Horsa for the night of the combat. From that point forward, there is no further contact with the outside world and armed guards parade around the perimeter of the camp. There is no going in or out, so every waking hour is spent on the minutest detail of the operation.

Before the battle for the Normandy beaches can begin, the battle for the bridges will need to be won. Before the battle for the bridges can begin, the near impossible landings will have to be completed. Second Lieutenant Tillett is given access to the wealth of air reconnaissance. In a daring daytime reconnaissance mission, some brave pilot flies past the German anti-aircraft guns and came close to landing in the fields beside the bridges, all the time filming the approach. The glider pilots get a really good understanding of what they are in for, particularly as they see how short the landing fields are, so a parachute is added to the rear of the glider to assist in the braking effort.

"We could see really every detail," explained Tillett. "We could see the design of the trenches, cut into the banks of the canal. We could see a pillbox on the end of the canal. We could see other German positions all around the bridges. Therefore, the detail that people were briefed on for this operation, was intense."

Before taking off, the team knows the name of the mayor, the name of the innkeeper, the location of every house, the location of every bush, the location of gun placements and the disposition of every slit trench.

"They had a marquis inside the camp," explains Private Allan (Horsa 95), "and laid out in there was a perfect model of the two bridges, with all the trees, and everything else there. And we were allowed to go up there as many times as we wanted and study this layout."

Corporal Parr (Horsa 91) and Private Edwards (Horsa 91) study the German model, paying particular attention to the defenses. The canal bridge is the heaviest guarded with a static anti-tank gun in a concrete pit on the east side and trenches radiating out. It was clear that if there was an attack on the bridges, the Germans expected that it would come from the east.

"Even if a pane of glass in one of the windows had been broken," explains Private Edwards, "we were assured that it would be shown!"

Major Howard (Horsa 91) will aim to land three gliders on one side of the canal and his second in command, Captain Priday (Horsa 94), will land three more gliders on the other side. They practice their assault conducting a dozen mock raids replicating the two bridge objectives. The whole force is quarantined in base at Tarrant Rushton, while the rest of the Normandy invasion force is sealed off in various locations across southern England. Howard waits as a dispatch rider comes by each day with a brown envelope, marked OHMS[25] on the outside, and containing a one-word message inside. All words are meaningless until June 4th, when the messenger delivers 'Cromwell'.

The men are in the mess hall when Major Howard enters and tells the men to 'black up!'. They proceed to return to barracks and grease their faces with cork. They then gather their equipment and await transport. No trucks come to pick the men up and they soon learn that weather conditions forced Eisenhower to call off the mission. The men return to the mess hall and watch a film appropriately called *Stormy Weather*. It is a movie about a negro soldier returning home at the end of WWI.

The outlook is only marginally better the next day, so Howard is not expecting the mission to be on. The rider comes by again and Howard is surprised as he reads 'Cromwell' for the second day in a row.

"The morning of the 5th was much brighter and we were informed that it was 'on' for that night," remembers Private Clark (Horsa 92). "The company had a day of rest. Sleep, however, was out of the question, we were all too keyed up."

---

[25] On His Majesty's Service

Around noon, the men are in the mess hall again when Major Howard arrives for the second day in a row to tell them to 'black up'. Major Howard also wants to talk to the troops about the payload. No 'live load' training has been carried out because as someone said, 'It's far too dangerous for the live load'. New equipment has been added along with a second Medic, so the Horsas will be slightly overweight. Howard has decided that he would rather drop a man than drop equipment. He asks for a volunteer to stay back.

"How about Wally Parr?" shouts out Private Clark (Horsa 92) half-joking.

Corporal Parr (Horsa 91) is always causing trouble, but he is very reliable in battle. Clark suggested his name because Parr is a friend and he is married.

"No bloody way! Not me Nobby, I'm going," replies Parr.

No one offers to back out of the mission, so Howard decides that they will go with the extra load. He asks the troops to make sure their wills are up to date and to write a letter to their loved ones, which will be mailed once D-Day is underway.

"You can now write to your wives, sweethearts, whatever and tell them, 'By the time you receive this card, I'll be in France'," Howard tells his men.

That night, the men don their equipment, gather their weapons and are trucked to Tarrant Rushton where six gliders sit ready to take flight.

"The airfield itself was absolutely teaming with people," recalled Private Clark (Horsa 92), "and everyone seemed to know where we were going, and this did concern me. There were cries of 'Good luck' all the way across and 'Godspeed'. I was absolutely convinced everyone in the aerodrome knew where we were going or certainly that the invasion was on. And this did concern me, considerably."

For over an hour, the men sit by the planes chatting or wondering around the other gliders. A jeep pulls up. It's the 'Padre', Captain Nimmo. He steps out onto the grass and sticks a small cross into the ground.

"We don't need a church, boys," Nimmo says, "come in and pray."

Nimmo leads the men in a prayer, wishes them well and then he is off again to visit another unit. The Ox and Bucks are sitting on the grass again, waiting. Finally, the pilots arrive.

"All right you chaps, don't you worry," calls out one of the pilots. "We'll get you there!"

Private Clark nervously approaches his pilot and asks him quietly "Ollie, do you think we'll make it all right?"

"You've got no worries; I can land on a six-pence" Staff Sergeant Boland (Horsa 92) answers.

An RAF officer comes around and gives the men a large iron pot of tea. When the men taste it, they are happily surprised to find that it has a good measure of rum in it. Shortly after that, the order comes to 'emplane'. Everyone gets up and enters the gliders.

"Good luck boys, see you on the other side," Major Howard says to the men as they board their gliders.

The Ox and Bucks can hear the emotion in Howard's voice. Gone was the usually stern tone that barked out orders from between his distinctly British teeth. While his words are encouraging, his face betrayed his concerns. Howard watches as his men board. The boarding process on the Horsa is unlike any passenger plane. A ladder is dropped straight down from the fuselage door and the men climb up the ladder carrying their full equipment to crawl into the Horsa.

"David had a school-boyish figure with puppy-fat on, you know," Private Clark (Horsa 92) recollected, speaking about Lieutenant Young (Horsa 92). "He was well overloaded, and as I say, he also had this large canvas bucket of grenades. God knows what would have happened if we had been shot up. We probably would have been blown up straight away."

As Private Parr boards Horsa 91, he takes a piece of chalk and names the plane by writing 'Lady Irene' on the side. Once onboard, the Ox and Bucks close the door and take a seat on the plywood bench inside the glider. They sit waiting for the sound of the tug.

At 10:45 p.m., the night before D-Day, outside Southwick House in Scotland, Captain Stagg is looking to the sky. The clouds are breaking up and he lets out a sigh of relief. His weather prediction is right.

At Tarrant Rushton, the bombers start their engines and the coup de main begins when the *first* glider feels the strain on the 125-foot tow rope and is pulled in the skies above England. With the full weight of the payload in the glider, the takeoff takes a lot longer than expected and the plane is almost at the end of the runway before it becomes airborne. The D-Day invasion is now underway.

"We were setting off on an adventure as the spearhead of the most colossal army ever assembled in the history of mankind virtually. I found it very difficult to believe it was true because I felt so insignificant ," explained Pilot Boland (Horsa 92) .

The first glider to take off is piloted by Sergeant Wallwork (Horsa 91) and his co-pilot Ainsworth (Horsa 91), both of the army's Glider Pilot Regiment, assigned to the 6th Airborne Division. For Ainsworth, this would be his third time crash landing behind enemy lines, having already done so in Italy and Holland. The 30-man wooden Horsa glider (often referred to as a 'flying coffin'), is towed across the Channel by Handley Page Halifax bombers. Five other Horsas follow Wallwork's Horsa 91, making up the mission total of 181 men (136 infantry, 30 engineers, 1 doctor, 2 medics and 12 pilots) flying over the Channel. Some equipment is moved off of Horsa 96 and the extra medic is on that plane.

The pilots and the troopers feel the additional weight. Despite all the practice runs with heavy load, there is still additional ballast on the flight. The glider is loaded with extra equipment for the battle and contingencies, such as Bangalore torpedoes and ten-man blow-up rafts (in case the bridges are blown up and the troops need to cross the river). The gliders proceed hidden amongst a squadron of bombers headed for France. They fly above the tail of the bomber-tugs, to avoid turbulence.

During training, boarding the Horsa was a bit of an adventure, with the men joking and exchanging wisecracks. However, boarding for the mission, there's hardly a word spoken and the Ox and Bucks sense the gravity of what lies ahead. In Wallwork's glider is Major Howard. Howard, a tall curly-haired, fit soldier sporting a tightly trimmed moustache, is 31-years old and is considered regular army. He had spent six years as a non-commissioned officer before joining the Oxford City Police in 1938. One year later, he was recalled back to the army. In 1942, he heard that the Ox and Buck were going airborne and he immediately volunteered. The day he told his wife that he had signed up for airborne assault, she told him that she was pregnant. Joy Howard gave birth to their first child in late 1942 and then to their second in May 1944. As the glider sails its way across the Channel, Howard's thoughts are a jumble of his personal life and his mission. Howard looks at his pilot and smiles. It was Wallwork that had given him confidence to start a mission with a crash landing. The air reconnaissance had returned photographs that looked like holes were being dug to plant anti-glider defense poles. Wallwork just laughed.

"Great," Wallwork had mused. "So, all we have to do is land in between the poles, which it will rip our wings off and slow us down, so we don't crash into the bridge. Perfect!"

Now Wallwork is flying Lady Irene to land on the same field where the German have been preparing their defenses. His cargo is Major Howard and some of the elite men of the Ox and Bucks. The men are bearing either standard Lee-Enfield rifles or Sten guns, along with heavier ordinance, bandoliers, field dressing and rations. Their kits weigh 80 pounds. They are silently sitting in the dark with their faces blackened with burned cork. Wallwork looks behind him and can only see sixty white eyes staring back at him. The flight time of one hour and 24 minutes is too long for the troops to be alone with their thoughts. The biggest question all the men have is 'Do the Germans know we are coming?'. Howard looks at the faces of the Ox and Bucks. 19-year old Private Edwards looks so scared that he might pass out.

"Personally, I was scared to death. I was literally sitting in my seat in the glider, and my teeth were chattering, my knees were knocking … I thought, 'this is my last time on earth, and I would probably die within the next hour or two'," recalls Edwards (Horsa 91).

Howard realizes that he needs to lighten the mood, partly to alleviate nerves and partly to avoid the building feeling of airsickness, something he is personally prone to. He leads the men in song and soon the atmosphere becomes lighter and the Horsa becomes filled with jokes, laughing and Player's cigarette smoke.

"The atmosphere in the glider was somewhat like a London tube train in the rush hour," remembers Private Clark (Horsa 92). "We were in good heart."

Being towed through moderately inclement air is more like rough sailing rather than flying. Flying in a glider is more susceptible to air pockets and the plane can suddenly dive down, or rise, without notice.

"Has the major laid his kit yet?" Corporal Parr calls out from the back of Horsa 91.

Parr is referring to Major Howard, who usually gets sick whenever they went up in a glider. On this trip, he didn't feel nauseous at all.

In Horsa 93, Lieutenant Smith leads the men in song, singing 'Immobile'. In Horsa 95, Corporal Howard leads the men in singing an old Jewish song:

"Abie, Abie, Abie my boy, vot are you vaiting for now?
You promised to marry me some day in June,
it's never too late and it's never too soon.
All the family keep on asking me vitch day, vot day,
I don't know vot to say,
Abie, Abie, Abie my boy, vot are you vaiting for now?'"

In Horsa 96, the mood is still more somber. The men sit in silence, smoking. The mission is even more daunting for the engineers of the 249th Field Company who have been assigned to the unit. They had practiced landing with parachutes, but this is their first time in a glider, and for some, their first time going into combat. Twin sappers, Cyril and Claude Larkin are sitting beside each other.

"For most of us this was our first time in action and there was almost no conversation in the blacked-out interior of the glider. No lights at all were permitted," Cyril Larkin recalled.

Suddenly, Sergeant Thornton (Horsa 96) starts to sing:

"Out on the plains down near Santa fe,
I met a cowboy ridin' the range one day,
And as he jogged along I heard him singing,
And as he jogged along I heard him singing,
A most peculiar cowboy song,
It was a ditty, he learned in the city"

When Thornton gets to the chorus, he has finally been able to change the mood on the Horsa. All the men know the song and join in:

"Comma ti yi yi yeah,
It Comma ti yippity yi yeah" [26]

As most of Britain goes to sleep, not knowing what June 6th would bring, the gliders cross the Channel to France.

"Do you realize that by the time you wake up in the morning, 20,000 men may be killed?" Winston Churchill says to his wife before they go to sleep that night. He will have a very restless sleep.

Despite all the planning, the mission design still requires a Channel crossing, pinpoint accurate glider piloting, an element of surprise, some

---

[26] Cow Cow Boogie - Benny Carter / Don Raye / Gene De Paul

strong close-range combat, very limited German counterattacks and a large share of good luck. The gliders leave Tarrant Rushton behind and they head for Worthy Down, then to Bognor Regis, then across the Channel to a point on the Normandy coast between Cabourg and Merville. In the darkness below the gliders are the flotillas of the seaborne invasion forces, including LCI 519 with Brigadier Lovat and Private Millin onboard. When the tugs arrive on the French coast with the rest of their squadron, the bombers turn slightly to the right.

"I think practically all of us, without exception, thought that we were on a suicide mission," said Private Edwards (Horsa 91). "What really frightened us was the 21st Panzer, which was a real battled-hardened group, within the area around Caen, six or seven miles from where we were landing. They told us they had about 350 tanks between them and we thought 'My God, they only need a half a dozen of those to come up the road and we're in trouble'."

Intelligence reports had come in just before the gliders' departure, indicating that the 12th SS Panzer Division and 21st Panzer Division (30,000 men and 300 tanks) are now in and around Caen. 180 men landing in gliders, with very little artillery, are going to be no match for the German forces.

The use of gliders is also a strong signal that this is a suicide mission. For Howard and his men, there is no return flight scheduled. They either succeed with the mission or they will die trying. The squad is equipped with the normal airborne ordnance. There are PIATs[27], two-inch mortars, Bren guns, phosphorus bombs and grenades. It is obvious to anyone reviewing this mission that the relief from the paratroopers, and subsequently the commandos, is essential if there is any hope of holding the bridge. This of course assumes that the glider force is able to take the bridge in the first place.

"Weather's good, the clouds are at 600 feet," calls out tug pilot Winged Commander Duder, "and we all wish you the best of luck."

At the Bénouville bridge, the German troops are just changing shifts. Private Roemer, a thin-faced, 18-year old boy with floppy blond hair, has just reported for duty. He salutes Private Bonck, a 22-year old conscript from Poland. It is midnight, and Roemer is now on sentry duty on the bridge, while Bonck is headed over to the bar in

---

[27] Projector, Infantry, Anti Tank Mk I – a British portable anti-tank weapon

Bénouville. Roemer is one of two sentries assigned to guard the bridge.

When they arrive above Cabourg, the tugs radio 'Cast off', signalling they have reached their destination. The songs and joking end immediately. There is the now familiar twang as the gliders detach, followed by a jerk on the tow rope, and then total silence.

"Having been towed across the Channel by a Halifax bomber," recalls Pilot Howard (Horsa 96), "we had to cast off at 6,000 feet and then make a silent approach to land in a specific field, in a specific part of a specific field, with absolutely no aids at all."

Winged Commander Duder is the tug-pilot pulling Horsa 91. He detaches his payload at the right time and four out of five of the other gliders follow. About a minute before Horsa 91 is released, Flying Officer Clapperton, tug-pilot for Horsa 94, releases his payload. He is too soon. The Horsas detach at 6,000 feet in this order: Horsa 94, Horsa 91, Horsa 92, Horsa 93, Horsa 95, then Horsa 96. None of the other glider pilots see Horsa 94 detach or descend.

The gliders start to drop, making very little noise for the outside world to discern as the roar of the tug bomber starts to fade. Full flaps are applied to slow the gliders down. Inside, the men hear the rush of air squeezing through the fabric covering the plywood frame. The men are all quiet and are aware that they have now passed the point of no return. Having no option but to descend, the pilots have to control the rate of descent in order to put the plane down in the right field. The flight down will take seven and a half minutes, five minutes on a course 212 degrees, then a turn starboard above Ranville. This flight path should bring the gliders on a course parallel with the canal.

"When I cast off, I couldn't trim the glider," recalls Pilot Howard (Horsa 96). "I was heavily overloaded and in fact, the load may have been wrong because the chaps just walked on and sat down. I immediately turned around and I called out to Lieutenant Fox 'send two men up from the back to the front, sir' and he did. Two men got up from the back to the front and it restored the trim. But otherwise, I was out of control initially."

The glider pilots need to avoid the belt of coastal anti-aircraft flak that the Germans are launching at what they believe are a squadron of bombers. After casting off, the bomber-tugs continue on to Caen and drop a light payload to complete the ruse that they are part of a rather ineffectual bombing mission. German radar might have been alerted if the bombers had reached Ouistreham and then turned around without dropping any bombs. The mission also relies on German radar not picking up the gliders which are constructed primarily of wood.

While still descending, the door is kicked open to assist in easy deployment after the landing. Speeding down to earth, the Ox and Bucks hear the rushing of wind across the plywood wings, so loud that it sounds as though they are going to tear off. In the darkness, fear enters the minds and faces of the men. It is challenging for the pilots to navigate as the lights below have been extinguished, thanks to the British bombing mission. The shifting clouds below are obscuring the waterways so all the piloting is performed following a predetermined script. Everything below is dark except the sight of Caen burning up the river a few miles. Some of the bombers have dropped their payload on the city and are now returning back to base.

The pilots use a stopwatch and a compass to gauge course changes and airspeed. They have not broken through the clouds yet and they are flying blind. Ainsworth (Horsa 91) counts down to three minutes and 42 seconds, then Wallwork steers right to catch the crosswind.

"I can't see the Bois de Bavent," Wallwork (Horsa 91) says, searching for the huge area of woodland.

"For God's sake, Jim, it is the biggest place in Normandy," Ainsworth retorts. "Pay attention."

"It's not there," Wallwork replied searching out to the darkness of the port side.

"Well, we are on course anyway," Ainsworth states. "Standby. Five, four, three, two, one, bingo. Right one turn to starboard onto course."

Strips of light from the moon shine through the clouds and highlight the silver waters of the river and the canal below. The pilots can now see the target.

"There it is," Co-pilot Boyle (Horsa 93) calls out to Pilot Barkway as he spots the bridges.

"It's alright now, Fred. I can see where we are," Pilot Howard (Horsa 96) said to Co-pilot Baack.

They were now at 1,200 feet and the waterways could be seen easily, as could the darker patches of orchards and woods. The pilots were all now looking at foreign soil. Staff Sergeant Howard thought that at this height, it looks exactly like the model that had been laid out by Lieutenant Tillett.

"I thought it all looked so exactly like the sand table that I had a strange feeling that I had been there before," Pilot Howard described flying over France with a strange feeling of déjà vu.

In each glider, the men are given the order to link arms to prevent being thrown around. There is a reason that the Horsas are nicknamed 'Hearses'.

"Link arms," calls Wallwork (Horsa 91).

"The drill when you come into land, is you link arms with the man either side of you … and you do a butcher's grip with your fingers, you lift your legs and you just pray to God that your number isn't up. And that's all you can do. You're entirely in the hands of those glider pilots," explained Howard (Horsa 91).

"Hold tight," calls out Wallwork, this time with a little more concern creeping into his voice.

Wallwork's Horsa glider, with a wingspan of 88 feet, hits the ground with a thump, still travelling at 90 miles per hour, rushing towards the metal bridge. At this point Wallwork is straining his eyes to stay focused through the bumpy landing. If there are any anti-glider poles or trees, crashing into them will kill the pilots and most of their passengers. The landing field is triangular-shaped, and the glider is speeding toward the most acute corner.

"Stream," Wallwork calls out hanging on to the yoke and trying to control the direction as the advancing plane careens across a bumpy field.

On instruction, the glider's parachute brake is deployed, a new procedure for this mission. This slows the glider down abruptly, but it also raises the tail, which pushes the nose down. The glider hurdles across the field, shooting up sparks as the lowered nose crashes through barbed wire fences. The wooden seats offer little comfort to the passengers. The glider loses its wheels and the metal skids on the bottom of the fuselage scrape along rocks and shoot up more sparks. At first Major Howard thinks that they might be on fire, but then the Horsa comes to a crashing halt as the nose of the glider buries into an embankment. The timber structured glider snaps apart and the wheels go flying forward. All at once, there is a deafening crack and a ripping sound, followed by complete silence.

The aircraft has landed 40-yards away from the bridge, resting up against the barbed wire that surrounds the area. The objective was to land close to the barbed-wire, and Wallwork had landed right on it. Better yet, there is a clump of trees in between the plane and the bridge, providing perfect cover. The glider could not have been placed in a more ideal spot to attack the bridge. There are no runway lights, or flares dropped, or lights shining from the glider. Everything has been performed by the moonlight shining through a break in the clouds. Wallwork is the *first* to land his craft in what Air Chief Marshal Leigh-Mallory referred to as 'the greatest feat of flying of the second world war'.

"When you land like that," explains Private Allen (Horsa 95), "you come down at such a speed and shock, that you're actually out of it for a few seconds, then you come to."

"Then some of the others began to stir," recalls Private Edwards (Horsa 91), "and the realization that we were not all dead came quickly as bodies began unstrapping themselves and moving around in the darkness of the glider's shattered interior."

The entire front of the glider is crunched and the men at the back are convinced there will be some deaths at the front. The hard landing has thrown Wallwork through the Perspex windscreen of his collapsed cockpit and on to the embankment. Wallwork is the *first* of the Allied invasion force to land in France. Wallwork, Howard and several of his men are concussed in the crash landing as the glider crushes together like a folding telescope. The time of the landing, 12:16 a.m., is captured as Howard's watch stops working. Howard's helmet comes down heavily on his head, leading him to momentarily think his eyes are injured.

"The dazed silence did not seem to last long because we all came to our senses together on realising that there was no firing. There was no firing! It seemed quite unbelievable..." recalls Major Howard.

Howard shakes off the effects of the landing and crawls through a jagged hole in the crumpled glider. There is moaning coming from outside the plane, from the pilot and co-pilot who have been thrown into barbed wire. There is no time to help them, the Germans might already be on their way. Lieutenant Brotheridge (Horsa 91) exits through a hole in the rear of the plane and comes around to the front.

"All right?" Brotheridge asks ready for action.

"Yes," replies Howard, still rattled as he looks around to see if the enemy is approaching.

Men come tumbling out of the plane. The door, which was opened during the landing, is completely gone. Men are crawling through the broken spaces of twisted material and plywood frame.

"Gun out," Brotheridge orders.

Private Gray jumps out of the plane and stumbles with the weight he is carrying. He has the Bren gun, so he sets it up and points it at the bridge.

"Come on boys this is it, come on," Howard calls out and heads for the climb up the side of the canal. He has shaken off the effects of the hard landing. Behind him he hears another Horsa scrape across the field heading towards him.

In two-minute intervals, two more gliders come crashing down.

"Christ, there's the bridge" calls out Pilot Boland (Horsa 92), as he attempts to control his descending aircraft.

Sparks are visible through the windows and Lieutenant Wood (Horsa 92) mistakes the result of metal skids on rock for enemy fire. The second glider crashes close to a pond and breaks in half. Wood is thrown out of the side of the glider where a newly formed exit appears. He is still clutching his canvas bucket filled with grenades. Boland (Horsa 92) is still in his pilot's chair as he turns around to see his passengers in both halves of the glider. The soldiers are in a daze but appear largely okay to him.

"The bridge is just in front of you. We're here. Piss off and do what you're paid to do," says Boland to the infantry.

Pilot Barkway (Horsa 93) crashes his glider across the field and hits a ridge of earth that hadn't shown up in any of the reconnaissance photographs. The glider takes off again, before it finally comes to a splintering stop in a pool of static water. The Horsa breaks in half. Pilot Barkway, Co-pilot Boyle and Lieutenant Smith are all thrown through the front of the glider. Smith is then run over by the glider as it comes to a jolting halt.

A Bren gunner, Lance Corporal Greenhalgh (Horsa 93), age 29, becomes the *first* of the Allied troops to die on D-Day. After the rough landing, Greenhalgh is ejected through the windshield of his glider into a nearby pond. He is unconscious as he is pulled under water by the weight of his kit. About half of the glider's infantry have been thrown out of the Horsa and scattered around the area. At the very least, the men are shocked and bruised.

Lieutenant Smith is groping around in the dark, covered in water and mud, and shock. He knows that his leg has been badly hurt when the glider ran over it, but he can still hobble. He looks for his Lee-Enfield bolt action rifle and finds somebody else's Sten gun instead. Smith hobbles out of the swamp to find eight of his men set and ready for battle.

"What are we waiting for sir?" says Lance Corporal Madge (Horsa 93).

Smith gives a quick nod and the men rapidly deploy. Part of the plane landed on top of a German trench and the sleep-drunk soldiers inside throw their hands in the air to surrender. One of the men from Horsa 93 arrives to march the soldiers out of the trench before the Germans can fully comprehend what is taking place. The *first* German prisoners are taken without a shot being fired.

The commandos from all three gliders, that landed beside the canal bridge, have now gathered themselves and are running to complete their objectives. In short order, they need to mark drop zones, clear demolition charges, clear slit trenches or pillboxes and launch the main assault to secure the bridges. Shaking off a severe concussion, Wallwork (Horsa 91) is still able to carry ammunition forward to Howard's men in preparation for the attack.

Despite the heavy landing by all three gliders, there is very little movement from the German infantry. The sentry at the Bénouville bridge, Private Roemer, has just started his shift. His posting at the bridge is his *first* assignment, the site of the *first* attack of the Normandy Invasion. Roemer barely knows how to hold his rifle. He sees the first glider crash into the field but with all the anti-aircraft fire, he thinks that a bomber has been shot down.

Corporal Parr (Horsa 91) and Corporal Gardner (Horsa 91) run across the road to where two dugouts lie, exactly where Lieutenant Tillett's model indicated. Parr opens the door, pulls the pin, throws in a grenade[28], then shuts the door. There is a tremendous blast and the heat rushes past Parr and Gardner. Parr then opens the door and Gardner sprays inside with his machinegun. The German resistance doesn't begin until

---

[28] A Mills Bomb No. 36

that *first* grenade signals the start of the conflict. The area around the bridge is now echoing with the sounds of grenades and gun fire.

"Come out and fight you square-headed bastards," Parr screams as he fights to get saliva back into his throat, then repeats his actions on the second dugout.

Howard's men are now rushing to the canal bridge. There is a large contingent of Germans stationed at the bridge, but the Ox and Buck have caught the Germans off guard. The German sentry, Private Roemer, is looking across the bridge when he sees a squad of painted black faces racing towards the bridge. He fires a flare into the sky and then dives off the bridge. Roemer lands in an elderberry bush at the side of the canal. Scared, he stays in the bushes, hiding from the British soldiers. Soon he is joined by Private Bonck, who as a Pole, has no desire to die for Germany.

Lieutenant Wood, age 21, had originally been scheduled to lead the men of Horsa 91 to the bridge. However, Howard decides to swap him to Horsa 92 and he moves Lieutenant Brotheridge, age 28, to take his place. The men from Horsa 91 are to lead the bridge attack. At the start of the war, Brotheridge was ready to become a professional footballer, playing for the Aston Villa Colts. He was a cadet in Howard's training company before the Ox and Bucks. Howard convinced Brotheridge to join the Airborne. When they storm the bridge, the Ox and Bucks are engaging in the *first* combat of D-Day, with Brotheridge being the *first* man on the bridge, the *first* to fire his gun at a German and the *first* of the Allied forces to kill an enemy soldier, on D-Day. The Lieutenant is fully aware of what the lead man on the lead team might mean, but displaying immense bravery, he still runs towards the bridge.

As Brotheridge heads the charge towards the steel bridge, shots from a German machinegun ring out splitting the night and hit him in the neck. Private Edwards (Horsa 91), running behind his platoon leader, tosses a grenade at the machinegun. He sees his lieutenant fall to the road near the edge of the bridge, in front of a café. Private Chamberlain (Horsa 91), the backup medic, is able to drag Brotheridge to a ditch.

Howard is directing the combat traffic from a ditch at the side of the road, west of the bridge.

"Baker, baker," calls Lieutenant Wood (Horsa 92), reporting with his platoon.

86   *Ian Moran*

Howard decides that the men from his glider are winning the battle for the bridge.

"David ... number two," responds Howard.

Wood now knows that he is the second platoon to arrive at the bridge, so he will proceed as planned. This means his platoon will clear the enemy defenses on the east side of the bridge. From the reconnaissance, Wood knew he would have to take out trenches, machinegun nests and one anti-tank gun.

"David, with all his boyish enthusiasm, he was a great leader," recalled Private Clark (Horsa 92), "and he went gallantly into action and we tore in like a pack of hounds."

Clark didn't even notice as he ran across barbed wire, but pain snapped through him and the scars on his legs would stay with him for the rest of his life. Clark lets out a scream.

"Shut up Clark," Wood calls out in the middle of the attack.

As they near the trenches, machineguns start to open fire.

"We better sling a grenade," Corporal Godbold calls over to Clark.

"We better not sling a 36, let's toss a couple of these stun grenades, otherwise we're going to kill our own blokes," answers Clark.

They throw two No. 77 stun grenades and a pair Germans exit their gun trench then run towards the bank of the canal. Godbold takes his Sten gun and fires at the fleeing enemy soldiers. The German gunners fall to the ground. Godbold doesn't have time to check the bodies until the next day. However, there were no bodies, so the Germans either escaped or fell into the canal.

"The poor buggers in the bunkers didn't have much of a chance," Lieutenant Smith said, "and we were not taking any prisoners or messing around, we just threw phosphorus grenades down into the dugouts there and anything that moved we shot."

The men believe they have cleared the enemy positions just as burst of enemy fire comes from a submachinegun[29]. It hits Wood in the leg leaving three 19mm bullets lodged into his bones. He is bleeding badly. Wood falls into the long grass. Extremely frightened, he is sure the German that shot him will come over and finish the job. He hears a soldier approaching and braces to use the bayonet on the end of his Sten gun. Fortunately, it is Corporal Godbold from his platoon, coming

[29] An MP 40 Schmeisser

to help. He fixes a rifle splint to Wood's leg and gives him some morphine. Wood finds out that his batman and his 2IC, Sergeant Leather, were both hit by the same round of fire. Corporal Godbold is now in charge of No. 24 Platoon. The task on the east side of the bridge has been completed in less than five minutes.

Everything is quiet on the west side bunkers but there are still some guns firing at the platoon. The attack on the bridge has been witnessed by five members of the German Fallschirmjäger Regiment 6. They try to sneak up on the British soldiers but are making more noise than the crashing of the gliders. They decide to stop and take a position in the woods, 100-yards to the north of the bridge. The five soldiers empty their pistols firing towards the bridge, but they never get close enough to hit anyone. After a few minutes, with their guns emptied, the firing stops and the Germans disappear.

"We stayed there near the bridge, roughly about a hundred yards, firing, and I more or less ran out of ammunition … I'm not a coward but at that moment I got frightened. If you see a para platoon in full cry, they frighten the daylights out of you … the way they charge, the way they fire, the way they ran across the bridge. Then I gave the order to go back. What can I do with four men who had never been in action?" recalled Feldwebel Hickman.

Pilot Barkway (Horsa 93) hears someone call out for a stretcher and he heads back inside the Horsa to grab one. A shot rings out and he is hit in the arm. He falls out of the glider and back into the pond. He passes out and his memory becomes fuzzy until he wakes up five days later in a hospital in England.

Lieutenant Smith (Horsa 93) crosses the bridge, slowed down by his injured leg. He looks into the ditch and sees Brotheridge bleeding from the neck. He is still alive. Just then, a German soldier throws a stick grenade at Smith. He feels the munition explode very near to him. Although his clothes are full of holes, Smith feels no damage to his body. He turns and sees the German trying to scramble over the back of one of the walls adjoining the café. Smith squeezes the trigger of his newly acquired sub-machinegun and he realizes that his wrist had been hit by the grenade burst. He is able to fire off a few rounds and he catches the German just as he is clearing the wall. He is confident that the soldier is dead as he watches the German fall to ground in front of the wall. Suddenly, he feels a great pain scream up from his right hand.

Smith looks down at his wrist to understand why he had been having a difficult time pulling the trigger. The grenade has scooped up the flesh right down to the bone. Dazed, Smith stares at his arm, noticing how flat the wrist bone looks. He realizes how fortunate he was to be able to operate his trigger finger. A head pops out of an upstairs window of the café. Smith spots it and slowly, painfully, fires off a few rounds at the figure in the window. He knows, from the intelligence that had been provided, that the German officers often frequent the café. Georges Gondrée, the café owner, pulls his head back in, not realizing that he would be dead if Smith was not struggling with his wrist injuries.

Howard is now standing in the middle of the road at the front of the bridge with his Sten gun poised to shoot any Germans trying to escape. Parr and Gardner come up from the side of the road, having just made sure that the dugouts were cleared.

"Who goes there," shouts the ex-Oxford City Police officer, Major Howard, as he swings around and points his gun at the two soldiers.

"Sir, it's us. Ham and jam, ham and jam," screams Parr, as Howard eyes them.

"Right. You've cleared those?" asks Howard, recognizing the two troopers.

"Yes, they're clear sir," Parr answers reaching the top of the road.

"Right, run, run, run. Get across that bridge," Howard commands.

As the two men run across the bridge, Gardner informs Parr of his mistake.

"By the way, you're not supposed to bloody shout out 'ham and jam'. You're supposed to call out 'Able'. We're 'Able', Horsa two is 'Baker' and 'Charlie' is Horsa three," reminds Gardner.

They reach the other side of the bridge and Parr finds Brotheridge lying in the ditch beside the road. Parr kneels down beside him and he puts his hand behind Brotheridge's head. The Platoon leader tries to say something, but Parr can't make it out. One of the forward troops comes back across the bridge to report the results of the combat to Howard.

"The Germans have been cleared on the bridge, but Brotheridge is hurt, sir," he says.

Howard's thoughts turn to the day he asked Brotheridge to take the lead in Horsa 91. Captain Vaughan (Horsa 93), the platoon's company doctor, was concussed when his glider crash landed. He is just now able to fight off his own injuries and establish a first aid post for men who are wounded by gunfire. There, he works to keep Brotheridge alive, but to no avail.

"He was looking at the stars, bewilderment on his face and a bullet hole in the middle of his neck below the chin..." recalled Dr. Vaughan. "All I could do was give him a shot of morphia. By then I had got some medical orderlies together and we carried him back to the RAP... David Wood I found near the anti-tank gun pit, his thigh shattered by machinegun bullets. He had no thought for himself but kept on asking how Den was getting on."

Brotheridge becomes the *first* British soldier to be killed by enemy fire on D-Day. In July 1944, his wife will give birth to their only child, a daughter, Margaret.

"He had never asked us to do anything that he would not do himself," laments Private Edwards who, like every man in his unit, has the greatest respect for Brotheridge.

The charge led by Brotheridge has had its desired effect. Some Germans have run away, some are caught sleeping in their bunkers and the few men that held their ground have been killed. The Bénouville bridge is now in the hands of the Allies and the Germans have failed to either defend it or blow it up. Smith takes over Brotheridge's platoon and puts them in a defensive position.

Another report comes into Howard from Corporal Godbold. Lieutenant Wood, who is leading the Horsa 92 chalk, is shot in the leg and incapacitated. Likewise, his 2IC, Sergeant Leather, has also been injured, so now there is another leaderless platoon. Howard's only other officer is Lieutenant Smith (Horsa 93), who hobbles at best and has a bandaged right wrist, the hand that he uses to fire. Smith feels exposed and asks Howard if he can get another platoon from the other three Horsas, not knowing that only two Horsas have landed by the other bridge.

Lance Corporal Tappenden (Horsa 91), Howard's radio operator, is on his radio but there is no response from the second bridge.

Horsas 94, 95 and 96 are supposed to land closer to their objective, the river bridge. However, Horsa 94 is released over the Dives River by mistake. To the glider pilot, the river looks like the maps, so he takes the plane down. The glider lands in the wrong place and the men find themselves too far east behind enemy lines. They will have to fight their way back to their objective location.

Beside the Orne River, on the strip of land between the two bridges, two out of three Horsas have landed. Pilot Howard (Horsa 96) finds the right field, the right landing spot and after avoiding a herd of unplanned cows, has a mild landing. The men from Horsa 96, under the command of Lieutenant Fox, land less than 100 yards from the Ranville bridge. Fox exits the glider to evaluate his mission status. Most of his men seem to be okay, except for himself, who broke his arm in the landing.

As he looks across the fields, Fox doesn't see any other gliders. The first glider was to take the bridge, the second glider was to clear the bunkers and he was supposed to be backup having landed third. It looks like his men will have to assume the role of the first glider. That means they will have to charge the bridge.

Fox recalled that they had planned for all different eventualities, "in case none of us arrived, in case one of us arrived, in case one of us arrived in the wrong place or at the wrong bridge, in case we had to carry boats from one bridge to the other."

Even though they had trained for various contingencies, it is still surprising to discover that the third glider had to perform the first task. The Horsa 96 chalk quickly survey the area and find three Germans fast asleep in their dugouts. Their rifles are stacked neatly nearby. Fox gathers their rifles and tries to wake the sleeping soldiers.

"Komm! Komm!" Fox orders as he shines his torch on the soldiers faces.

"Fuck off," one of the Germans responds, thinking it is a joke.

The German soldier rolls over to go back to sleep.

"It never occurred to him that this was the enemy," said Fox. "It took the wind right out of my sails. Here was a young officer, first bit of action, first Germans I had seen, giving them an order and being taken no notice of. It was a bit deflating."

Fox leaves Sergeant Thornton to complete the wake-up duty, then he heads for the bridge with the rest of the troops.

"I suppose I could have shot them all," recalled Thornton, "but I don't believe in murdering people in cold blood, so I put my Sten gun on to automatic and fired it along the bottom of the bunks. They moved like greyhounds."

Pilot Howard stays back and empties the glider with co-pilot Baacke. They stack the munitions at the side of the Horsa, keeping an eye open for approaching Germans. Apart from a herd of cows, the two pilots are alone in a field. Suddenly, Howard hears gun fire. The battle for the second bridge has started. A few German sentries on the bridge have been alerted by the sounds coming from the first bridge.

"It was, fortunately, very lightly defended," said Private Woods (Horsa 96) describing the defenses at the Ranville bridge.

The German soldiers manage to fire a few rounds at Fox's men using an air-cooled machinegun[30]. The glider troops dive for cover in ditches beside the road leading to the bridge. The young Germans are too inexperienced to hit anyone. From 150 feet away, Sergeant Thornton (Horsa 96) fires a two-inch mortar towards the bridge. Thornton will get a reputation that day for launching extremely accurate shells shots. He hits the very centre of the bridge with the first shot. The men from Horsa 96 proceed with a full assault on the bridge.

"Dear old Thornton had got from way back in his position a mortar going, and he put a mortar slap down, a fabulous shot right on the machinegun, so we just rushed the bridge, all the chaps yelling, 'Fox, Fox, Fox, Fox'," recalled Fox. His chalk's call signal just happened to match his name; an unfortunate coincidence that would have him turning his head all night.

Thanks to Thornton's shot, all the enemy has either been hit or they have run away. There is no further resistance and the battle is over in less than two minutes. The men fighting at the Bénouville don't even notice the sounds of the skirmish at the Ranville bridge.

Lieutenant Sweeney is in charge of the chalk in Horsa 95. Their glider hits an air pocket on the way down and lands short of the target, 500 yards away from the bridge. Sweeney hears firing in the distance to his right … the fight for the Bénouville has started. He then hears firing straight ahead … the fight for the Ranville has started. Sweeney assumes that Horsa 94 is taking the bridge, so he gathers his men and starts to run towards the bridge. He hears the German machinegun firing, and then a mortar blast. By the time the troops from Horsa 95

---

[30] A Maschinengewehr 34

make their way to the bridges, ready for a fight, the position has already been secured.

"How was it?" Sweeney asks Fox.

"Well, so far the exercise is going fine, but where the hell are the bloody umpires," Fox muses, thinking back to his days in training.

From landing to securing the bridge, it is under five minutes.

"I went racing across with my heart in my mouth, eventually coming to a halt, a bit disappointed... We were all worked up to kill the enemy, bayonet the enemy, be blown up or something," Sweeney lamented.

Now the troops set about fixing a position to hold the bridge. Sergeant Thornton (Horsa 96) and most of Sweeny's platoon, take their position on the other side of the bridge. Thornton and a few others are in a German trench on the east side of the bridge, watching for any German counterattacks.

Howard's radio operator, Tappenden, still hasn't heard anything from the other three Horsas.

"Anything from four, five, or six?" Howard asks for the fourth time impatiently.

"No, no, no," Tappenden answers, frustrated.

Finally, Fox comes on the radio to deliver the good news. The river bridge is under their control and no troops are lost. It is only when Fox and Sweeney come over to the Bénouville bridge that Howard realizes Horsa 94 has failed to make it to the landing area.

Ninety minutes after taking off from RAF Tarrant Rushton, Howard's men have not gone gently into that good night. They have crashed their way behind enemy lines and completed the first part of their mission. Both bridges are secured, however two men have been killed in the battle, 14 were wounded and one glider is still missing. However, none of the men knows what happened to Horsa 94.

As soon as the Bénouville bridge is secure, the Royal Engineers go to work and check under the bridge to ensure that the Germans have not rigged the structures to explode. Georges Gondrée and his wife Thérèse, own the Café Gondrée and live on the top floor. The café sits beside the Bénouville Bridge. The Gondrées have been supplying information to the French Resistance and they have indicated that it looks like the Germans had placed explosives under both bridges. Captain Neilson (Horsa 92) informs Major Howard that both bridges had been mined, but the explosives have not been attached to a hellbox detonating device.

After clearing the bridges, the engineers proceed to check the other areas they have been assigned.

"We had an aerial photograph on the Saturday before we went over and there was a disturbance or something, altercation in the road, just about seven or eight feet from the actual beginning of the bridge" recalled sapper Cyril Larkin. "My Engineer Officer had detailed me to check that out. What I found was a light-hearted thing. A horse had stopped and deposited its job there!"

Cover is provided for the sappers, as they crawl under the bridges. Any motion, especially near the Ranville bridge, is still dangerous. The German infantry has not been cleared on the far side of the Ranville bridge and they continue to hold their position. They start to take shots at anyone who crosses the bridge. This is the line that the Ox and Bucks will have to maintain. Howard's men are now isolated behind enemy lines in the middle of the night, and all they can do is wait. The orders now are 'hold until relieved'.

With a limited supply of weapons and ammunition, the Ox and Bucks aren't prepared to withstand an armoured attack. The first line of relief should come from paratroopers, but the paratroopers will not bring any heavy artillery. The permanent relief will come after the beach landings, when the commandos march inland to link Howard's men to the beach forces. However, the commandos will have to first land and face the German defences at the beach. Hopefully, Brigadier Lovat's reinforcements will arrive before the Germans can mount a serious counterattack on the bridges.

If the Allies can hold the bridges to bring their armour inland, then the Germans will want the bridges blown-up. If the Germans can get control of the bridges to bring their armour to the beaches, then the Allies will want the bridges blown-up. From the seaside to Caen, these two bridges are the only remaining bridges that can support the weight of a Panzer tank. If the German tanks cross the bridges, it will result in a huge loss of Allied lives and the eastern flank of the Normandy Invasion will be at risk. There is a lot riding on the ability of less than

200 men being able to hold off whatever the German army can send to the bridges.

Howard has his men move the Sten guns around to various positions and the men fire tracer bullets into the air to give the impression that the force is larger, with more artillery, than it actually is. Howard, Smith, Fox and Sweeney feel very exposed. The Germans are now over the initial surprise and are coming down from the village of Le Port, about 300 yards away. They start to sneak towards the bridges through the backs of houses and gardens, and they take up positions as snipers. When they see the bridges, they are surprised to see how few British troops are at the bridge and the German infantry is confident that the bridges will be taken back as soon as the Panzers arrive. In the meantime, the German infantry will try to stop the British as best they can, by killing them one at a time and not letting anyone advance or retreat.

The line down the Orne River is to be the eastern flank for the invasion. Weeks before D-Day, the RAF has blown up several bridges, leaving only the Bénouville and Ranville bridges. If the bridges are to be controlled, they will also need to establish a bridgehead beyond the Ranville bridge, to ensure that German troops can't attack the bridge position and breach the flank.

Major Howard tells his radio operator to send the success message 'Ham and Jam'. 'Ham' is the signal that the Canal Bridge had been captured intact and 'Jack' means that it is captured but destroyed. 'Jam' is the signal that the Ranville Bridge was captured intact and 'Lard' means that it is captured but destroyed. Thus, the message is 'Ham and Jam'.

"Hallo Four Dog. Ham and Jam. Ham and Jam," Tappenden calls into his radio set[31].

There is no response.

Four Dog is Brigadier Poett, the tall, well-groomed leader of the 5th Para Brigade of paratroopers. This experienced part of the 6th Airborne Division has also had limited success with the jumps that evening. All the British paratroopers belong to the 6th Airborne Division, which is named the 6th to fool the Germans into believing there are five other divisions. Poett's radio operator Lieutenant Royle, age 21, is dedicated to radio communications and should not have

---

[31] A Murphy Radio Wireless Set No. 38

engaged the enemy, so he should be waiting for the status report. No response might mean that something went wrong with the paratrooper landings. Poett was to jump with a small contingent of paratroopers, and the rest of his men would follow later. As the Brigadier, he is landing first and will co-ordinate the remainder of paratroopers. Even though he is experienced, after he lands Poett has no idea where he is. He looks for his men but can only find one of his pathfinders.

"Hallo Four Dog. Ham and Jam. Ham and Jam. Ham and bloody Jam."

Still no response. Tappenden continues the message for the next half hour. What Tappenden doesn't know is that Royle did engage with Germans on landing and he was killed in action. Even Poett is unaware that his radio operator is dead, so there is no one on the other end to receive the 'Ham and Jam' message. An offshore ship overhears the message and the information on the initial success is relayed back to Britain. The commandos that are approaching by sea, know that the bridges have been secured, but the paratroopers that are behind the German lines are not aware of the status at the bridges. If the bridges were not taken, Brigadier Poett will have to implement the backup plan to have paratroopers attack the bridges. The next batch of paratroopers will be landing in half an hour with inflatable rafts in case the contingency is enacted.

Major Howard gives up on the radio and decides to send a signal the old-fashioned way. He takes out a whistle and blows three short blasts, followed by one long one. His signal for 'V' in Morse code, V for victory, travels across the quiet night air and is heard by dozens of paratroopers, most of whom do not know where they are. Poett is lost after landing. Fortunately, there were no Germans in sight. He rubs his finger across his thin mustached upper lip as he contemplates which direction to take.

"It was too dark to see the church or any of the landmarks on which we had been briefed," recalls Poett. "but I could see the exhaust of the aircraft disappearing and I knew that it would be going over Ranville … After getting rid of my parachute, I moved in the direction of the flight of my aircraft, and sure enough I came across one of my men and he and I set off in the same direction. Then almost at once, to my right, the silence and the darkness was transformed: All the sights and sounds of battle – explosions, firing, signal lights and so on."

Poett approaches the bridges slowly, as he is unsure if Howard's men have been successful. As he arrives at the bridges, with one paratrooper, they exchange passwords. Sweeney is there to greet him, just as the skies start to fill with the arrival of hundreds of planes filled with more paratroopers.

"As I entered the bridge area," recalled Poett, "I heard the roar of aircraft behind me, a comforting sound in the night sky. It was the main body of my Brigade beginning to come into the DZ I had just left."

The main thrust of paratroopers will establish the bridgehead to the east, so Major Howard pulls Lieutenant Fox's platoon over to west to the canal bridge. Lieutenant Colonel Pine-Coffin lands east of the bridges with his men of the 7th Battalion Parachute Regiment. Thanks to the distinctive Ranville Church's detached tower, which provides a strong orientation point, the troopers should have an easier time getting organized. However, poor weather, low visibility and high winds, combine with inexperienced pilots lead to men dropping further behind the enemy lines. Paratroopers will have to fight their way back to their units, slowing down the relief for the bridges.

The Gondrées had been anti-German since the start of the war. At first, they expressed this passively by not providing bunk space in their home for German troops (their children unnecessarily occupied every room). Then as the war waged on, the Gondrées became more daring in their resistance tactics. Thérèse was born in Alsace and is fluent in German. She hadn't let anyone know her fluency, so this allows her to overhear German conversations at the café. The information gathered includes where the German defenses are placed and where the gliders can land without encountering Germans.

Thérèse passes the information to Georges, who relays it on to Madame Lea Vion the Director of the Maternity Hospital and a resistor, who gives it to Eugene Meslin of the French Resistance in Caen, who supplies it to the 6th Airborne Division Headquarters at Brigmerston House on Salisbury Plain (codenamed Broadmoor but called the Mad House after the Broadmoor psychiatric hospital), which delivers it to the Airborne Division Headquarters, which informs Howard at RAF Terrant Ruston, who gives it to Lieutenant Tillett to build into his plans and models, which the Ox and Bucks review before take off.

As more small groups of paratroopers finally begin to arrive in relief, Howard's men can begin clearing houses. They move slowly through small isolated houses on the west of the canal, to ensure there are no German snipers. The clouds shift to reveal the bright moonlight, making the searches easier, however there is always an inherent danger in this task. One of the soldiers knocks on the café door, bracing in case of enemy fire. Howard's men are still suspicious that the Germans have been using the establishment. When Georges and Thérèse finally answer the door, the Café Gondrée, beside the Bénouville bridge, becomes the *first* French home liberated on D-Day.

Lieutenant Sweeney approaches a small lone house, in between the café and Bénouville. With his Sten gun readied, he knocks on the door. An old French couple come to the door and see the soldier with his blackened face. Sweeney asks where the Germans are holding out. They don't respond. He realizes that they don't understand him, so he uses the French that has been given to him.

"Pour la liberation de la France," Sweeney says.

The couple in fact understood Sweeney, but after four long years of German occupation, they are afraid to speak any English. They are fearful that this could be the Gestapo attempting to rout out any Allied sympathizers. The couple were too afraid to talk, so they retreat back into their house and close their door. Sweeney decides there is no risk and he moves on. Later that day, the elderly lady will be walking in a free France for the first time in four years. When she spots Lieutenant Sweeney again, the old French lady will run up to him and this time she will give Sweeney a big kiss.

The bridges were to have been guarded by Germany's 736th Grenadier Regiment[32]. The unit is commanded by Major Schmidt and based one mile away at Ranville. Schmidt's standing orders are to blow the bridges if they come under attack. When the attack on the bridges begins, Schmidt is dropping his girlfriend off. Driving in a halftrack[33], being led by a motorcycle escort, he is on his way back to home as he approaches the bridges. The two vehicles drive right past Sweeney's men and onto the Ranville bridge. Sweeney watches the German vehicles race passed with no concern for the lack of German guards. On the other side of the bridge, Corporal Jennings (Horsa 95) open fires and tosses a grenade at the vehicles, killing the motorcyclist

---

[32] German 716th Infantry Division
[33] The vehicle was an SdKfz 250, not a Mercedes convertible, and Schmidt was not sitting in the back, eating leftovers, drinking wine, etc., as often cited

and forcing the halftrack off the road. Schmidt and his 16-year old driver, surrender immediately to Private Woods (Horsa 96).

"A German officer was also at the scene and immediately surrendered to me, passing over his revolver," explains Woods.

Both Schmidt and the boy are injured, but Howard's men are not set up to take prisoners.

"The wounded we treated the same as one of our own wounded," stated Private Allen (Horsa 95), "but we didn't intend to wound, we intended to kill them, but we wounded them."

During questioning, Schmidt starts off with the defiance of Germany's superiority. Soon he realizes what is taking place and he knows that he will face severe punishment for failing the Reich. Schmidt pleads with Dr. Vaughan to shoot him.

"He harangued me about the futility of this Allied attempt to defeat the master race. We were undoubtedly going to end up in the sea he assured me with complete conviction..." Vaughan recalled. "He ended his lecture by requesting me to shoot him. This I did – in the bottom – with a needle attached to a syringe of morphia. The effect of this, it seemed, induced him to take a more reasonable view of things and in about ten minutes he actually thanked me for my medical attentions."

Doctor Vaughan's morphine puts Schmidt under but when he comes to, the Ox and Bucks learn that he is the commander responsible for the two bridges. There is some discussion among Howard's men as to whether or not Schmidt had been lured away from the bridge by French Resistance. Whether it was a purposeful act or shear serendipity, the German defenses were not on full alert without a leader.

Two hours after the Horsas have landed, things are quiet enough for Howard's men to hear the ominous sound of German Tanks rumbling in the nearby village of Le Port. Howard's men have very little firepower and a lack of suitable ammunition to repel tanks. The Number 81 grenades, that can be used to attack tanks, can't be found. Most of the PIATs had been rendered useless in the gliders' rough landings. There is only one working PIAT, which is moved to a forward position. The PIAT guns are short-range weapons that essentially launch a bomb.

"Oh Christ! If they're sending tanks in against us, we haven't got no chance at all," says Private Allen (Horsa 95).

The Gondrées' intelligence had indicated that the tanks in Le Port were part of the highly experienced 125 Regiment of the 21st Panzer Division commanded by Major Hans von Luck. With his jet-black hair slicked back and his immaculate uniform displaying his iron cross, Von Luck was a proud Prussian and a professional soldier. Since his arrival in Normandy, he had always remained east of the Orne River, so it likely won't be von Luck in Le Port. As a cadet in pre-Hitler Germany, von Luck's instructor in tactics was Captain (now Field Marshal) Rommel. Von Luck became a close friend and protégé of Rommel's. Although the German Army is expecting an invasion, they are not ready for it to be at Normandy. In fact, Rommel placed von Luck near those specific beaches, because of the unlikelihood of the invasion landing there. Major von Luck had led tanks into Poland in 1939, then into France in 1940, then to the outskirts of Moscow in 1941, and finally he led Rommel's extreme flank in Africa from 1942 to 1943. As a reward for his faithful service, Rommel decided it was time for von Luck to get an easy assignment: just south of the beaches of Normandy in 1944.

"We didn't expect the invasion in Normandy, because the distance was very long, there were a lot of cliffs, difficult to overcome," von Luck would confess later when discussing his Division's readiness.

Tanks can be heard starting up, followed by the clanking and grinding of the German armour taking to the road.

"To my horror," recalls Lieutenant Smith (Horsa 93), "I heard the rattle of tank tracks coming down the road from the Le Port direction. I remember feeling very, very helpless because there we were without an anti-tank weapon, except for the one we'd given to Dennis (Fox). With my platoon only about seven or eight strong, and Brotheridge's 20-odd people, and I thought this is going to be it."

Smith's troops are looking at him to see if he is going to react to the sounds of the tanks. His face doesn't betray his fears. There are two vehicles in the small convoy, a tank and a halftrack with an 88mm on the back. The lights of the lead vehicle are spotted hesitating at the T-junction at Le Port. There is some hope that the tanks are on night exercises and might turn right, but then slowly, they start turning left towards the canal bridge. It is inevitable that they will soon realize that the British have landed at the bridges. Howard's men are ill-equipped to combat a line of tanks.

Immediately upon landing, Lieutenant Colonel Pine-Coffin's regiment is tasked with gathering their gear and heading straight to relieve Howard. Pine-Coffin lands, bundles his chute and slowly stands erect. Being over 6-foot tall, Pine-Coffin makes an easy target and he is already brandishing a scar on his right cheek from a previous battle. Looking around, he can't see even one other paratrooper. His men are scattered throughout the landing area and have to orient themselves in the fields to the east of the bridges. Once landing in France, the paras are supposed to go to the rendezvous. Pine-Coffin makes his way there and just like most of the other paratrooper Battalions, many paras have failed to make it by the appointed time. He is only able to locate a quarter of his men and even less of his armoury. Hearing the battle for the bridges and the constant barrage of sniper fire, Pine-Coffin decides to head out. He is fully aware of the challenge that Howard will be having and some help early would be better appreciated than a larger contingency arriving too late. Also, there is still a chance that his men will have to attack the bridges.

Pine-Coffin and Lieutenant Richard Todd arrive at the bridges at 3 a.m. Seeing a few paras arrival, the Ox and Bucks know they are no longer alone in France. Pine-Coffin, who reports to Poett, now assumes command of the bridge forces. He arrives just in time to witness the *first* German counterattack of D-Day, as German armoury heads towards the bridges from Le Port.

Sergeant Thornton, one of Fox's men, is in a trench east of the canal bridge when he sees the approaching convoy. He grabs the only anti-tank gun, runs over the bridge and up the road towards the tanks. Private Clare (Horsa 96) follows him. Fortunately, there are no Germans snipers in position there as they run across no-man's land. The two men dive into a ditch about thirty feet from the T-junction and they lay motionless in the pitch black, waiting for the convoy. Other Ox and Bucks are following but have to take cover as the German armour approaches.

"Off we went up the road with Sergeant Thornton leading this time, not knowing we were into no man's land, because, although we knew the road and we knew which was the Mayor's house and so on, we didn't know what to expect," explains Lieutenant Fox (Horsa 96). "A window went up on the house on the T-junction and someone called out in French. My reply was something like '*Nous sommes l'armée de liberation*' and we started to take up various positions. I stayed inside the church, protected by the church gateway. Then we heard the sound of tracks coming and I crouched down beside this wall – there was nothing else I could do.'

One man is needed to fire the anti-tank gun and the other needed to reload it. The PIAT gun takes up to 30 seconds to reload, and although they have two bombs available, Thornton and Clare know they might only get one shot off before the German troops start to fire back at them. Other than fire their rifles at the tanks, they have no other plan to combat the return fire.

It's 2:00 a.m. The two men wait in the ditch until the convoy is just starting to pass them. Fortunately, the first vehicle is not a Panzer. It is a captured French vehicle, which has more vulnerability than the German armour. Better yet, there is no infantry accompanying the convoy. Thornton is 'shaking like a leaf' when he lets go the first shot. It is his second 'great shot' of the day. Despite having a reputation as slightly inaccurate and only good for close range, the two-and-a-half-pound bomb penetrates the lead vehicle. The shot is meant to delay the convoy by taking out the first vehicle, but it hits some ammunition inside. Machinegun clips explode and hit grenades, grenades explode and set off the tank's shells.

The result is a massive fireball that lights up the night 'like a large fireworks display' with explosions continuing for half an hour. It is a great victory, but the sound of the driver trapped inside is extremely unsettling as he screams for a full 15 minutes. Four other men jump out of the vehicle and are captured by Private Clare. The *first* German armoured vehicle is destroyed about four hours before the beach landings start. The other German tank comes to a halt and assuming the Allies are equipped with some very large, accurate anti-tank guns, the tank turns and retreats. The destroyed vehicle burns for a half hour, lighting up the road to Le Port. The Germans will delay any counterattack, at least until the sun comes up and they can try to assess the British artillery. The burned-out carcass of the French halftrack sits right at the final crossroad before the bridges and is now blocking the road in every direction. Thornton will receive the Military Medal for his quick reaction and incredible courage.

As more men from the 7th Battalion of paratroopers slowly start to arrive at the bridges, Howard's men immediately begin to taunt them. They were due at 2 a.m. and it is now closer to 3 a.m.

"Where the hell have you been?" Private Woods calls out jokingly.

The paratroopers begin to develop the bridgehead and clear more positions. The night becomes reasonably quiet, as men make their way to the bridges from the five parachute battalions to the east and one to the west.

Generalleutnant Richter, the commander of the German 716th Division in Caen receives reports that paratroopers have landed in his area and there was some minor combat. He relays the information through to General Marcks, who was born in 1891 ... June 6, 1891. He has a birthday celebration scheduled for that day. Marcks has trouble convincing the command chain that this is not a decoy. By June 15th, the 716th Division will have lost sixty percent of its soldiers.

As daybreak approached, any motion near the river bridge takes the risk of becoming a target for German snipers. Since the Allied forces are no longer advancing, the German forces are content to fire machineguns and mortars in what seems like a never-ending supply of ammunition. The snipers are very accurate and crossing the bridges becomes dangerous.

"I remember lying in a ditch, in this little gully-way between the two bridges," recalls Lieutenant Smith (Horsa 93), "having my wrist bandaged by one of our first aid people. And a sniper bullet came cracking over my right shoulder, and hit this fellow in the chest, who was actually bending over me, and knocked him clear into the road. The bullet went straight through him. Strangely enough, he survived and came with us to Germany. But I remember him lying in the road and I expected the next bullet from the sniper to be coming and get me in the back of the neck because I couldn't get down any lower. That wasn't a very pleasant moment. The sniper, as they sometimes do in those sorts of situations, he shoved off. We never found him."

"That's not cricket," shouts out Dr. Vaughan seeing his medic, Lance Corporal Gregory (Horsa 93), has been hit treating Lieutenant Smith. He shakes his fist at the trees, but the sniper is gone.

Suddenly, there is a roar from the coast and the sound of sniper fire at the bridges is almost completely drowned out by the naval bombardment that precedes the beach landings. The 16-inch guns feel like an approaching freight train as the earth starts to rumble from the power of the naval shelling.

The ground between the two bridges offers some relief from the snipers as the canal trees block the view but crossing the bridges remains extremely treacherous. Slowly but surely, the original force and the paratrooper reinforcements are being wounded or killed by the German infantry. Captain Vaughan orders Lieutenant Smith to check-in to the aid station. Although he is the last of the three Horsa Lieutenants available to lead the troops, Smith can no longer run or fire a gun. When he checks-in, his finger is unable to pull a trigger and his leg is now giving up function.

While on patrol around the perimeter, Howard's men catch two Italians in the field near the gliders. They are taken prisoner and questioned. The two men are labourers from the Tadt Organisation, which essentially supplies Germany with slave labour from Italy. The men started working early in the morning and are there to erect poles in a field near the crashed gliders. The Italians confess that the poles are being put in place as anti-glider devices. Britain had already demonstrated how successful gliders could be with several stealth glider attacks, including in Italy. The poles are to be put in place around the bridges to prevent the type of glider landings that had just occurred the night before. The poles that are to be planted, have been nicknamed 'Rommel asparagus' by the Allied troops.

Howard decides that these men are labourers, not soldiers, so they pose no threat. He gives them a share of rations and then releases them. To his surprise, the men return to their work in the field. They are questioned further, and they confess that they have been tasked with finishing the job by the end that of day, June 6th. Not realizing that the gliders have already arrived and believing that the Germans might inflict consequences if the job is not completed, the two men prefer to go back to work in the field. They continue to work, even though the invasion is happening all around them. Everyone is amused when they pass the field and see the two men working on an assignment that is clearly one day too late.

"Silly Buggers," Corporal Parr (Horsa 91) muses.

When he gets back to England, Flying Officer Clapperton records the results of his mission in the flight log: "*Operations, 'Coup de Main', loaded Horsa tow (troops), high release at Ouistreham - - bombed powder factory at Caen*".

He doesn't report anything unusual about the glider release. As far as Clapperton is concerned, everything appeared to go as planned. Even

Staff Sergeant Pearson, the pilot in Horsa 94, doesn't realise that his glider has been released too soon.

"At 2350 hours, thirty minutes before we were due to land, I stopped smoking and had the lights put out for fear of enemy fighters," Priday recalled. "We checked our equipment and weapons, and I wondered whether our grenades would explode if we had a heavy landing. I said nothing of this. I stressed the importance of shouting as we came into land, since I did not want deaf men to deal with when we reached the ground. I again went into the cockpit and kept a running commentary going of all I saw. I didn't see very much, for it was a dark, cloudy night. At this stage, about 0005 hours, I ordered safety belts to be put on and gave a reminder about holding on to one another and lifting the legs clear of the floor for the landing."

Captain Priday, Major Howard's 2IC, is descending down to land in France, but he is headed for the wrong river. On board the glider is No. 22 Platoon D Company, commanded by Lieutenant Hooper. Pearson sees the silvery reflections of the water below and he heads down to make his approach. The glider sets down crashing on to the left bank of the Dives River. It is a rough landing, but it's the softest of the six Horsas. Had this been the right bridge, the landing would be praised for its accuracy. They are thirty-five yards from a bridge, the wrong bridge. They are seven miles away from the right bridge, and none of the men know it.

The troops get out of the glider with no injuries. Since the plan is for this contingent to be the first glider at the bridge, as planned, Priday leads a charge to their objective. They capture the bridge without firing a shot and are pleasantly pleased that the bridge is guarded even lighter than anticipated. There is only one German sentry at the bridge and on seeing the charging troops he leaves his helmet on the parapet and runs away. Everything gets very quiet very quickly. Priday watches for other men from other gliders. No one arrives.

Priday and Lieutenant Hooper listen for sounds from the canal bridge, but everything is still extremely quiet. Something is wrong. As they survey the area, there are indications that the model might not have been that accurate. The bridge is slightly different, the land surrounding the bridge is different, and the road leading to the bridge is different. No other gliders are arriving. It is just occurring to Priday that maybe they have captured the wrong bridge. He splits the troops up to guard the road at each end of the bridge, while he tries to figure out where they are supposed to be.

The German sentry has run for reinforcements and a German counterattack is launched at the bridge almost immediately. The men of Horsa 94 come under rifle fire. A burst of machinegun comes past Priday and hits Private Everett. Everett, the unit's radio operator, is killed instantly. Priday can see dark figures approaching and takes a position in the grass near the bridge.

After the firing stops, Lieutenant Hooper sets out on a 'recce' to evaluate the German positions. The next time Priday sees Hooper, he is approaching with his boots tied around his neck. He is marching with hands above his head, captured by two German soldiers. They have machineguns pointed at Hooper's back. Priday is on one side of the road with his rifle drawn and Lance Sergeant Raynor is on the other. They exchange glances as the Germans march closer with their prisoner. The two Germans are trying to evaluate how many troops they are up against. The rest of the platoon are hidden, faces blackened, in the ditch right beside Hooper.

"Jump Tony!" Priday and Raynor call out together.

With that, Hooper dives for the ditch as Priday, Raynor and the troops emptied their magazines into the two Germans. The enemy troops fall to the ground, and one squeezes the trigger on his submachinegun[34] spraying bullets. One bullet shreds through Raynor's bicep, missing the bone, and another scatter of bullets rips Priday's map case in half. Raynor will gain the reputation of being shot by a dead German. At this point, the platoon is defending the wrong bridge, with no radio operator, ripped up maps and no reinforcements on their way.

Priday questions the pilots to get a description of what they saw when they were landing. There is another smaller bridge in the opposite direction, but it is not the canal bridge. Priday is able to determine they have landed further to the east, and he realizes they have no intelligence on how many Germans are stationed near this bridge. The men of Horsa 94 will need to abandon their position and try to find the real bridges. However, they will have to wait until daylight, otherwise they could march right into the enemy lines. The men set up a defensive position for the night, each man keeping a keen

---

[34] A MP40 Schmeisser

eye for any movement. Priday starts to worry about the men at the Ranville bridge, who he realizes are 30 men short.

The sun rises very early in June in Normandy, so the gray light of dawn is not long after they had taken their position. Private Clive spots a Frenchman on an early morning walk with a young boy. They are approaching the bridge from the east, unaware that they are about to cross into a warzone. Clive runs over and warns the man to stay away from the bridge. The Frenchman is helpful and able to convey exactly where they are and how to get to the right bridges. The men of Horsa 94 are almost eight miles away from their objective.

The fields on the east side of the bridge are swampy and flooded. The Dives is a small winding river surrounded by meadows and willow trees. Part of the Atlantic Wall defense is to flood the valleys of the Dives and create a marsh that would slow down attacking infantry. However, it would have the opposite effect for escaping infantry, making them difficult to track and slow down troops on the hunt. The swampy land is sparsely populated and should make it a good escape route.

German troops from the smaller bridge to the east, are now making their way towards the Horsa 94 chalk. Germans in the trees to the west start to fire. Priday realizes that the Germans might fire at each other if his men disappear. He decides the swampy water will aid their escape route, but they need to get going before the light of day leaves them fully exposed. One by one, the men slip down to the fields and start moving. Priday is the last man down. They head through the flooded fields toward the town of Robenhomme.

The sun is now up. As they wade through the flooded fields, they still cannot hear the sound of the battle for the bridges. Along the way, they find other confused and lost paratroopers, as well as the bodies of those that did not make it.

"We saw a lot of Paras drowned in this water," recalled Lance Sergeant Rayner. "They had so much equipment on, they didn't have a chance, poor buggers. There were a lot of Paras who did join our party."

As they pick up paratroopers, it is clear that their training was not as robust as the men of the Ox and Bucks. The paratroopers struggle with working their way across the terrain. At places, the marsh water is extremely deep and non-swimmers have to be pulled across with ropes. After three hours, exhausted, they head to a farmhouse to confirm their location. The farmer is helpful, but Priday did not want his men to enter the house in case they left any sign that they had been there. The Nazis were known to execute any civilians that assisted the Allies. Priday explains who they are and confirms that they are heading in the right direction for Robenhomme. The troops head to a thatched outbuilding to regroup before setting out again. Before they are ready, they hear the sound approaching motors. Everyone takes cover in the small thatched building.

A German patrol on motorcycles and sidecars pulls into the farm. The patrol parks their bikes less than 20 yards from the outbuilding. On seeing his first sight of enemy troops, one of the paratroopers wants to have a shot at the handful of Germans. Priday stops him. The Ox and Bucks men ready their guns in case there is action, but Priday does not want to initiate any engagement. They have an objective at that moment, and it is not to fight one small patrol of German motorcycles. The other men of the Ox and Bucks could be dying at the bridges waiting for the extra firepower of Horsa 94. The Germans enter the farmhouse. Tension mounts ad the glider team braces to see if the farmer will give away their position. Priday's chalk ready for combat, but no Germans come out of the farmhouse. There is another rumble, then more motorcycles arrive. This is not a patrol after all, it is a full motorcycle troop. More than 30 motorcycles come to the farm and everybody goes inside the farmhouse. Priday and his men just have to wait it out.

Two hours pass and the Ox and Bucks restlessly feel the day slipping away from them. Their muscles are getting tight with the lack of movement. Finally, the first Germans exit the house. Guns are readied again, as the nerves of the Ox and Bucks are on edge. Eventually, the enemy troops all come out and leave, one by one. The French farmer has not given up their position. The men can now continue their trek to Robenhomme. Once they arrive at the small village, they meet up with some Canadian engineers and other paratroopers who are on different missions but have become separated from their units. Lance Sergeant Raynor finally has his arm looked at by a medic. Now they have maps and can head to the bridges. The platoon sets out with the other stragglers who had made their way to Robenhomme. They head down drier roads, eluding several German patrols along the way. There seems to be a lot of German movement the closer they come to the bridges.

It is well into the night before Priday's chalk finally reaches their
original objective. As there are still Germans in the area, they approach
the bridges slowly from the east. They do not want to get shot by either
enemy or friendly fire. Horsa 94 is over 24 hours late and the other Ox
and Bucks are no longer expecting them. When the troops from the
other gliders realized that it is Priday and his men, they let out a big
cheer. The men of the other five gliders were surprised and delighted.
Howard is particularly joyful as he had assumed the worst for the men.
It is 3 a.m. on June 7th when the six glider chalks are finally linked up.

On the morning of June 6th, the German counterattacks are
continuing to mount at the bridges. The rising sun shines light on the
positions of Howard's men, and they become easier targets for
Germans snipers. Pilot Howard, and his Co-pilot Baacke, are talking
with one of the Ox and Buck troops. The trooper is standing right in
between the two pilots as a sniper shoots the man in the middle. The
man immediately falls to the ground dead. Howard realizes how stupid
they had been to be standing up.

The relief troops of the 7th Parachute Battalion are trying to clear
sniper locations. B Company meets tough resistance in the Hamlet of
Le Port. A squad of Germans are inside the church tower and are
sniping in all directions. It is a challenge to take them 'en masse', so
Corporal Killeen sneaks across yards and through houses until he is
beside the church. Killeen, an Irish paratrooper, fires a PIAT bomb and
hits the belfry, obliterating it. The tower crumbles down on top of the
German infantry. At the bottom of the tower, Killeen finds 12 dead
German soldiers. A devout Catholic, Killeen, removes his red
paratrooper hat and prays for God to forgive him for destroying the
Lord's house.

"I walked across to the church, and I reckoned it was safe by then,"
recalls Killeen. "I went to the church, but oh God I was sorry to see
what I had done to a wee house of God, but I did take off my hat when
I went inside."

Corporal Parr (Horsa 91) and Private Gardner (Horsa 91) move into a
gun pit[35] and start to analyze the large German anti-tank artillery. From

---

[35] 5 cm Kampfwagenkanone 39 L/60 - a German 50 mm calibre tank gun

the air reconnaissance, they knew that the gun was there, they even know the gun's calibre, but they had not received any training on how to operate it. Not being familiar with the equipment or the language, they are trying to determine how the gun functions. Parr has figured out how to aim the munition, but the firing mechanism is not where he expects it to be.

"What's this do?" Gardner asks, pushing a red button on the opposite side.

The gun unexpectantly fires a 2-foot long shell in the direction of Caen and delivers a pretty significant explosion, letting out thunderous reverberation in the gun room.

"I want nothing else to do with this," Gardner says as he feels an ache in his eardrums.

He leaves Parr to put his newly found expertise to practice. Parr starts loading and firing anti-tank bombs wherever he thinks there might be a sniper location. He shoots three shells through the water tower and it crashes down killing the two snipers that were laying on top. Then he shoots at the chateau down by the canal bend, where he is sure a sniper is firing from the top floor. Major Howard barges into the gun pit. He was already on his way to tell Parr to keep the noise down so he could contact the paratroopers, but now he is furious as the chateau is the local maternity home. He yells at Parr for 'making a bloody racket' and tells him to stop firing, especially at a hospital. As soon as Howard leaves and heads back across the bridge, Parr returns to firing on any place he thinks he sees unwanted movement.

"Seeing London, Bristol and other places bombed to smithereens," Parr explains, "it gave me the greatest personal delight on D-Day, to sit behind a German captured gun, firing German ammunition, up German arseholes. I thoroughly enjoyed every minute of it."

Corporal Bailey (Horsa 91) comes down to the gun pit to watch Parr firing the gun. While Parr loads a shell, Bailey starts to boil water for a tea. It takes 20 minutes for the little Tommy flame to bring the water to a boil. Just as the water starts to bubble, Parr lets fire another shell blast. Soil comes crashing down from the roof of the gun pit and lands in Baily's tea. Baily is furious with Parr and chases him around the gun.

"I think I was in more danger from Bill Bailey that day, on that bridge, than I was from any of bloody Germans," recalls Parr.

At this point, the German plan is no longer to recapture the bridges, it is to destroy them. The German sentry, Private Roemer, is still hiding in the bushes with a Private Bonck. They see two German gunboats approaching the Bénouville Bridge from the direction of Ouistreham. The boats are probably fleeing the armada that is now approaching the beaches, but they stumble across the British who have captured the bridge. The lead boat fires a 20mm gun at the bridge.

"Grab the PIAT Nobby," Private Godbold (Horsa 92) calls out to Private Clark (Horsa 92).

Godbold and Clark race to the bridge and take a position directly in front of the gunboats. The German boats are firing, but they are not quite in range yet. Godbold fires his last remaining PIAT bomb and it lands right in the boat's wheelhouse. The boat loses control and crashes into the east bank of the Orne River. Much like the tank convoy, the other gunboat turns and retreats, back towards the coast where the Normandy Invasion is now fully underway. Godbold races down to the river and takes the German crew prisoner. The boat skipper rants so much about how the Germans will annihilate the English on the beach, that Howard orders him gagged.

In an attempt to remove the bridges, Germany sends in a single seat, single engine fighter plane[36]. The pilot approaches with the sun behind him, hedge hopping until he gets to the canal, then continuing to fly low, he releases a single massive bomb. Men are diving for cover as Howard and Tappenden look straight up at the quickly falling shell. The bomb scores a direct hit on the Bénouville bridge, however it fails to detonate and the explosive rebounds off the superstructure. The shell bounces to the side of the bridge and lands in the canal, leaving a big dent on the bridge's counterweight. The Ox and Bucks stare at the bridge and the bomb in disbelief.

Two German frogmen are then dispatched. They come down the canal from the German naval base in Caen. They are being propelled by a torpedo-type underwater propulsion device. Their mission is to detonate the bomb that the plane had dropped, which is now sitting in the canal beside the Bénouville bridge. As the frogmen approach through the calmness of the canal, the challenge of controlling the propulsion device has made the approach too obvious. One of

---

[36] A Focke-Wulf FW190

Howard's keen-eyed men catches sight of the air bubbles and a British sniper dispatches the frogmen.

Another boat is spotted, this time heading down from Caen. Private Parr is still in the Tobruk gun pit looking for targets to shoot at. He is told to spin the gun around an aim at the patrol boat coming down the canal. Using the charts on the wall, Parr believes he has worked out the right range, so he lets go a blast. There is a loud bang and Howard is inside his temporary HQ yelling 'Paaaaarr!'. The shell misses, but the shot gives Parr enough information to work out the range. When the boat reaches 300-yards, Parr lets go another blast and this time the shell finds its target. Crippled and taking on water, the patrol boat turns around and heads back to Caen.

The Horsa 95 chalk are defending the Ranville bridge, when they hear some movement in the trees. They call out for the password (the answer should be 'V Victory'). When no answer is given, Corporal Howard (Horsa 95), Private Clark (Horsa 95) and Private Wood (Horsa 95) open fire, killing six Germans. Unfortunately, they have also killed a paratrooper that had been taken hostage. The firefight continues for most of the morning but then suddenly ceases for a few minutes at the sight of an elderly Frenchwoman.

"A woman dressed in black, as women of a certain age do in France, with a basket over her arm, walked between us and the Germans," recalled Corporal Bailey (Horsa 91). "Everyone on both sides stopped firing and stared. And she was gathering her eggs! She stooped over not three feet from my firing position and gathered one in. When she had completed her task and strolled off, we resumed firing."

A Spitfire squadron is spotted on a low flyover. Howard's men signal that the bridges are in British hands. No more that 200-feet above the ground, three fighters perform a full 360-degree revolutions on their longitudinal axis, the victory roll. Another plane flies down and drops a bundle of newspapers. Howard's men let out a great big cheer. For a few moments, they are not thinking about their chances of holding the bridge. They are riveted by *The Daily Mirror* and the cover story that Rome has fallen. Spitfires and Hurricanes now keep a patrol around the bridges. This will provide protection against heavy artillery.

The war diary of the 6th Airborne Division is as follows:

– Horsa 91: Landed at apex of triangular fd (X) close to br. Ran into mud and barbed wire.
– Horsa 92: Landed behind No. 4 Airldg A Tk Bty RA. Hit wire and mud. Pilots fought with party. Saw Sgt Oxf Bucks KO tk with PIAT
– Horsa 93: Landed correctly in X but hit bank. 1 passenger killed, MO concussed, some injured.
– Horsa 94: Tug mistook R DIVES for R ORNE and glider landed on br 218761 on R DIVES. Got back to own lines via BASSENVILLES - BOIS DE BAVANT - RANVILLE.
– Horsa 95: Landed 500x North of Br in LZ "Y". Found br taken when arrived.
– Horsa 96: Landed near hr in correct LZ "Y" in fd full of cows.

Howard looks at his watch. He has no idea how long it will take for the commandos to get there, but he understands what his orders are. 'Hold until relieved' means there is no retreat. Keep firing at any Germans that approach the bridge as long as there is a man alive. Howard and his men have accomplished their initial mission and the first engagement of D-Day has been successfully completed. However, they are now taking heavy casualties as the German counterattacks are mounting. Brigadier Lovat's men will need to arrive soon. If Lovat fights through the beach landing and successfully navigates the subsequent cross-country march, then the bridges can become the path to the liberation of France and Europe.

5. Overlord's Piper

And now this soldier, this Scottish soldier,
Who wandered far away
And soldiered far away,
Sees leaves are falling
And death is calling
And he will fade away in that far land.[37]

Inside landing craft LCI 519, there was nothing the commandos could hear over the clamour of the engines. As the morning approached, the throbbing of the boat's pistons began to slow down. The sudden calmness woke Piper Millin. Brigadier Lovat was already back on deck peering into the knifing wind. He had slept fitfully in Commander Curtis' bunk. Millin went to the hatch, opened it up and could immediately feel the outside winds blowing cold and heavy. Looking across the silvery dawn with the freezing cold drizzle in his face, there was little to see except the murky silhouettes of hundreds of ships of all sizes. Millin couldn't yet distinguish the shoreline, so he closed the hatch and headed back below.

On deck, in the pilot's room, Curtis described the sea to Lovat, calling it 'lumpy'. The weather was different than the last time Lovat

[37] Scottish Soldier – Andy Stewart

was on deck. The shelter of the Isle of Wight was gone, and the choppiness of the Channel was all around the landing craft. Through the dark of night, Lovat thought to himself 'Now the parcel is in the post and out of my hands'.

Lovat looked ahead, watching for his stretch of beach. Coordinated landings were planned over a 50-mile, heavily fortified stretch of Normandy beaches. The five main beach areas are codenamed (west to east) Utah, Omaha, Gold, Juno and Sword. Sword beach is a five mile stretch on the French coastline running from Lion-sur-Mer to the west, to the village of Ouistreham at the mouth of the Orne River. Sword beach was then subdivided into four sections from west to east: Oboe, Peter, Queen and Roger. Queen beach was a large three-mile sector that was subdivided again into Red, White and Green beaches. Lord Lovat's commandos were to land on Sword beach, at the Queen sector, in the Red zone.

Sword beach was actually Colleville-sur-Orne[38] beach. The small village of Colleville-sur-Orne was dotted with small hotels, vacation homes and tourist locations located just above a short seawall and a paved promenade. For many of the men who about to land, this would be their first time in France. The beach landing was about nine miles away from the city of Caen, one of Normandy's major hubs and the birthplace of William the Conqueror. Field Marshal Montgomery's objective was for the British troops to take Caen … on the very first day. This was a very aggressive objective since there were German Panzer divisions in the area of the beach.

By 1944, Hitler had become a hypochondriac. He took 28 different pills and injections every day and Field Marshall Göring nicknamed him 'Der Reichsspritzenmeister'[39]. On June 5th, Hitler took a sleeping pill and he remained shuteye through the Allied landings. News of the invasion had reached the Berghof, Adolf Hitler's headquarters in the Bavarian Alps, but nobody wanted to wake the Führer unless there was a confirmed emergency. Over the past few weeks, Hitler had been awoken several times because of false invasion information. The attack on Normandy could be a feint or maybe a small-scale attack.

"Has the Führer been woken up?" asked Albert Speer, Hitler's Minister of Armaments and War Production.

---

[38] Renamed to Colleville-Montgomery after the war
[39] Master of the Imperial Needle

"No, he always receives the news after he has eaten breakfast," Hitler's staff answered.

Hitler had told Rommel that he wanted to be consulted before there was any movement of the Panzer Divisions. Accordingly, the tank movements performed exercises but restricted their movement to the area around their immediate positions and there was a general order not to advance. The only person who might have acted against the order was Rommel, but he wasn't in France that day. Until Hitler woke up, there could be no significant tank movement, and even then, someone would have to convince him that this was the undeniable invasion.

"When we realized the landing of paras and of gliders, on this very night we were immediately alarmed, but we could not move, restricted by this order," Major von Luck later commented on the standing order not to move unless authorized. "Unfortunately, Rommel wasn't there. He was on his way to see Hitler and our Division Commander wasn't there, he was in Paris."

In fact, there was another standing order for the Panzers that allowed them to engage and attack if there was an air landing. However, this had never been communicated to von Luck. 18 kilometres south-east of Caen, the deadly 12th SS Panzer Division was an hour away from the beaches when they saw the bombardment to the north. However, they were also prevented from advancing.

"At first we started moving north, but we had the order to stop," described Untersturmführer Siegel of the 12th Division. "We were held in this area for the next 12 hours, because our headquarters was not sure if this was a real invasion or only a diversion."

The British plan for Sword beach on D-Day was first to land tanks with infantry to mark paths. Next to land would be the commandos who had to push inland to the bridges. Finally, the British Army 3rd Division would land to provide the bulk of the infantry. Lovat's 1st Special Service Brigade[40] would land No. 4 and No. 6 at H-Hour+75, while the others would land at H-Hour+105. In the morning light, the commandos were greeted by a dune with a row of white houses that looked like the bottom row of some very bad teeth. Many of the beach houses had already been bombarded. Ironically, less than a mile from the landing point is the entrance to the Orne River where there sits a

---

[40] Consisting of No. 3, No. 4, No. 6 and 45 Commando Royal Marine unit

monument erected to commemorate the British failed invasion of Normandy in July 12, 1792.

Once ashore, the first objectives were to move inland, take control of the small seaside village of Ouistreham, and march the commandos to reinforce the paratroopers.   Once they reach the bridges, some commandos would remain there to reinforce the paratroopers at the bridges, while others would continue to march inland to reinforce the paratroopers at the Merville battery and establish the bridgehead.

Lovat's plan was to land at the beach, leapfrog the beach defenses, take out any German opposition they ran into, and then establish full control of the bridges.   British casualties were already starting to mount.   The men in the gliders had paid the first price of the invasion. Paratroopers were next to take casualties.   Then there were deaths on the boat trip to the beaches, as the naval mines put in place by Germany had successfully sank several ships and landing craft.   The Nazi defenses had imparted the first naval casualties of D-Day before the Germans even knew there was an invasion.

Higher than normal tides, due to the rough weather, made the sighting of the German defenses more difficult.   As the landing craft came ashore, they had to avoid the underwater obstacles that included long pointed metal extrusions, mounted to the sea floor during low tide and facing towards the incoming ships.   Many of these sharp steel rods had mines latched to them.   They were also placed strategically such that if boats successfully avoided them, they were directed towards natural defenses such as sand bars.   Many boats were already getting stuck on the sand too far from the shoreline.   The result was the disembarking infantry landed in deep waters and drowned with the weight of their kit.

Commander Curtis understood the importance of the commandos' mission, and he was determined to land the troops at the right beach at the right time.   The twelve landing craft increased speed and headed to Sword beach.   Landmarks were obscured by low clouds and smoke from the advanced bombing missions.   Curtis had to fight through a strong westerly wind and incoming tide that was threatening to push the boats to the east.   As they reached the beach, they were pleased to see the ruined chateau that was one of their key landmarks.   The boats slowed down to thread their way through the German sea obstructions of Rommel's Atlantic Wall.   While the rising tide would assist in unbeaching the landing craft, it also meant that the German defenses were only partially visible.

Off to the left, east of the landing craft, a ship erupted into flames in a massive explosion and sank. The ship had come in contact with an enormous mine. All the boat pilots had already been informed that the Germans had mined the coast, but the sight of the blast was still alarming. The explosion was followed up by the sky being lit up with the blood orange flames and then slowly sliding back to darkness, all in under two minutes. The flotillas were being led by minesweepers, but the pilots knew that it would be very difficult for the sweepers to clear every mine, especially with the incoming tide. The sappers would clear shorter obstacles and leave any that were greater than four-feet six-inches for the Royal Navy clearance units. As the tide rose however, the Navy was skipping some obstacles that appeared to be in the sappers' range. The confusion left hundreds of obstacles untouched.

The commandos were on the eastern flank of the five-beach assault. After landing, the immediate task was to take the beach, knock out any batteries that are still active and take a position to hold the beach. If their flotilla was taken out by mines, there were no reserves scheduled to follow-up and take on the commando mission. It would be a very thin green line. Lovat's plan had to be executed on all fronts.

Soon, the other commandos started waking up. The men gathered their gear, threw their rucksacks on their backs and then headed up to the deck carrying their artillery. Millin came through the open hatch to find a much brighter world outside. The beaches of Normandy lay underneath an early morning mist that was being consumed by black smoke. The rain of the previous day was now a drizzle. Millin's landing craft was heaving in the waters that broke before the shoreline.

The commandos could hear the full force of the naval bombardment that signalled the beginning to the campaign from the sea. The landing on the beaches was preceded by an aerial bombardment, followed by a naval assault for two hours. The battleship *HMS Diadam* was behind the commandos firing with a deafening sound. All guns were blazing towards the land above the Normandy shore. When the ship started firing, it was unfortunately hitting directly on Sword beach. The captain ordered all water and fuel to be move to the starboard side of the hold, tilting the ship on an angle, allowing the long-range guns to reach as far as three miles inland. The Germans had already started to fire at the shoreline and very quickly it became challenging to see the beach.

"The Germans welcomed us with a lot of guns firing," recalled French Commando Corporal Gautier, "but we realized that we were going free. The Airforce came to cover the beach in smoke, we landed in smoke."

German mortars started taking aim at the commandos' landing craft whenever the smoke cleared. They were using high armour-piercing shells meant for tanks. The landing craft commanded by Curtis, and carrying Lovat and Millin, was hit twice. Fortunately, the shells went through the metal of the gun shields without hitting any sailors or commandos. Had the Germans used exploding ammunition, the 4,000 gallons of fuel would have destroyed the vessel and killed both Lovat and Millin before they even reached the beach. To the right, another landing craft was also hit, but this time the shells hit the engine and pierced four petrol tanks. Miraculously, the vessel didn't explode either, otherwise it could have had a chain effect.

"When we got up on deck, my God, all hell had let loose … all hell had let loose," remembers Private Treacher. "There were guns firing from the boats, there was aircraft flying out, there was bullets flying around. We were about 800 yards out to sea."

One of the three landing craft that was carrying the French commandos was hit by a shell and it started to sink. Some men were wounded, and others were killed before they had even started to fight back for their homeland. A few made it to another landing craft and continued to head ashore.

The commandos had arrived at Sword beach. Millin could only see smoke and mayhem, rather than the coast of the French seaside, with its gently rising hills sloping behind a strip of sand. The beach was fifty yards from the shore to some sand dunes and a seawall. Behind the wall there were fields, a few small seaside bungalows and a small hotel about 100 yards in. The hotel had been converted into a German bunker with heavy guns on the bottom floor, machineguns on the middle floors and rifles or mortars on the roof. Not far inland, was Ouistreham, a small fishing port in Normandy. Before the infantry landed, there was only one road leading off the beach and a few small footpaths. Soon the dunes would be bull-dozed and new routes would be formed to access the fields for the arriving infantry and armoured vehicles. First however, the beach had to be secured.

"Good morning commandos, and bloody good luck," the signalman relayed from *HMS Stork*.

"Thanks, think we are going to bloody well need it," Lovat had the LCI 519 signalman reply.

Lovat looked to the coastline and then back to Commander Curtis. Curtis had just spent seven hours at the helm, in the dark. Lovat wished he had come on deck earlier. Lovat thought the commander looked like he could have used the company as he tried to navigate through the mines at night in the rough water. In fact, Curtis had a feeling of elevation brought on by a sense of duty. He was aware of the importance of the day, the importance of the mission and the importance of his cargo. Curtis hoisted his battle ensign and raised the flag to signal the flotilla to move into arrowhead formation.

A landing craft from the East Yorkshire regiment that was tasked with marking the beach was headed back to England. Lovat had Curtis steer the flotilla towards the craft and Curtis picked up his megaphone.

"How did it go?" Curtis called out.

"It was a piece of cake," replied a sailor on the quarterdeck of the passing ship.

The sailor flashed a 'V' for victory and continued on. Lovat and Millin both looked forward to Sword beach. There was a dark grey smoke from the purposeful smoke screen laid down by the RAF, as well as thick black smoke coming from the British tanks that had been hit by anti-tank weapons. Millin thought that the beach did not look like a piece of cake. Lovat was also thinking that the beach 'did not look all that inviting'. There were infantry lying with their heads down in the sand not moving, providing easy targets for the German snipers and machine-gunners.

"If you wish to live to a ripe old age – keep moving," Lovat reminded his men.

The commando troops were acting abnormally normal as they 'got dressed for the show'. They readied their kits, checked their weapons, loaded their magazines, ensured their grenades were primed and put 'one in the spout' of their rifles. The full kit meant a tommy gun, 100 rounds of .45 in ammunition, four 3-inch mortars, four grenades, a shaving kit, a clean vest, pants and cigarettes. Lovat ordered the men to remove their steel helmets and put on their green berets.

"It was a crazy order," Private Owens said, "but we all obeyed it. All through the war, we never wore a tin hat. You could pick us out anywhere."

The berets were the signature headgear of the commando units. They never wore metal combat helmets (or brain buckets as they were routinely referred to). Some of the men thought wearing the berets rather than the combat helmets was a little crazy but Millin preferred the beret as it was a better fit with his kilt.

Commander Curtis used the large chateau on the eastern end of the beach as his guide. Despite the rough waters, in a practically unsteerable boat, he had managed to get the commandos to the right spot on the beach.

"I'm going in," Curtis told Lovat.

Everyone was on deck staring across the cold. The closer they got, the more they took in. The scene on the beach was depressing with some of the earlier landing craft entangled in German naval obstacles and destroyed tanks that had been forced into the mine path by the anti-tank screen. There were already dead bodies floating on the shoreline from some of the troops that had landed with the tanks. The waters of the channel were thundering around as waves crashed into the boats. The commandos were instructed that once landed, they were not to stop, not even for injured men. They had an objective and it was an assault not a rescue mission. Others would follow to gather the injured. The smoke and mist were hiding the German infantry guarding the Normandy beaches. Millin wasn't thinking about the location of the rifles, machineguns and large artillery that were getting ready to take aim at the landing troops. He was only thinking about making it ashore.

It was June 6, 1944. D-Day. A miserable, cold, grey day. The start of the European invasion that would once and for all establish if the Allies or the Axis would win the deadliest war the world had ever known. There was a driving, bitter, cold air that morning as the troops held for the order. Millin took his pipes out of the box and assembled them. This time there would be no tuning. Millin didn't bear a rifle. He was going to pipe the men ashore. Standing on the landing craft, Millin could hear the noise of machines, explosions and wounded men calling for help. There were flashes of light across the grey sky, coming from the ships and some from the land.

"It was impossible not to be thrilled by the happenings round about. Aircraft scurried to and fro across the dawn sky, all independent – and all beautifully ours. Shells from the warships *HMS Warspite* and *HMS Ramillies* were screaming overhead, destroyers fired salvo after salvo, and soon we heard a new sound – the roaring swish of missiles from the rocket ships. The whole coastline was now under a thick pall of smoke," Lieutenant McDougall recorded.

The naval bombardment proved accurate, effective and unrelenting. The *HMS Warspite* alone would consume 300 shells[41] in 48 hours. In contrast, the RAF bombings to neutralize the major defenses had failed. Not all the intelligence on the German positions had been accurate. On Omaha beach a coordinated attack successfully took out a line of telephone poles which was thought to be large gun barrels. The night bombers had failed to disarm most of their targets near the beach. The German guns were ready for the invasion, even if Germany was not. The Royal Navy continued to shell locations that had already been hit, however the navy was also blasting German positions for the first time. The naval attack was much more accurate as 15-inch shells flew over the landing craft and exploded beyond the beach.

Royal Navy: All the coastal cities inland from Sword beach were being bombarded by the Royal Navy Force 'S':
- *HMS Warspite* was firing at Villerville,
- *HMS Ramillies* was shelling Bénouville,
- *HMS Roberts* was bombing Houlgate,
- *HMS Arethusa* was blasting Le Mont and then Merville,
- *HMS Frobisher* was bombarding Riva Bella,
- *HMS Dragon* was hammering Colleville-sur-Orne, and
- *HMS Danae* was besieging Ouistreham.

The coast was carpeted with a barrage of naval salvos.

The RAF failure to adequately bomb the beaches would also make it harder for the landing soldiers. They had expected to be able to take cover in the holes created on the beach by the previous night's bombing, but the aircraft had even failed at this task. Fortunately, German defenses to the east of the beaches were cut-off from effectively firing at the invasion by a smoke screen laid down across the water by the RAF[42]. The German 5th Torpedo Boats emerged through the smoke screen to engage with the Royal Navy. The German

---

[41] 375mm
[42] 88 Squadron

flotilla launched 18 torpedoes at the Royal Navy battleships and then headed back to Le Havre before they could be effectively fired upon. Every torpedo missed the battleships, however one torpedo cut between the *HMS Warspite* and the *HMS Ramillies*, and struck a Norwegian vessel.

Millin readied himself to play. He wondered if his playing would be effective over the cacophony of war. The placid sound of the early morning waves lapping on the French shoreline was completely drowned out. All the natural sounds were being smothered by the firing of naval missiles, the roar of passing planes and the start of a violent barrage of enemy fire. The German shells were landing at a midpoint between the landing craft and the Allied destroyers. The sound of the Nazi shells overhead would provide a great motivator for the troops to get off the boat and get to shore as quickly as possible. A German salvo hit a ship behind the commandos' landing craft. The ship caught fire and unbeknownst to the commandos, 168 men died.

At H-Hour, the invasion started first at Omaha beach, then the invasion worked its way down from west to east along with the tides. The British RAF air reconnaissance[43] had built up a set of one million photographs detailing the location of batteries and gun positions, however some of these guns would be moved by the Germans shortly before the invasion.

First ashore at Sword beach were the 25 amphibious tanks[44]. The tanks of Royal Engineers were known as 'Hobart's Funnies', named after their commander, Major General Percy Hobart. These specially-designed tanks took the lessons of Dieppe into their construction, so they were more amphibious and equipped with flails. The beach mines were targeted to take out infantry. As the Funnies drove over the sand with the flails spinning, they exploded mines and absorbed the smaller explosions. Soon, the German artillery was aiming for the tanks with some success, so the tanks had to fire back at the German strongpoints before they had successfully cleared all the mines.

Next, on queue, the commandos that had made it to the Normandy coast, were waiting to head ashore.

---

[43] Using Bristol Blenheim planes
[44] 13th and 18th Hussars

Landing Craft: 200th Flotilla, Convoy S9 and 9A:
- LCI 506: badly damaged but took the crew from 531 and managed to complete its mission.
- LCI 517: snagged an obstacle and began to take in water just offshore.
- LCI 518: struck by a shell in the mid-section and then again at the landing ramps. Men were killed by both shells.
- LCI 519: took two shells but made it to shore and was waiting for H-Hour.
- LCI 524: beached under fire and took casualties. It would take a direct hit and sink on the way back to England.
- LCI 530: No. 45 Commando A Company, watched their stern-side as two shells hit another vehicle carrying B Company.
- LCI 531: hit and sank.

15 of the 24 landing vehicles landed and were ready for the commandos to go ashore

Lovat was counting on the skirl of the bagpipes to motivate his men to wade ashore towards the German guns. Other commanders would also use something familiar to inspire their men. In Captain Hutchinson Burt's landing craft, the No. 4 commandos sang *Jerusalem*. Major King of the 2nd Battalion, the East Yorkshire Regiment, read Shakespeare's Henry V just before coming ashore.

> *On, on, you noble English! whose blood is fet from fathers of war-proof... Be copy now to men of grosser blood and teach them how to war! The game's afoot: Follow your spirit.*

Curtis picked up speed to get the troops as close to shore as possible. He rammed the landing craft scraping sand on the bottom of the boat in about four feet of water. LCI 519 came to a jolting stop. The commandos should be able to make it ashore from there, then Curtis would rely on the incoming tide and the lighter load to help free the craft.

"Ashore is a line of battered houses whose silhouette looks familiar from the photographs," recalled Lieutenant Young. "They must surely mark our landing-place. On the beach, a few tanks creep about and fire occasional shots at an unseen foe. Ouistreham is not much more than a thousand yards to port now. Somewhere on the front are the guns that are shelling us; the flashes are plainly visible every few seconds. The craft slows down..."

It is 7:40 a.m. and Lieutenant Young's LCI hit the sand just offshore. The ships' signal men were receiving and relaying a message via flags.

"It's from King George and Winston Churchill, sir," the signalman tells Lieutenant Young. "It says: Good luck. May God be with you."

Young looked at the shells screaming both ways above the craft, then heard another landing craft echo in an explosion of metal followed by shrieks. A tank landing craft on Young's port side was hit. As it burned, the ammunition started to erupt throwing metal in all directions. The screams came from the crew trying to escape the shrapnel from the munitions. Young felt too anxious to fight and too vulnerable to sit in a boat offshore waiting to start the war.

"What are you waiting for?" cried Young the boat's skipper.

"There are still five minutes to go …" replied the Captain, a young RNVR officer.

"I don't think anyone will mind if we're five minutes early on D-Day," responded Young.

The nervous young naval officer gave the order to drop the ramps and four sailors lowered the metal gateway to D-Day. The oiled chains clanked for a full minute and then Young's men left the craft to become the first commandos to enter the water.

At 7:45 a.m., H-Hour+75, the order came down to drop ramps and go ashore. A horn blew and Curtis called out "Lower away." The ramp at the front of LCI 519 was cranked down and through the mist and smoke, the French shoreline could now be seen.

On LCI 527, Lieutenant Colonel Dawson waved the Frenchmen forward on his landing craft. Brigadier Lovat had instructed Dawson to let the French commandos have the honour of being the first to set foot in France. As they hit the shoreline, the commandos quickly removed any waterproof covering they had on their rifles and start firing.

"That's it lads, open them up for us," one commando called out on Lovat's LCI 519.

"Right lads, when we hit the beach, get clear as soon as possible and head for the road up ahead," a commando behind Millin called out.

Reality set in for the young piper.

"I either survive this, or I don't," Millin thought, his face betraying several hours of seasickness.

The boats were far enough away from the shoreline that the commandos would need to wade ashore in three to four feet of water, laden with 80-pounds of equipment, holding their rifles above their head. This would leave them open to a hailstorm of fire from German batteries.

The ramps were lowered and immediately the German bullets could be heard cutting through the water close to the landing craft. This was followed very shortly by mortar explosions. The landing craft disgorged the commandos one by one into the sea. The British commandos balanced down the ramps, into the water, and headed towards the shoreline. There were no screams or violent anti-German chants even though many of the men getting off the boat were about to make the last charge of their short life.

The Nazis had fortified the area at Sword beach with relatively light defenses, mostly beach obstacles and fortified emplacements consisting of machineguns and mortars, placed in the sand dunes and some of the shoreline hotels. However, there were also a few very substantial guns in the area to protect the beach. There was a 75mm guns located to the east across the Orne River in the town of Merville. The night before the invasion, Lieutenant Otway had successfully taken control of the Merville gun battery, so no shots were fired on the beach. There was also a very large 155mm gun located farther east at Le Havre, which was pointing out to sea. On D-Day, the large gun in spent the morning trying to sink the *HMS Warspite* but it failed to hit the battleship even once. It could have caused significant harm if the large gun had been focused on the beach instead. This left a few large guns that were placed inland. These 88mm guns were capable of supporting the beach defenses, but they did not have a direct view of the beach and would require radio support for aiming.

Sword beach was also protected by mines and antitank ditches. For infantry, the German troops consisted of the 716th Infantry which was capable of acting in both defensive and offensive operations. In addition, the 711th Division was just across the Dives River. In case of a sea invasion, there was a defense system where the German Army could set the shore on fire by igniting a flow of petrol. The Germans tried to ignite the sea, but nothing happened.

"A French resistance movement man[45] came and cut the cable," recalled Lovat, "which was rather kind of him, or we would have been set alight before we touched down on the beach."

---

[45] Monsieur Lefevre of the French Resistance

The commandos disembarked to find infantry already pinned down. The first tanks that were supposed to clear the mines on the beach had arrived with some infantry, from the South Lancashire and East Yorkshire regiments, to help move the debris. Once the tanks had cleared an area, the infantry would mark the path with thick white tape. However, the Yorkshire infantry was carrying out their first beach landing, so they did not have the training or experience in their troop DNA. Even the commandos had never landed on a beach that was defended as heavily as Normandy, but at least they had been trained in the challenges of a beach landing.

When the Germans started firing, someone gave the Yorkshire and Lancashire infantry the order to take cover and the troops started to dig into the beach. Once the troops lay down in the sand, it was a real challenge to get back up with the weight of an 80-pound kit on their back, especially for men who had never practiced doing this before. The result was instant target practice on the beach and the infantry was cut down. The tanks continued to do their job, but when the commandos arrived, they were greeted by carnage ten feet from the shore and no clear path markings.

"I often wonder whether they were sort of put there, as sort of gun fodder, to distract their attention for us to go in," remarked Private Spearman, commenting on the number of bodies that were already on the beach when he arrived, "because we were always the people that went in first, to do a sharp, quick raid and get out again. It seemed to change here, they put those East Lancashire people in there first … of course, if you elongate yourself on a beach, you elongate the target."

After cutting down the first wave of infantry, the German vantage on D-Day must have been daunting. The infantry, largely Hitler Youth and older soldiers, were witnessing the largest sea-borne invasion in history from the receiving side. The sea was covered with a pall of battleships, cruisers and landing craft. The sky was filled with bombers and fighters. The beach was being rapidly covered by commandos, more infantry and armoured vehicles.

The specially converted American Sherman tanks, part of Hobart's funnies, were officially called Duplex Drive tanks. When the tanks became known as DDs, the troops started to refer to the amphibious vehicles as Donald Ducks. They emerged from the water bearing their massive guns toward the shore. Soon, the Germans would also need to contend with a piper standing among the onslaught of fire power.

The Germans did not retreat. They aimed their defensive forces at the landing Allies. The commandos would have to get to the shoreline, then navigate across a beach that was still laden with mines and barbed wire, designed to direct troops into the line of machinegun fire.

"We hit the beach, and the ramp went down," described Corporal Nield-Siddall, "and I had two young boys with me, two young marines as a signal unit. They were carrying the radio sets and we landed in about four feet of water. It was up to my chest and I was considerably taller than these two lads, and they were up to their necks. Of course, the disturbance of the water from the shells and the sea and everything else, I had to virtually bounce them ashore ... we got on the beach, which was covered in bodies, and tanks, and smoke, and the smell ..."

Brigadier Lovat stood on the left ramp facing the shore. He looked over at Millin standing on the right ramp holding his pipes up high. Lovat was thinking back to the intelligence briefing when he said 'The Ouistreham end of Sword looks like a hot potato; the town is strongly garrisoned, but please knock out the battery in double quick time'. He hoped the Merville battery has been put out of service as he nodded at his piper, then charged down the ramp into the Channel waters. Watching the six-foot Brigadier Lovat enter the water, Millin gauged the depth so he knew how high he had to hold his pipes to keep them dry.

Before Piper Millin could start down his ramp, someone came retreating back up Lovat's empty ramp. The commando was picked off by a German sniper bullet that hit him in the head. The beret had offered no protection in real warfare and Millin watched the commando fall off the ramp into the French waters. Moments before, the soldier had said 'Well, cheers then,' and descended the ramp. Now the piper watched as the body sank out of sight. He had witnessed his first fatality at Normandy. Still retching from seasickness, Millin took the grotesque sight as a sign to get moving and he jumped into the cold waters.

Carrying his bagpipes above his head, Millin toppled over from the weight of his rucksack. Before he could fall face down into the water, someone grabbed him from the back and set him straight. His father's kilt began to float around him 'like a ballerina's tutu' as Millin got his footing and started to head towards shore. The water washed away the sickness from Millin's clothes and the chill of the water cured any further bouts. He quickly pursed his lips, inflated his bag and brought the blowpipe up to his mouth to begin playing. Paddling through the surf he played *Hieland Laddie*, a tune based on a poem by Robbie Burns. It was of one of Brigadier Lovat's favourites and used for a quick march. Millin proceeded to pipe the remaining commandos from his LCI ashore, in fine Highland style. Brigadier Lovat, firing his antique non-service issue Winchester hunting rifle, turned back around and gestured an ever-so-slight smile of approval to Millin.

Anyone watching this scene would have believed that they were watching a Hollywood movie, except this was not a movie, yet. The scene appeared so outlandish that the movie audience critique would probably be: 'that would never happen'. But it did happen. The performance was truly one of legends. The tall, handsome figure of Brigadier Lovat, holding his rifle above the lapping waves, as he strode through the waves, cutting a wake for his piper behind him. The young piper dressed in his father's kilt parading to shore as he played a march to keep the men on a quick pace as they headed inland. Like an ancient clan chief and his piper, Lovat and Millin led the men into battle, seemingly without any concern for their own safety. Green bereted commandos were not unfamiliar with acts of courage and bravery, but even these men were fittingly impressed by the fearlessness and almost blatant display of disdain for the Nazis defenses. The audacity was true theatre, except the explosions and rifle fire discharging through the early morning mist, were very much real.

Over one million men would land on the beaches of Normandy that month, but only one would be wearing a kilt. At the water's edge, Millin passed by an officer from the East Yorks who was badly injured. The piper's tune had come to an end and he dropped the blowpipe out of his mouth.

The theatre had concluded. Millin lowered his pipes as he stepped onto the Normandy sands. The piper crouched down beside other commandos as they surveyed the land to determine where the German fire was coming from and what route would lead them to the beach exit. A mortar exploded behind them. At this point, the piper was very aware that he was not carrying any weapons, except his ceremonial sgian-dubh[46].

"The commandos proceeded to land quite calmly," Commander Curtis recalled. "Every minute detail of that scene seemed to take on a

---

[46] A traditional highland knife that is kept sheathed in the righthand knee-high sock.

microscopic intensity, and stamped in my memory is the sight of Shimi Lovat's tall, immaculate figure striding through the water, rifle in hand and his men moving with him up the beach to the skirl of Bill Millin's bagpipes."

Men continued to come ashore. William Spearman, John Mason, Fred Mears, Anthony Rubinstein, Thomas Yates, Jim Kelly and Joe Patterson, all landed at Sword beach. The men were met by the chaos of war, the sound of the pipes and the dead bodies of the East Yorkshire regiment washing limply backwards and forwards. The sight impacted every man who had to endure it and would never fade from their memories.

Private Spearman, who as a commando had lived through the horrors of Dieppe, said, "I was shocked by the number of bodies – dead bodies, living bodies and all the blood in the water, giving the appearance they were drowning in their own blood for the want of moving."

18-year old commando Private Mason found himself "running through piles of dead infantry who had been knocked down like ninepins".

Corporal Mears was "aghast to see the East Yorks lying in bunches, it would probably never have happened had they spread out", then gloomily he thought "they would know better the next time."

Second-Lieutenant Rubinstein waded ashore further west with the Canadian troops. He could see the men of his unit struggling in the high water all around him. His friend Lieutenant Yates was drowning, but Rubinstein looked forward and pushed to shore. The orders were 'not help anyone and just get to shore', a considerable ask for a 19-year old to bear. For the decades that followed, Rubinstein would re-examine his decision with the conflict of natural human impulse to help another versus his duty to country or the necessity to follow orders. Yates died in the waters of Normandy.

Corporal Kelly, a 24-year old commando from Liverpool, faced fire as soon as they lowered the ramps of his LCI.

"In our group there would be about seven of us," recalled Kelly. "Within six paces of getting on to the sand, there was only me standing up. The others were all down, and I got told to get off the beach."

"There was a man standing there, in his full naval uniform, dead smart," recounted Kelly remembering the bizarre, surreal image, "and he were directing traffic off the beach. 'Come on, off the beach'. He wouldn't let anybody stop. 'Get off. Get off.'"

Captain Patterson, Medical officer, passed the body of a commando that he recognized, knowing that the dead man's letter to his wife said, 'I am no hero, I did not volunteer for this lot'. Patterson's day was filled with trying to stabilize and triage wounded soldiers, while he avoided mortar and gun fire. As he was leaving his LCI, he was hit by shrapnel, but fortunately 'it hit nothing important, I just swore and carried on'. He described in detail what the challenge was like as he struggled to save Lieutenant Glass:

> *I saw Donald Glass at the water's edge, badly hit in the back. I went to him and started to cut away his equipment. As I was doing so, I was conscious of a machinegun enfilading us from the left front. In a minute I was knocked over by a smack in the right knee, and fell on Donald, who protested violently. I tried my leg, and found it still worked though not very well. I got Hindmarch to open a stretcher and put Donald on it. I looked round for help, but the only other standing figure anywhere was my batman, who was working on his own with drowning wounded in the water. He smiled and waved to me. I tried my leg again and took one end of the stretcher. Hindmarch is a big strong fellow, between us we began to carry Donald up towards the wire. At the finish I was beat, and just lay and gasped. We took the stretcher from Donald, we knew we would be needing it later, and left him in a hollow in the sand.*

The once serene French beach had been transformed into a monstrous array of steel and wooden obstacles emerging from the smoke. Lovat was impressed by the height of the obstacles. The two-dimensional air reconnaissance photographs did not give a sense to the size of the structures. The enormity of the structures was accentuated by the continuous and unrelenting sounds as shellfire hit the beaches, mortars exploded, bullets cut the air and men were screaming in pain.

Millin spotted Brigadier Lovat standing upright brandishing his walking stick. With Lovat's brazen stance, Millin didn't even think of trying to duck the fire and he approached the Brigadier just as Lovat was getting an update.

"Good news sir. The paras have captured the bridges at the Orne," one of the senior officers informed Lovat. The Orne is the river in Normandy that discharges into the English Channel at Ouistreham.

Lovat looked over, saw his piper and smiled at the Private.

"Give us a tune piper," Brigadier Lovat called.

While British regulations forbade pipes being played on the front lines, the Highlander Lord Lovat still believed in the tradition of pipes leading the troops into combat. The pipes were an instrument that could boost morale, send signals along the lines and spark fear in the mind of the enemy. The power of the pipes and their ability to rise 'people to the occasion' had been proven in Scotland's history. Lovat knew that this war would not use the same type of combat tactics that were used in the Great War. There were no trenches lined with armies facing each other. Without these static lines, there were no troops waiting to demoralize the British troops by shooting their piper first. The commandos were prepared for constant movement warfare and there might be a place for the bagpipes once again.

Millin was sure the Brigadier must have been joking, so he called back "What was that, sir?"

"Would you mind giving us a tune?" Lovat requested again, not an order but a request.

Still thinking it was a joke, over the sounds bullets that screeched through the air and splinters rattling off the landing craft as mortars exploded, Millin responded "Well, what tune would you like, Sir?"

"How about *The Road to the Isles*?" Lovat responded.

Scottish tradition was to have a piper demonstrate the bravery of his platoon by piping his comrades into battle. Brigadier Lovat was a fan of this tradition and thought this was the time and place for the pipes. Millin reminded the Brigadier about the Army regulations that forbade the practice and specifically stated that the bagpipes could only be played at the rear of the combat area. However, he was rebuked by the brigadier.

"Ah, but that's the ENGLISH War Office. You and I are both Scottish, and that doesn't apply," stated Lovat.

"Now, would you want me to walk up and down, Sir?" Millin asked continuing to play along.

"Yes," replied Lovat. "That would be nice. Yes, walk up and down. That would be lovely."

Lovat was serious. He wanted Millin to play and he would worry about the consequences later. Millin realized that the Brigadier was not asking in jest. He raised his pipes up slowly watching for a reaction from Lovat, but he saw a gesture of approval.

Millin took three deep breaths, then he began to 'strike his pipes'. The procedure to start the bagpipes requires eight beats, which Millin instinctively counted in his head. As he counted, eight beats in five seconds, the war drifted away from him:

One, two: The piper stood by the shoreline with the three pipe drones rising over his left shoulder. The tallest drone, or pipe, soared from the bag, reaching skyward, tucked between the neck and shoulder muscles. The two shorter pipes lay further down the shoulder and were tied to the tall drone with a colourful cord. Millin's drones were made of African Blackwood, which was aged for fifteen years and then drilled lengthwise through the center. The bag was hanging below the drones on the piper's left-hand side. The piper's left hand was positioned on the chanter, which was connected to the bag. His right arm was stretched down smartly by his side, giving the appearance of standing at attention. The blowpipe was in his mouth and he looked straight forward as he started to silently inflate the bag.

Three: The piper brought his right hand across and up to the bag.

Four: The piper continued to blow into the blowpipe to inflate the bag, which now bulged full of air.

Five: The piper pushed the bag with his right hand forcing the air through the three drones which started a sustained howl. The bass note and two tenor notes, all tuned to an 'A', were not quite tuned to Millin's standards but they were more or less in pitch.

Six: The piper tucked the bag under his left arm and swung his right hand in position on the chanter.

Seven: The piper squeezed the bag harder under his arms and began to play an 'E' note on the chanter.

Eight: The piper played a quick grace note, followed by two pickup notes to start the tune.

On the next beat, Millin began to march along the water's edge and he fingered *The Road to the Isles* on his chanter. He paraded along the shoreline as the waves of men and water rushed towards him.

Brigadier Lovat smiled when he heard the skirl. He turned and even he was impressed when he saw Millin stepping over mortar holes and bodies as he paraded with his pipes. The German guns backed off for a moment. Capitaine Kieffer, who had just been injured by some shrapnel from a mortar blast that hit his landing vehicle, heard the break in the firing and used that time to drag himself ashore and join his unit.

Commandos and infantry continued to disembark from the landing craft. Some had to carry the bulky and heavy equipment; 3-inch mortars, stretchers, Bangalore torpedoes and telescopic ladders. The troops were greeted by German artillery fire, and the sounds of Millin playing the pipes. His 'show no fear' gesture encouraged the soldiers to run towards the fire despite knowing that 75 percent of the early group might not make it back home. The motivated commandos came running past Millin on both sides, laughing and giving him the thumbs up. Some tanks had been hit by the anti-tank munitions and were burning on the beach. A fresh boat of disembarking commandos ran ashore and were taking cover behind the burning tanks. The constant pock of the barrage of mortar bursts, and the thick smoke screen, disoriented the troops on their rush to the beach. The skirl of pipes helped to guide the soldiers to shore.

"That's the stuff, Jock," one commando called out as he marches ashore.

A Sergeant came to the water's edge and put his hand on Millin's shoulder.

"What are you fucking playing at, you mad bastard? You are attracting all the German attention. Every German in France knows we're here now, you silly bastard," the Sergeant said, then he ran up the beach to take his position behind the low seawall separating the beach from the land.

Millin smiled with the thought that this one must be English, and he must be new to the unit. 'Mad Bastard' was the nickname the unit had for Brigadier Lovat.

At the seawall, the men started cheering and let out a big 'Hooray'. Millin continued to squeeze air through the drones past the pipe reeds. The water of the English Channel lapping around his boots was beginning to flow with red streams from the carnage. Millin didn't miss a beat as he stepped over the bodies of the men that had failed to reach safe cover. Some corpses began to float out to sea as the incoming tide made the beach area smaller. The bodies became entangled on the Nazi obstacles placed in the water.

A couple of German Messerschmitt airplanes arrived and started to strife the beach. Right on schedule, British Spitfires arrived to chase the German aircraft after only a few minutes of firing. A formation of rocket firing Typhoon aircraft roared by as it returned to England to refuel and re-arm.

The Germans that could hear Millin were confused by the sound. The Germans that could see the piper were perplexed by the sight. Germans notably disliked the sound of the bagpipes and the 'ladies from hell' that played them. Millin marched along the shoreline for the third time and he finished his third stanza of '*The Road to the Isles*', then he let the song wind down and took his mouth off the blowpipe. For a moment, he looked and took in the scene in front of him. Bullets flashed past him on his left, then on his right.

Piper Bill Millin had witnessed horrific beach scenes, including the death of some of his commando friends, men he had been training with for several years. The unlucky men of the East Yorks were no longer making any sound, but they were still contributing to the sights and smells surrounding the piper. These were memories that would stay with Millin for the rest of his life. With fear pulsing through his fingertips, the young piper brought the blowpipe back up to his lips and started playing '*All the Blue Bonnets are Over the Border*'. The pipes were drowning out the sound of enemy fire for many of Millin's fellow commandos, but the piper could feel the ground shudder as the mortar fire hit the sand near him.

Malindine E G (Lt) War Office official photographer, Imperial War Museum

Lord Lovat addressing the No. 4 Commando unit (1943)

War Office official photographer, Evans, J L (Capt) - The Sun newspaper, credited to Imperial War Museum

Private Bill Millin plays for 45 Commandos as they wait to depart for the Normandy
Invasion (June 2, 1944)

Evans, J.L. (Capt) No. 5 Army Film and Photo Section, Army Film and Photographic Unit. Imperial War Museum

Captain J. L. Evans' famous photo of the June 6th Landing on Sword beach, Queen – Red. On the left, Private Bill Millin is about to disembark, while Brigadier Lord Lovat can be seen striding to the right of the line of commandos (June 6, 1944)

BHC 007014

Reinforcements (the 51st Highland Division) arriving at the Bénouville (Pegasus) bridge. Horsa No. 91 can be seen on the right, crashed on the other side the canal on the right (June 1944)

Twentieth Century Fox

Peter Lawford and Pipe-Major Leslie DeLaspee as Lord Lovat and Bill Millin in The Longest Day (1962)

https://www.pikdo.online/media/ByYUk0HoPeo

In 1984, a French tourist spotted a man in a kilt in the Café Gondrée. She approached and in her flickering Englished she asked if he was Bill Millin, the famous piper who landed at the beaches. She was a great admirer of John's and he told her his story then posed with her (1984).

Bill Millin at home in Dawlish, Devon, England (2008)

John Millin plays the bagpipes in front of the "Piper Bill" statue, in
Colleville-sur-Orne (Colleville-Montgomery), France, as a lone Spitfire flies by (2013)

6. The British, the French, X-Troop & the Piper

And the beast on the hill he looks like a king,
Then we pull on our packs and the sea rushes in.
And we hit the beach, we're pinned down by fire,
The bullets, the smoke, the call on the wire.
And Lord Lovat stands and calls for a tune,
From the Piper.[47]

Before unbeaching landing craft LCI 519 and returning to Britain, Rupert Curtis thought about the men he had just dropped off. The landing craft commander recalled "In my heart, I wished Lord Lovat and his men Godspeed as they moved across the fire swept beach with piper Bill Millin's bagpipes giving everyone's heart a lift."

Unbeaching and manoeuvring astern was always going to be a challenge, but now that the tide was covering most of the obstacles and mines, the task became harrowing. When the port engine failed, the sailors were lucky to make it out alive. Once the craft was clear, they set off on a westerly course, parallel to the shore, where Curtis said he had 'a grandstand view of the invasion beaches'.

---

[47] Fraserburgh Train – James Studholme, Police Dog Hogan

On the return trip back to England, LCI 524 after carrying commandos to shore, took a direct hit and blew up in flames. The high-octane fuel tanks ignited, and the craft disintegrated. A U.S. Coastguard Reserve boat managed to get close enough to the burning landing craft to save five men. The rest perished. With only one engine, LCI 519 limped home.

Philippe Kieffer was a Haitian-born, bank director in New York City, who immediately enlisted into the French Free Navy on September 2, 1939, at the age of 40. He volunteered for the commandos and put his fluency in both English and French to good use. Kieffer founded the 1er Bataillon de Fusilliers Marins commando unit, which also trained heavily under Lord Lovat at Commando Castle. The French commandos were all also volunteers. This meant that they were going to do what they had to do and had time to think about it before signing up.

Kieffer's commandos crossed the Channel on LCI 523 and LCI 527, sharing landing craft with No. 4 Commandos and Lieutenant Colonel Dawson. When Brigadier Lovat left No. 4 Commando unit, Dawson was promoted to command the unit. Dawson was a Francophile and a fluent French speaker. Lovat had told him to look at the French commandos, their 'eyes were bright, for they were going home…'.

"French fellows, be the first to enter your country," Dawson said on LCI 527, giving Kieffer's unit the honour of being the first to leave the landing vehicles.

The immediate mission for Kieffer's men was to capture the concrete casemate that they landed in front of. Unfortunately, the landing craft took a direct hit from a shell, killing three officers and injuring several others before they had made it to shore. Kieffer was one of the injured men taking a chunk of shrapnel in his left leg. He heard the sound of the bagpipes, which reminded him of all his training efforts in the Scottish Highlands. Kieffer had performed all the training exercises alongside his men. He pulled himself up and made it to shore. He refused medical evacuation and instead led the 'bérets verts' to take Ouistreham and marched all the way to the Bénouville bridge. On June 8th, he was finally taken to a hospital ship to have the shrapnel removed from his leg. He returned to combat to continue the leadership of the commandos on June 14th. He died at home in France in 1962.

J. L. Evans was a photographer for the Army Film and Photographic Number 5 Unit. He was assigned to land on Sword beach in Brigadier Lovat's landing craft, and then follow the commandos inland to the Bénouville Bridge. On D-Day minus 3, Captain Evans captured an image of Millin playing the pipes for the entertainment of the troops. When they arrived at Sword beach, Evans took one of the unit's most iconic photographs as he snapped the moment that Millin departed the landing craft to enter the Channel waters.

If the story of Lovat and Millin was ever said to be a myth, Evans' photograph would put an end to the debate. He managed to capture Millin leaving the landing craft with his bagpipes held high, following Lovat who is striding through the waters marching a column of commandos ashore. On the beach, the tanks of the Hussars can be seen clearing the minefields.

Evans left the landing craft and headed for cover on the shore. He was lying behind one of the dunes while Millin was marching along the beach, but with bullets and mortar fire filling the air, he didn't dare take his camera out at that point. Evans proceeded with the commandos for their assault on the villages to the south and continued to capture their success on film.

Tom Duncan was 20-years old when he left the Gordon Highlanders to volunteer for the commando team. He endured the challenging training at Castle Commando and had proved himself worthy of the green beret. He landed on Sword beach as part of the 1st Special Service Brigade. Private Duncan was part of the second wave of commandos to disembark. When his land ramps dropped, Millin was already piping on the beach and the earlier wave of troops were just making their way inland. The sands were being bombarded continuously. Duncan said that many of the early troops had already been 'cut down, suffering horrific injuries, as mortar bombs screamed down like flocks of partridges'. The men who had been hit before they could make their way out of the water, were struggling to drag themselves in faster than the tide was rising.

When asked to describe the scene at Sword beach, Duncan said "I shall never forget hearing the skirl of Bill Millin's pipes. It is hard to describe the impact it had. It gave us a great lift and increased our determination. As well as the pride we felt, it reminded us of home, and why we were fighting there for our lives and those of our loved ones."

Duncan survived the landing, made it inland to his rendezvous point in a swamp, then the commandos proceeded with their assault on the German defenses. That day, he was wounded by a German grenade and returned to Britain to recuperate. He would return to France two months later to take part in the advance on Caen. Duncan passed away in Aberdeen at the age of 91, in 2012.

Patrick Gillen was 18-years old when he enlisted in 1940. Born in Galway, Ireland, Gillen volunteered for the commandos and was posted as a sergeant in Commando Unit No. 6 when they landed at Sword beach. Bagpipes could be heard above the thunderous noise of the Allied planes, tanks and battleships, as well as the German artillery and constant barrage of sniper fire. Following the sound, Corporal Gillen raced passed Millin and made it to shore, stepping foot in France for the first time in his life. The Germans had held this area for four years, so they had established excellent sniper locations. Gillen concluded that life and death depended on his ability to move fast and not be a target for the snipers.

Gillen remembered Colonel Mills-Roberts telling the commandos, "If you want to see your grandchildren then get off faster than Jesse Owens."

The No. 6 commandos had made it to the beach but were slightly late because the landing craft had challenges avoiding the German defense obstacles. Brigadier Lovat was yelling at Mills-Roberts for not being on time and Gillen listened his response.

"With respect sir, we were where we were supposed to be at the right time, it was the navy that got us here late," Mills-Roberts said.

The No. 6 commandos dug in and held off the German counterattacks, at both Sword beach and the bridges, for 42 days.

Holding the beach allowed Allied reinforcements and equipment to come ashore and push inland. Gillen continued inland through France and marched into Germany, where he met up with Russian forces at the Brandenburg Gate. He would continue his military career, retiring as the Commandant with the Field Artillery unit in 1982. In 2014, Gillen was awarded France's highest military honour, the Chevalier de la Legion d'Honneur. He passed away later that year.

Before the war, George Fraser worked as a ghillie on Lord Lovat's estate. Encouraged by Lovat and like his father before him, he joined the Lovat Scouts at the outbreak of war. Sergeant Fraser was subsequently recruited by Lord Lovat again, this time as a volunteer in the Commando unit, to help with the training of snipers. Sergeant Fraser, 29-years old and a proud young Scotsman, felt honoured that his landing craft had been piped out to sea by the sound of Millin's pipes. He came ashore on D-Day, rushing past the piper to find safety with the No. 4 Commandos. The No. 4 unit fought to liberate Ouistreham and then joined up with Lovat just before arriving at the Bénouville bridge.

On June 9th, George's unit returned to the Ouistreham battery, where he searched the area and helped carry the wounded to the Regimental Air Post. When his Troop moved on, he remained with the medical section assisting in the evacuation of the casualties. George rejoined his Troop the following day and continued to fight against the German counterattacks on Ouistreham.

The Germans had taken a house and were clearly getting prepared to launch an assault on the commandos. George looked through the sights of his rifle, but the Germans were careful not to be seen. With that, the sniper put a bullet through each of the windows of the house, hoping that a ricochet might take out a German or two. When the German assault was finally launched, George directed the troops to repel the attack, which eventually ended in a victory with a fierce bayonet fight. Towards the end of the engagement, George was shot and killed. He was awarded the Military Medal for his bravery and leadership. Brigadier Lovat made his way to the orchard at Hauger for George's burial.

"The whole performance was carried out swiftly in respectful silence, in keeping with the hush of a golden evening. We left the battlefield, as it were, on tiptoe," recalled Brigadier Lovat.

Like all commandos, Sergeant Fraser had filled out a will before leaving for combat. His will was witnessed by his 23-year old brother, Duncan, who was also with the Lovat Scouts. Duncan was killed later that year in Italy. Duncan is buried in Italy and George is buried in France.

Maurice Chauvet, a Frenchman, was 25-years old when he landed on the beach in Normandy. Chauvet was a quartier-maître[48] with the Kieffer Commando unit. Chauvet had boarded his landing craft near the Hamble river to the tunes from Lord Lovat's piper, then he proceeded out to sea to great cheers brought on by Millin's piping. When his small landing craft hit the sand, its ramps were pushed open and he saw his homeland for the first time in almost three years.

The French commandos immediately faced the machineguns firing from the left. On the bridge, four sailors were hit and wounded. A 75mm mortar shell screamed right over Chauvet's head and blew up the ramps of the landing craft next to his. He didn't know at the time but the mortar had just hit his commander's boat, and Kieffer was injured by some of the shrapnel. As Chauvet jumped off the craft and onto the sand, he was overwhelmed by his return to his native land. Sword Beach was under the control of Generalleutenant Richter who took control of the area in 1942. His 716th Infantry Division had 8,000 men to control the entire area north of Caen, but now the sand below Chauvet's boots was once again French. He was a Frenchman in France fighting for the return of his country and this part of the beach was now his.

As the 1er Bataillon de Fusilliers Marins unit formed an eastern flank, Chauvet heard the drone of the pipes. Among all the explosions and bullet fire, Chauvet knew that Lovat, Millin and the commandos had followed the Free French to shore. Suddenly, Chauvet noticed that the Germans were no longer firing at them. He concluded that the bagpipe music had reached the Germans and for a few seconds, they

---

[48] A quartermaster, the equivalent of a corporal.

stopped firing. He thought they probably couldn't believe their eyes … and their ears!

Chauvet and the Free French commandos proceeded inland and fought their way to help in the taking of Ouistreham and then Bénouville. Of the 170 French commandos, 11 were killed and 30 wounded on the first day, and 144 would be killed or injured in the Normandy Invasion. Chauvet survived the war and became a filmmaker. When he attended D-Day memorial services, he would wear tartan trews under his French tunic in honour of his training time at the Commando Castle and his attachment to Lord Lovat's commandos. In 2008, French President Nicolas Sarkozy designated Chauvet an Officier de la Légion d'honneur at a ceremony in Ouistreham. Chauvet lived to be 91-years old.

Edward Treacher landed on Sword beach with the 45 Commandos of the Royal Navy. Treacher was called Eddie by his wife, but all the commandos called him Tommy. He had been through all the training at Achnacarry, received his green beret and had been presented his 1st Special Service Brigade patch by Brigadier Lovat.

Approaching Sword beach, at 400 yards out, in the midst of the resonating sounds of the naval battle, a shell hit the mid-section of Treacher's landing craft. There were 23 casualties including 11 dead on the boat before the ramps had been dropped. The smell of death started to encompass the beach. The remaining commandos had to step over bodies and shuffle into position, with the floor of the boat swimming in blood.

"We had to walk through the blood on this boat and it was really running over the deck and it was in a terrible state," Treacher recalls.

Four Navy matelots move to the front of the boat to drop down the ramps. Before they could get the ramps lowered, another shell hit, this time on the bow of the boat. All four matelots were killed, decapitated in the explosion. Private Treacher looks behind him at commando bodies, then up front at Navy bodies. A lieutenant charged forward with three sergeants and pushed the ramps down. They were still 300 yards from shore as they struggled with the metal ramps. The ramps were twisted and mangled, but the four men were able to get what's left of the front of the boat lowered before another shell hits the landing craft.

"How are you Jasper?" Treacher asked another commando jokingly.

"How am I Tom? How am I," replied Private Higbee. "I reckon I've broke both me legs. I can't get up. I can't walk."

"Oh well, I'll see you when I arrive back," Treacher responded as he jumped off the landing craft and into the war.

"Yea, that's alright. I can't get off this boat," Higbee sighed.

Treacher knew Higbee would be okay, as long as the landing craft wasn't hit a third time. He smiled at Higbee and set off for the shoreline. He was carrying 85 pounds of kit and the water was deep. For a brief moment, it was a relief to get out of the pool of blood on the boat, but then Tommy got a view of the scene on Sword beach.

"When we got down on that beach, the beach was aw … there was bloke laying dead, there was dead in the water, you've never seen anything like it." recalled Treacher. "These East Lanks and East Yorks, they went in before us. And aw … that was in a terrible state. As we landed, they were shelling us, they was machinegunning us, everything, they were throwing everything at us. And I tell you, it was absolutely bedlam, but our orders were: get off the beach as soon as you possibly can … and Bill Millin at the time, he was piping us to shore. He was piping on those beaches ashore and he was playing his pipes."

One of the war's strangest events occurred when Peter King became bored waiting for the invasion of Europe and decided to take matters into his own hands. Sergeant-Major King, a regular soldier, was assigned to the Dental Unit and had seen very little action. He applied for a transfer but was turned down. In 1942, King, who was 26-years old, convinced a 19-year old dental assistant, Private Cuthbertson, that they needed to be proactive. So, the two impatient warriors wrote a letter to Prime Minister Churchill advising him that they were launching Operation Wild Dog and they were going to invade France. And they did.

The two men stole weapons, grenades and a boat and sailed across the Channel to France. They blew up railway tracks, cut communication wires and generally caused havoc for Germans across the French countryside. After three days, they stole a French boat and set sail for home, expecting a hero's welcome. However, their boat broke down and they were adrift in the Channel for 12 days, before being picked up by Air-Sea Rescue.

The return of the dentist unit escapees was not the hero's welcome that the two had anticipated. Initially, they were treated likes spies, then they were charged with theft and leaving their ranks. They were court-martialled for their efforts.

Demoted, King was stripped down to a Private and posted in Scotland. When Lovat heard of King's exploits, he asked Lieutenant Colonel Vaughan to post King to No. 4 Unit. In the commandos, King rose up to Troop Sergeant-Major. On June 6th, 1944, King invaded France for the second time. Running past a piper on the shores of Normandy, King charged inland and within the hour was fighting his way to a Military Cross for outstanding courage.

Stanley Worsley was a Marine in 45 Commando unit and a member of E company. His platoon was onboard LCI 519, along with Brigadier Lovat and Private Millin. Stan advanced to the beach alongside Millin, who piped the commandos from LCI 519 ashore. Stan survived the march through the waters, across the beach of Normandy and then the advance seven miles inland to the bridges at Bénouville. His company bogged down marching through a marshy field that had been flooded by the Germans. They were fired on by German mortars but fortunately, many of the mortars failed to explode as they spattered into the bog.

After crossing and taking a position on the east side of the bridges, E company settled in at the end of D-Day. On June 7, 1944, Worsley was reported missing in action. That week, his mother and father were at home in a Manchester subdivision, when they were informed that their youngest son was 'Missing on war service'. Later the status was updated to 'Reported to the Admiralty as Prisoner of War in German Hands'. POW No. 80157 had been taken to Marlag und Milag Nord concentration camp, located around the village of Westertimke. Because of its location 50 miles from the shores of the North Sea, the camp was used largely for British Merchant Navy and Royal Navy prisoners. Fortunately, Stan was not identified as a commando because he wore naval badges on his uniform.

The camp was split into two parts, Milag for Merchant Seaman and Marlag for Royal Navy prisoners. Marlags were for sailors and Stalags were for soldiers. The Marlag prison was well organized with thousands of men living six or eight people per hut. There were enough captives that there were a few doctors in the camp. There was an entertainment committee that performed in a large communal area. There was a library with 3,000 books. The food was reasonable and eventually the soldiers received regular Red Cross parcels. Tins of corned beef would be merged to create a feast. The Red Cross also passed letters back home, although everything was censored.

Whenever a new prisoner entered the camp, he would relay the news of the war. When Worsley arrived, he announced to camp that the Western front had begun at Normandy. Each man entering the camp brought news of Allied success. Eventually, one man on a work detail managed to come back with a radio receiver. As France fell, then Belgium, then Luxembourg, the sailors and marines were able to feel that the drive to Germany was well underway.

In early April 1945, with the threat of the approaching Allied forces, one hundred SS-Feldgendarmerie arrived and marched over 3,000 prisoners out of the camp and headed east towards Lübeck. The next day, as the column of men were headed through Germany, an RAF fighter came in and strafed the column mistakenly killing several prisoners. On April 16, before the prisoners reached their destination, Worsley managed to escape, and he made his way back to England by the end of the month.

Joe Pasquale was 25-years old on D-Day. Lance Corporal Joseph Pasquale had previously landed with Lord Lovat in Dieppe. Both he and his younger brother Domenic (the commandos called him Jim) were with the Royal Army Medical Corps and had been assigned to the No. 4 Commando unit.

Joe came ashore to the sound of distant bagpipes on D-Day with a particular determination. Winning the war was even more important to Joe ever since Domenic had been captured at Dieppe. Domenic had decided to stay with a few wounded men to ensure that they cared for when their capture appeared inevitable. Domenic was only 19-years old when he was taken prisoner. Joe imagined the push into Germany and seeing his young brother's face when he was freed from the prisoner of war camp.

On the eastern flank, Joe rushed ashore to the safety of a wall by a large chateau. Joe had married Jean Carter the previous year. Jean would learn that Joe was killed in action two days later. However, Jean was spared the details of how a German mortar was dropped from the Chateau and took most of Joe's head off.

Joe's mother, Winifred Pasquale lost her husband in 1940. She was then informed that their son Domenic was missing in action at Dieppe in 1942, then their daughter-in-law told them her other son Joseph Jr. had been killed in action at Normandy in 1944.

After being captured at Dieppe, Domenic Pasquale spent most of the war in Stalag VIII-B in Lamsdorf, Germany. After three long years, he still imagined returning to his parent's house in Liverpool. Once home, he would learn about all the war's great battles through the stories his older brother would share with him. Domenic didn't learn about Joe's death until he was released from the POW camp at the end of the war.

Phillip Wellesley-Colley was born in London and was 25-years old on D-Day. After joining the Royal Horse Artillery, he met and married Valerie Canning. That same year, the couple gave birth to their daughter, Angela. The following year, in 1943, Wellesley-Colley volunteered for the Commandos and he earned his green beret.

Lieutenant Wellesley-Colley led a detachment of the No. 4 Commando unit, off their landing craft and onto Sword beach where Millin was playing. Behind him was young Private Roy Maxwell, age 21. A machinegun bore down on the men and the lead man took the brunt of the damage. To Maxwell's shock and horror, he watched as his lieutenant fell. Wellesley-Colley was one of No. 4's first casualties on Sword beach. In December, Valerie gave birth to Elizabeth, their second daughter.

Lieutenant Wellesley-Colley was buried at the Commonwealth War Graves Commission's Bayeaux War Cemetery. In 2019, on the 75th anniversary of D-Day, an emotional Roy Maxwell visited the grave of his fallen friend. On D-Day, Maxwell thought of the lieutenant as an older man, leading the way off the beach, now he thought of Wellesley-Colley as a young man, cut down before his life had even begun.

"Yes indeed. There we are mate," Maxwell said as he patted the top of the headstone. "I remember him a very decent man. Yeah, he was a young fellow you know. I can remember calmness before it started, and then all hell broke loose."

Maxwell shed a tear for the man that led him ashore and bravely took enemy fire.

Ken Sturdy was 24-years old when he landed at Normandy. He was a signalman for the Royal Navy and was landing on the beach with the 41st Commando Royal Marines. His job would be to send vital messages back to the ships. Radio signals were not always reliable in 1944, so Ken could manually request position changes in naval bombardments using flags. As he left his landing craft, he dropped his rifle. He was very aware that he was entering a war zone without a weapon and was extremely nervous. Sturdy was guided to the shore that day by the sound of Millin's pipes. Bullets flew past but he knew he couldn't pause, even when fellow commandos were falling around him.

"Among all the noise and bedlam going on I could hear bagpipes. I thought I had imagined them, and it wasn't until later that I realised I really had heard them," Ken said. "It's strange how the sound of a bagpipe carries even above this tremendous noise level."

Once ashore, Ken ran past the piper and dove for cover quickly into a ditch. He reached inside his jacket for his cigarettes and realized that he didn't have any matches. He turned to another soldier who had also made it to the same ditch.

"Have you got a match mate?" Ken asked.

The other soldier had also followed the sound of the pipes to shore. He turned and smiled warmly at Ken. The soldier was Ken's younger brother, Norman. The two brothers hadn't seen each other in over four years. They had been guided to the same ditch on Sword beach, guided to safety by the sound of the pipes.

"What are you doing here?" Norman responded jokingly.

In the middle of the bedlam, Ken and his brother turned to watch the piper's performance and they caught up with each other. Ken learned that his brother signed up at Padgate in 1942. A mortar exploded near the shoreline and the two men looked towards the piper to see if he had been wounded.

"Bill marched boldly with his pipes in a situation that was quite unbelievable," Ken remembered. "It was in the heat of battle, there was a lot of gunfire and he was unarmed except for his pipes and his dirk. It was certainly heroic. People were dying around him and he was in the most alarming situation so he must have been a very cool young fellow."

Another procession of commandos was greeted by the bagpipes and then a naval officer came over to order the Royal Marine Commandos to get off the beach.

"I can remember a Beach Master," recalled Ken, "he was a navy officer I think, and he had of all things a bulldog on a lead. It made me think of Churchill of course. And he was yelling 'Get off the beach'. His instructions of course as beach master was to clear that beach and get people over the seawall because the Germans had the range of that beach."

Years later, Ken Sturdy met Bill Millin and told him that he could remember hearing the pipes as he came to shore.

"We talked about armament," Ken recalled, remembering that he had dropped his rifle. "All I went to shore with was my pistol, you see and he said, 'My pipes were my weapon'."

In 2015, Ken's heroism was recognized as he was awarded the Légion d'Honneur from France. Ken Sturdy passed away in Calgary in 2018 at the age of 98.

In 1943, 21-year old Harold Pickersgill, was working on the invasion plans for a newly formed reconnaissance regiment. Private Pickersgill's assignment was to draw relief maps based on aerial photographs. A mistake in a map, could cost a soldier his life. Working for over a year on simulations in Scotland, Pickersgill had no idea that he would be one of the soldiers that would land in France, follow a piper inland, and never return to Great Britain.

On June 6, 1944, Pickersgill came ashore at Sword beach as part of the 3rd Infantry Division. His platoon followed behind Lovat's men, as they marched forward, with Millin piping the troops inland. When they arrived at a crossroad, Pickersgill took a motorcycle and headed west to his post. He was stationed for a month at Mathieu, a little village midway between the Channel and Caen.

In Mathieu, Pickersgill, who had high-school French, met a Norman girl, who had high-school English. As the story goes, 'they took one look at each other and fell in love'. Before he left Mathieu, Marie-Genevieve placed a rose in Pickersgill's motorcycle helmet. Towards the end of the war, Pickersgill returned to Mathieu, this time with the gruesome task of exhuming and identifying the dead while waiting for the creation of the military cemeteries.

"A huge trauma for him but it was the price to pay to be with Mom," said Pickersgill's daughter emotionally.

Harold and Marie-Genevieve Pickersgill were married and lived in Mathieu with their five children. Pickersgill worked for thirty years in the maritime trade. In 1998, Pickersgill was buried in Mathieu, beside Marie-Genevieve who had passed away four years earlier. Not far away, in Herman-sur-mer, they dedicated 'Harold Pickersgill Avenue' in honour of the love that triumphed through war.

When Russell Dunkeld was 18-years old, he was in LST[49] 304, one of the first landing craft to land on Sword beach. After the tanks left the landing craft, Dunkeld, a stretcher bearer, went ashore to convey wounded soldiers back to the landing craft for evacuation. With shells and mortars exploding all around him, Dunkeld was clearing the first round of young men from the East Yorkshire Regiment, as Millin piped the commandos ashore.

The music continued to drone when Dunkeld came across a boy about his age. He had a bullet hole where his appendix was. The soldier was lucid and talking away. He spoke very romantically about his home and his girlfriend. The bagpipe tune came to an end with Dunkeld holding the soldier's hand as he passed. Dunkeld gathered the boy's dog tag and letter to home, then moved on to another wounded soldier. Millin started up another tune, this time marching along the shoreline.

---

[49] Landing Ship – Tank

Dunkeld, who was 5-foot 3-inches, darted back and forth through the enemy fire onto Sword beach to retrieve the injured. After the war, Dunkeld didn't like to think about Normandy. The scenes, especially in those first few hours would be imprinted in a dark cavity in his mind. He would remember one young man who was blown off his motorcycle by a mortar bomb.

"Here, hold this," a surgeon commanded.

It was the boy's foot. Dunkeld held the foot while the surgeon sawed it off. When he was finished, the surgeon scowled at Dunkeld.

"Don't just stand there looking at it, get rid of it."

The surgeon moved on to another of the wounded, leaving the 18-year old Dunkeld to dispose of the foot. He flung it in the sand and then stretched the young soldier to the landing craft for the long ride home.

Dunkeld accompanied the young soldier and consoled a landing craft filled with wounded men on the trip back to England. In June, July and August, Dunkeld crossed the Channel 25 times in LST 304 to pick-up his wounded comrades, injured enemy soldiers and civilians. He received the Legion d'Honneur from France. Dunkeld died, a great-great-grandfather, in Lancaster at the age of 90.

19-year old Ted Owens was part of the No. 41 Commando unit that came rushing past Millin on the west side of Sword beach. Coming ashore, he witnessed the dead bodies and wounded men flailing on the beach. This was when the young man realized that this was not a game. The sea was full of battleships and the shore was filled with the roar of tanks, making 'one heck of a noise'. However, as Owens went down the gangway, he heard a different sound – a piper, playing his bagpipes.

"I don't know if he was crazy or brave," said Owens, "But you can imagine the men. Shut your pipes, stop drawing attention to us!'

Behind Owens, a tank came to shore with heavy rotating chains on the front to disperse mines. Many of the commandos were running up behind the tank, so Ted joined them.

"Concentrate your fire on the hotel," a voice called over the tank's loudspeaker.

Owens saw an abandoned tank, so he ran over and crawled to the top of it. He laid down with his machinegun and aimed his sights at the hotel. Owens could see men moving inside, so he fired five or six shots. He had disturbed the wasp's nest and the Germans launched a mortar towards him. It exploded less than six feet away. Shrapnel came down on top of him and he felt a white-hot pain as metal entered his left shoulder, his back and his chest.

Owens was knocked off the tank and was still conscious when he realized he was paralyzed. He could still hear the sound of the pipes as he lay in the sand trying to remain conscious. He was in terrific pain, trying to hang on to life. After a while more commandos came marching past his frozen body.

"This poor blighter's had it," one of the passing commandos said.

Another commando turned his body over to retrieve the Owens' will and dog tags but was startled when he saw the Private's eyes move. He had successfully been able to remain conscious.

"Oh God, he's alive!" exclaimed the commando.

They patched Owens up as best they could and gave him a morphine injection. He was taken by stretcher back to a landing craft then transported to a Canadian hospital ship. After three months, Owens was discharged, and they sent him back to join his unit in France. Owens and his unit liberated Pont-l'Évêque, a village about 25 miles from where he was injured. It was there that the 19-year old had his first glass of champagne. The next major offensive for his unit was at the Battle of the Bulge, where Owens would take a bullet in the throat. Before the unit continued its charge into Germany, Owens was sent back home to Pembroke Dock, Wales.

In 2019, he attended the 75th anniversary of D-Day, with the German bullet still lodged in his throat.

John Airy was a Private in the No. 3 Commando unit. His landing craft came ashore at Sword beach ten minutes behind Lovat and Millen. He didn't hear any pipes and his memories of landing was just the horrific scenes of carnage.

50 years after D-Day he recounted his recollections of the landing: "There was spasmodic shelling on the beach as we arrived. Many bodies lay sprawled all over the beach, as young men of the East

Yorkshire Regiment who had been in the first wave of the landing, now lay mutilated or dying."

The No. 3 Commando unit landed and marched inland to join up with Lovat's beloved No. 4 Commando unit. Before they had even spotted Lovat and his men, they could hear the bagpipes playing in front of them. Airy holds pleasant memories of hearing Millin's playing in the middle of the invasion.

"Our next task was to meet up with the 6th Airborne Division who were holding the bridgehead over the River Orme. By 2 p.m. with Lord Lovat at our head, his Piper playing a cheerful tune, we then crossed the bridge under heavy sniper fire."

Across the bridges, Airy volunteered for a stretcher party to move the wounded back down the line for safety. He came across a German patrol and was surrounded by Germans in a wood. Captured, Airy was transported across Germany into Poland, Stalag VIIIA. As a commando, the young Private was interrogated and put into solitary confinement. He was then marched further across Poland, in 'near Arctic conditions' and put to work in a Polish sugar factory for 12 hours a day. He laboured at the work camp for over a year and he received a ladle of soup and 1/5th of a loaf of bread per day. In February 1945, the Russians freed the POWs and Airy made his way to Germany where he was finally rescued by the Americans and made his way back home.

The French were the first of the commandos to land on Sword beach. Robert Piaugé, 24-years old, was on Sub-Lieutenant John Berry's landing craft when they hit the beach. Berry waved Piaugé forward to get ready to go ashore. He was less than two miles from his mother, who lived in Ouistreham. His mother was against him joining the war. She had lost Robert's father to his wounds in World War I.

The landing craft hit a beach obstacle, got hung up and was turned around. Piaugé jumped into the Channel water only to find himself in deeper water than he had anticipated. In the mist and smoke, surrounded by the splashes of mortar blasts and bullet fire, Piaugé was disoriented. In the deep water with explosions on all sides, he couldn't tell which direction was inland. He followed the skirl of the pipes and waded ashore. He was the third Frenchman to arrive back to France.

Mortars continued to blast the shoreline as Piaugé walked his first steps on French soil after four long years. He had made it ten steps towards his mother's house, when a mortar exploded beside him. The shrapnel filled the air. Piaugé's friend, Lance Corporal Flesch, who came ashore right behind him, was hit and fell to the sand immediately. Piaugé was stunned as he felt like a brick had been thrown at his back. He looked down to see his body had been completely punctured with fragments of metal. Piaugé dropped beside his friend.

A medic was on the scene shortly. He pronounced Flesch dead and moved on to examine Private Piaugé. The medic looked at his wounds and said 'fini', knowing that Piaugé was still alive. He gave Piaugé a shot of morphine, but didn't spend any more time on him, instead he moved on to the next man who looked like he might live.

"I began to cry. Not out of sorrow for myself, nor because of my wounds, but at the great joy that I felt at being back on French soil."

Piaugé lay in the sand, looking up at the sky, listening to the bagpipe music, waiting for what was next. He thought about his mother, then about his father who had died from his wounds in the previous war. As the morphine took effect, Piaugé passed out. He was picked up by a medic then carried out on a stretcher to an LCI that transported him to a hospital ship. He was treated for his wounds and eventually recovered in a hospital in England.

Bobby Piaugé survived his injuries and visited his mother in Ouistreham before the end of the war. Piaugé met Lucie Coquelet in Ouistreham and they got married. The couple lived in a seaside apartment, where, from his living room window, Piaugé could look out at the beach where he landed and almost died in 1944. Piaugé lived out his days in Ouistreham and when he was buried in 1998, he still had twenty-two pieces of steel in his body.

Etienne Webb wasn't supposed to land on Sword beach. He wasn't even supposed to land on the shores of Normandy at all. He was a bowman on a landing vehicle that was carrying an assault team to the west side of Roger beach. Their job was to drop off the soldiers and return to England to repeat the process.

"We caught one of those obstacles and it ripped the bottom of the craft like a tin-can opener," Webb explained.

The landing craft was ripped open and sank. It was every man for himself as Webb started to swim ashore. He had been injured by shrapnel. Wounded, Webb didn't want to come completely inland until he could see a clear path. He was not armed. Other men from the boat followed Webb as he headed diagonally, swimming to Sword beach, where he decided to come in, to the sound of bagpipes.

"What in the bloody hell am I going to do now?" thought Webb. "There was all this activity, bugles sounding, bagpipes playing, men dashing around, the commandos coming in off a landing craft and just moving off the beach as if it was a Sunday afternoon, chatting and mumbling away at whatever they were going to go through to do their little bit of stuff."

The beachmaster spotted Webb and the wounded men from his landing craft that were following him ashore.

"Keep out of the way, keep out of trouble and we will get you off," the beachmaster said.

Webb watched as the piper played and Lovat's commandos disembarked and cleared the beach with a constant stride and well-rehearsed efficiency.

Webb watched in amazement as the occasional mortar landed on the beach and the commandos just continued their tasks, ignoring the threat. Within half an hour, the fighting on the beach had all but stopped and the commandos had pushed the fight inland. Three hours later, a landing craft took Webb and his mates back to England.

Peter Masters, 22-years old, landed on Sword beach with the No. 10 Inter-Allied Commando unit. The unit was raised in 1942 with 10 distinct troops. One of the strangest troops within the group was Troop No. 3, under the command of Captain Hilton-Jones. The troop consisted of men who were technically enemies of Britain. Known as X-Troop, the men were largely Germans and Austrians, with a few Romanian, Hungarians and Czechoslovakians. The unifying language in the Troop was German.

Masters, like many of the men, was Jewish. Born Peter Arany, he lived an uneventful life in Vienna, Austria until 1938, when the Nazis took power. Soon his family was forced to wear a yellow star with 'Jude' scrolled in the centre. Masters' family decided to chance everything and narrowly escaped the regime to relocate to England that same year. After being held in a British internment camp, Masters was eventually released, whereupon he immediately volunteered for the new commando units. He took the name Masters and burned all his Austrian identification.

At Achnacarry, Masters studied the German Army. He knew its weapons, its vehicles, its organization, its documents, its methods and especially its mentality. He studied tactics, army language, slang, drills and commands. The troop would be used as reconnaissance for the commandos, so surveying and reporting techniques were part of their training. On D-Day however, he would serve as a translator for Brigadier Lovat. He would use a bicycle to be more mobile and cover more ground.

"I concluded that at twenty-two I had had a rich, full life and therefore could not complain if it were to end then and there," thought Corporal Masters. "But before that, I, who had been harassed by the Nazis, intimidated, and targeted for extermination, would at long last have the opportunity to strike back. What's more, I felt well trained and definitely a better-than-even chance, I would have to look upon the rest of my life as a bonus."

Masters and his unit were part of the first wave to land on Sword beach. He was the second man in his unit to disembark, and he carried his rucksack, a tommy gun with a thirty-round magazine, 200 spare rounds, two fragmentation hand grenades, two smoke grenades, a change of clothing, a blanket, two days' rations, a full-sized spade, and a 200-foot rope to haul inflatable dinghies across the Orne waterways if the bridges were blown. In addition, he had the challenge of having to carry a folding bike ashore.

"Nobody dashed ashore," Masters remarked. "We staggered. With one hand I carried my gun, finger on the trigger; with the other I held onto the rope-rail down the ramp, and with the third hand I carried my bicycle."

The man in front of him was cut down by machinegun fire, so Masters was the first from his boat to make it ashore. He had been told to look for the windsocks, which would both guide him and instruct him. There were no windsocks. At first, Masters thought the smoke and mist was concealing the markers, but the men of the East Yorkshire Regiment who were supposed to place the windsocks, were all dead, dying or wounded.

Trying to orient himself, Masters followed the skirl of Millin's pipe. Masters came to a dune and he lay behind it. Beside him, he saw Troop 3 skipper, Captain Brian Hilton-Jones, and he instinctively saluted, giving away the position of the higher ranked officer. Years later he would still anguish over this mistake, it was probably the only salute given on the D-Day beaches. Fortunately, the German snipers didn't pick it up. Masters made it ashore and linked up with his troop. He wouldn't remember hearing the pipes, but he knew they had led him ashore.

"Piper Millin, the bagpiper who had piped us ashore … I hadn't heard him until then, and I didn't hear him pipe even then," Masters wrote.

Brigadier Lovat was at the assembly area, directing and urging the troops on as Master approached. Masters saw Millin, who had just finished piping on the beach, march over to Lovat. Masters noticed how calm the Brigadier looked as he stood in the centre of the combat pandemonium.

"He seemed to be a man perfectly at ease, and shots and the noise in general didn't seem to bother him at all. 'Good show, the Piper,' he said as Piper Millin came dashing up. Millin was panting and catching his breath, dragging the bagpipes as well as all his other equipment. 'Come on, get a move on, this is no different than an exercise,' Lovat called out. He was very calm. He carried no weapon other than his Colt .45 in his holster [Lovat had handed his rifle to a soldier who had dropped his in the water]. He had a walking stick, a slim long stick forked at the top. It's called a wading stick in Scotland."

An hour later, Corporal Masters was approaching the village of Le Port with the unit that he had just been assigned to. As instructed by Hilton-Jones, he asked the troop leader, Captain Robinson, several times if he needed a reconnaissance patrol. Robinson just kept dismissing him. The soldier was in no need of the near comical appearance of Masters and his gear. Masters' heavy load felt easier to carry, now that he was on his bicycle. However, the sight of a fully grown, over loaded soldier, wiggling his way across the dirt roads, did not inspire confidence.

Suddenly in the valley just before Le Port, there was an eruption of machinegun fire as shot rang up from the village. A commando was killed by the shots and everyone took cover. The troop was pinned down without knowing where the shots had come from.

"Now there's something you can do, Corporal Masters," Robinson said, finally giving Masters his reconnaissance assignment. "Go on down to the village and see what's going on."

"Well, it isn't very difficult to tell what's going on," Masters commented.

Masters could see there were snipers in the town, but he would go take a look if that was what was required.   He envisioned a reconnaissance patrol so he asked how many men he should take.

"No, no, I just want you to go by yourself," the Captain replied.

"I will go around the left here and please look for me to come back in a sweep around the right-hand side," Masters replied, unphased by Robinson's request.

"You don't seem to understand what I want you to do," said Robinson. "I want you to go straight down the road and see what is going on."

It was then that Masters understood what Robison was asking. He wanted him to be visible so Masters would draw the fire. Unsure how many Germans were waiting to fire from the houses, he was to head down the road and expose the Nazi position.

"I figured my head was on the block," Masters recalled in 1997, "but we had been trained to improvise."

Corporal Masters boldly rode his bicycle through the street shouting in German.

"Everybody out!   Come out! You are totally surrounded!   Give yourselves up!   The war is over for you!   You don't have a chance unless you surrender now!" cried Masters, tying to imitate something he saw Cary Grant do in *Gunga Din*.

As the Germans stuck their heads out the windows, they saw Masters and were slightly stunned before they started to fire at him. He dove for cover and Robinson's troops open fired on the exposed German positions. After clearing as many snipers as they saw, Masters rejoined the troops and they continued their trek to link up with Major Howard's men.

After the war, Masters became a prominent television art director and U.S. government graphic designer. In 1997, he published a memoir about his time in the X troop called *Striking Back: A Jewish Commando's War against the Nazis*. He died playing tennis at age 83, near his home in Bethesda, Maryland.

George Henry Kirby was an able seaman on the HMS Princess Astrid. On D-Day, he was assigned to pilot an assault landing craft to Sword beach. He dropped his ramp and unloaded troops from No. 4 Commando unit, part of Brigadier Lovat's troops. Looking to the shore, he saw a man in a kilt, a sight that he would never forget.

"I will always remember Lovat's piper in one of the boats going ashore, who I believe to be Bill Millan, piping the troops to battle," the pilot recounts.

Kirby made several trips to the beaches of Normandy in June 1944. On each of his subsequent voyages, he would relay the story of the crazy piper to the amusement of men who were crossing the Channel and trying to summon up their own bravery before entering battle.

Harry Drew, born Harry Nomburg, was assigned to X-Troop. He was a Central European Jew. He went through the commando training and like his fellow X-Troop soldiers, he changed his name to conceal his background. Drew was 21-years old when he waded ashore at Sword beach, wearing his green beret and holding his Thompson submachinegun above the waves. He knew this tommy-gun quite well and had fired thousand of shots, using a twenty-round magazine. When readying his kit, he was given a thirty-round magazine.

"Alas, nobody had informed me that when filled with the thirty rounds of .45-caliber bullets, the magazine would get too heavy and therefore easily come loose and drop off," Private Drew said. "It therefore should never be loaded with more than twenty-eight rounds. Not knowing, I filled it all the way with the result that the magazine got lost in the water and I hit the beaches of France and stormed the fortress of Europe without ammunition. I would be far lighter than I had expected."

Reaching the shore without ammunition, he heard the skirl of bagpipes and headed diagonally across the sand to the west.

"I noticed a tall figure stalking just ahead of me," Drew said, remembering the sight of Lovat and his piper. "At once I recognized the brigadier and, getting close to him, I shyly touched his belt from behind while thinking to myself, 'Should anything happen to me now, let it at least be said that Private Drew fell by Lord Lovat's side'."

Drew headed inland with the commandos and as he crossed the seawall, he was immediately greeted by two Wehrmacht soldiers. The two men had approached to surrender to him. Drew, who was fluent in German, spoke to the two enemy soldiers. He figured that the men would have been filled with propaganda and lies, so quoting yesterday's newspapers he informed them that the Allies are were 15 miles from Rome. The Germans laughed and told Drew that they had already heard on their radio that Rome had fallen.

At that point, Drew decided to turn the two men over to a professional interrogator. He marched the men over to where Corporal Masters had come to shore. Drew left the two prisoners and continued his advance to link up with Major Howard's men at the bridges. After the war, he returned his name to Harry Nomburg, married in Haifa, Israel and lived until 1997 in New York City.

René Rossey was only 16-years old when he volunteered for the British 8th Army in Tunisia. After fighting for a year in North Africa, he heard about the French-speaking Commandos and immediately signed up. He was the youngest commando to land on Sword beach.

As one of Kieffer's Commandos, he was given the honour of being one of the first to go ashore and set foot in France. Nicknamed 'le petit Rossey', René carried a rucksack that was two-thirds his weight as he pushed ashore. As part of the KG platoon, Private Rossey also had to carry a 30-pound Vickers K machine gun. The French Commandos received some of the heaviest shelling that morning. From the moment they left their landing craft, there were mortars aiming at the soldiers coming down the ramps. Rossey made it to shore and took a position in the sand where the defensive bombardment prevented him from making it to the seawall. Fortunately, LCI 519 landed and Millin came ashore.

"We were pinned down on the beach, many of our comrades dead or dying," Rossey recalled, "but when Lovat's piper walked up and down the beach, piping his lungs out, the Germans seemed stunned, as if they'd seen a ghost. They briefly stopped firing and we made it to the barbed wire at the top of the beach."

Private Rossey fought with the Marine Fusiliers as they overpowered Nazi blockhaus bunkers, captured Ouistreham and marched to the Bénouville bridge. Rossey was only 19 when the war ended and he returned to Tunisia … penniless, jobless and homeless. In 1954, he moved to France where he worked for Total Petroleum, a company founded by Kieffer. René Rossey passed away in 2016.

Georges Gondrée was 46-years old on D-Day. After having worked for many years at Lloyds Bank, he was fluent in English. He and his wife, Thérèse, bought Café Gondrée in the French community of Bénouville in 1934 and by the time of the Invasion the couple had three daughters, Georgette, Arlette and the newly born Françoise. The Gondrées had provided some of the critical intelligence that allowed for the Bénouville bridge to be taken.When the Horsa gliders landed, Thérèse woke up.

"Get up! Can't you hear what's happening? It sounds like wood breaking…" she said, as she shook her husband.

Suddenly, there was some machinegun fire and explosions. Georges stuck his head out of his window to see where the sound of explosions was coming from. Georges watched as the German sentry on the bridge called out 'Parachutists!', his eyes widening with fear. Georges' head was spotted by Lieutenant Smith (Horsa 93), who fired a few rounds at him. Smith's aim wasn't the best at that time, as two minutes before, his wrist was ripped down to the bone by a grenade blast. Georges couldn't tell if it was Germans or Allies that fired at him, but either way he pulled his head back in. Smith missed Georges, but the bullets went through the window and ricocheted off the ceiling to hit the headboard of the bed below, where Thérèse was lying with her daughters. After that, Georges took his family down to the cellar for shelter.

Corporal Parr (Horsa 91) ran past the café and his eye caught movement as he stood on a metal grate. Hearing a giggle, he looked down and saw six eyes staring up at him. It was Thérèse, with her daughter Arlette in her arms and her other daughter Georgette standing beside her. Parr was concerned that the cellar was not safe from grenades or mortars, so he tried to coax them out but Thérèse did not speak English. Parr tried giving the elder girl a bar of chocolate.

Thérèse suspected that Parr was a German pretending to be British, so she threw back the chocolate bar, convinced it was poisoned.

The firing continued into the morning when finally, British soldiers with blackened faces abruptly entered the café brandishing their machineguns. At first Georges thought that he had been caught passing on intelligence and the Germans had come to take him away, but this time the soldier spoke with a distinctly English accent. When he heard the cockney slang, Georges knew that they had at last been liberated. Georges burst into tears of joy and Thérèse kissed the paratroopers. Thérèse's embrace was so tight that she wound up with camouflage black on her face, which she wore proudly for days. The café became the first liberated house in France.

Knowing the positions of the Panzer tanks, the Gondrées couldn't understand how this small contingent of British soldiers was going to be able to hold off the German Army. The family stayed, huddled in their café listening to the battle rage on, until suddenly they became aware of the sound of bagpipes approaching from the north. The sound was glorious to them as it meant the British had landed at the beaches. Georges came outside to witness the arrival of Lovat and Millin.

7. Dudelsackpfeifer

Back 'n forth I piped away
Many soldiers fell that day
Battle raging all around
And the allies held their ground![50]

Millin continued to pipe on the shores of Sword beach. He marched the entire length of the beach, three times, and had passed hundreds of corpses that were rolling in the surf. He could feel the earth shake under his feet with each mortar blast in the sand and in the water. Most of the commandos from his unit had disembarked and the landing craft heading back out to sea were now being replaced with new vehicles. Millin was stepping across a body, when he caught the ghastly sight another soldier's body floating to shore. The piper stopped playing.

"I stopped playing the pipes as I passed between two dead soldiers lying at the water's edge," Millin recounted sorrowfully, "one with half of his face blown away."

Millin let the air out of his bag and he focused his eyes back towards the land. He had forgotten about his seasickness and had been mostly

---

[50] My Head is Filled with Music – The Real McKenzies

distracted from the horrors on the beach. Now, the piper was no longer in his own world, he was now back in the middle of a war. He lowered his pipes and quickly headed inland to catch up with his unit.

The commandos were quick to clear the beaches. They had trained in the procedures with dozens of landings in Achnacarry and then again on the south of England.

"We cleared the beaches straight after we hit them," explained Private Fussell, remembering how the infantry had not been trained for beach landings. "Unfortunately, some of the infantry units of one of the brigades, who'd landed along with us, part of the infantry training was to … once you land dig in. Well, that was not what we were taught in the commandos. Our idea was to get the hell out of it, as quickly as you can, as fast as you can and as far as you can. So, one or two of our officers shouted at these chaps 'For God sake don't dig in here, you're going to get shelled and mortared, we're going to get counterattacked. For God's sake get clear of the beach and get to the other side of the road'. Anyway, these chaps didn't know what to do. They followed us, which is probably just as well."

Millin reached one of the small paths leading off the beach. There were a dozen badly injured men lying wounded at the entrance to the path.

"Are the medics here, Jock?" one soldier asked seeing Millin approach wearing his kilt.

Millin didn't know but he told them not to worry and that the doctors would be coming soon. He moved to take cover behind the low seawall where he had seen his unit earlier. Behind him, Millin heard the sound of a tank approaching from the beach with its flails sweeping for mines. The tank was headed toward the small path and toward the injured men. Millin got up and waved his hands frantically to get the attention of the tank. The commander was looking out of the top of the tank with his steel helmet just barely visible. Keeping his head down from oncoming fire, the commander didn't notice as the tank crossed the small path straight over the injured men. Seeing the injured men die, crushed underneath the enormous machine, one of their own, was the most traumatic event Millin would see in Normandy.

John Snagge reported at 9:32 a.m., the first report of the invasion provided by the BBC:

> *This is London. London calling in the Home, Overseas and European services of the BBC and through United Nations*

Mediterranean, and this is John Snagge speaking. Supreme Headquarters Allied Expeditionary Force have just issued Communiqué No. 1. Communiqué No. 1: Under the command of General Eisenhower, Allied naval forces, supported by strong air forces, began landing Allied armies this morning on the northern coast of France. I'll repeat that communiqué. Communiqué No. 1: Under the command of General Eisenhower, Allied naval forces, supported by strong air forces, began landing Allied armies this morning on the northern coast of France.

The world now knew that the Allied Army had launched its attack to free Western Europe, even if the German High Command considered the radio broadcast a poor attempt to fool them. At noon, Prime Minister Churchill addressed the House of Commons. He reported that D-Day had begun. He described the airborne landings behind the enemy lines and that thousands of troops that had landed on the beaches.

"I cannot of course commit myself to any particular details. Reports are coming in in rapid succession. So far, the commanders who are engaged report that everything is proceeding according to plan," Churchill told the House, then he added, "And what a plan!"

One of the most challenging tasks after clearing the beach, was assigned to the commandos under Major Porteous. Porteous was still suffering from his injuries to his right hand, inflicted during the Dieppe raid. His task was to head to the eastern side of Sword beach, Queen – Red, and destroy a German base in the tower of a medieval fortress. Once the tower was neutralized, along with a smaller battery, he would lead the commandos to link up with Lovat to help relieve Major Howard's men.

The attack on the tower was always optimistic and Porteous lost a quarter of his troops just getting to the seawall. That sector of the beach was not cleared or marked sufficiently, so the remaining obstacles directed men through minefields while mortar fire hailed down and machinegun fire sprayed out of a pillbox. The commandos used smoke bombs to disguise their movement and they made their way to the tower battery. Despite the intelligence that had said otherwise, there was no infantry at the bottom of the tower and there were no guns there. The 'guns' that were picked up in the air reconnaissance, were telephone poles.

"We learned afterward from a Frenchman that the battery had been withdrawn about three or four days before D-Day and had been resighted some three kilometers inland," Porteous recalled. "As we got into the position, they started bringing down fire on the old battery position. We lost a lot of chaps there."

The Germans were using the tower as a lookout point and the observers on the top of the tower were radioing targets to an inland battery. The commandos tried the stairs inside the tower, but Germans dropped a grenade. They tried a PIAT missile, but it failed to buckle the ten-foot walls. They tried to reach the Germans with a flamethrower, but the tower was too high. Time was ticking away for Howard's men at the Bénouville bridge, so Porteous decided to leave the tower alone. There mission had been to take out the large guns that didn't exist, so in a way that objective was accomplished. The commandos set out for the bridges.

"We were still soaking wet, carrying our rucksacks, we really looked like a lot of snails going on. But we met no Germans, except a few dead ones lying about," Porteous recalled.

On the road to the bridges, they ran across several civilians. At one farmhouse, a Frenchmen approached the commandos.

"It was very sad, a man rushed out and cried, 'My wife has been wounded. Is there a doctor?' At that moment I heard a mortar bomb approaching. I went flat and as I got up, I saw his head rolling down the road. It was kind of awful. Luckily, I had gone down faster," Porteous lamented.

As they passed a field of strawberries, the commandos walked through the field and began eating the berries. All they had in their stomachs was soup from the previous night's onboard dining, and many of the men had been unable to keep that down. A French farmer came running out and started screaming at the liberators. No one understood what he was yelling but they got the point: no strawberries for breakfast. For four years of German occupation, the Germans had never managed to take one strawberry from that farm. Porteous' men continued on their way to the bridge.

The No. 4 French unit was assigned to destroy a blockhaus bunker at the edge of the beach. Precisely to plan, their landing craft beached directly in front of the German defence. Once they made it to shore, they rushed to the firing blockhaus and threw a grenade through the door. The Germans surrendered the position very quickly. Once the

German defense was taken, as planned, the commandos swung left and took the remaining German positions from the rear. All the strongpoints had been designed to fire towards the sea.

Corporal Gautier searched the beach house behind the blockhaus to make sure there were no Germans. He found a man and woman hiding in the basement, the first two of his countrymen that he had come across. They asked him what was happening and were surprised when he answered in French.

"Rester sous couverture. Nous sommes sur un raid de commando. Cette fois, nous sommes là pour rester,"[51] Gautier told the couple.

The commandos returned to the beach to pick up their heavy packs, with four days of food and ammunition, then continued towards Ouistreham.

Things were starting to settle down on the beach. The South Lancashire Regiment was very proud that they were the first ones to brew tea on Sword beach. More medics were now disembarking and starting the gruesome task of sorting through infantry that was either killed or wounded. Some men were with the South Lancashire and East Yorkshire regiments, which had attempted to mark the beach, and other men were from the first commandos that had raced ashore. The medics had their hands full tending to the wounded and moving them off the beach.

The infantry at Sword beach had the best medical support in any battle in history. There was a ship designated as the water hospital. There were 70 landing craft that are designated as water ambulance. There were doctors, stretcher-bearers and five blood transfusion units. Medics were supported with a thousand refrigerated bottles of blood. They also had Alexander Fleming's discovery, penicillin.

A big burly Scotsman was one of the medics who was carrying a soldier who had been shot in the legs.

"To think they could miss a big bugger like you," remarked the wounded soldier, "those fucking Germans …"

As the soldier made light of the German's poor aim, the last commandos were making their way to Brigadier Lovat's rendezvous point.

---

[51] Stay under cover. We are on a commando raid. This time we are here to stay.

"We crouched beneath the eighty-pound Bergen rucksacks and, we hoped, beneath the flak the enemy were hurling at us," recalled Captain Harper-Gow. "When we reached the sand-dunes at the top of the beach I looked up and saw Lovat standing, completely at ease, taking in the scene around him."

Brigadier Lovat was greeted by the mayor of Colleville-sur-Orne, who headed down to the beachfront dressed in his full mayoral regalia. Five clear exits had been established from Sword beach, so the troops were making their way inland faster as most of the mines had been cleared, and the tide was depositing men closer to the seawall. The sand beach was churned with tank tracks and covered in a mix of carnage, rubble and burning armoured vehicles. Brigadier Lovat settled in and greeted each of the commandos as they made their way ashore in small batches of 10 or 12 men.

"Good morning gentlemen," Lovat said to each of his men.

"There he stood! It was unforgettable, the way he stood, with his piper behind him and his Fraser-Lovat badge gleaming in the sunlight. I'm surprised he wasn't shot then and there," said Sergeant Saunders.

Saunders, from Troop X, remembers watching the Brigade leader and thinking that he looked as if he was at a grouse shoot on his Scottish estate. Every now and then Lovat calmly brushed sand from his polished brogues when bursts of machinegun fire got too close.

"And his piper behind him … weh, weh, weh … they must have had tunes for going into battle because he kept repeating it," continued Saunders.

Lovat watched to ensure that the different units were headed out to complete their various objectives, as follows:

- No. 3, led by Lieutenant Colonel Young, would head to the bridges to link up with the 6th Airborne Division.
- No. 4, led by Lieutenant Colonel Dawson, would head out to liberate Ouistreham.
- No. 6, led by Lieutenant Colonel Mills-Roberts, would capture some beach defenses then head to the Merville gun battery to ensure that the paratroopers had successfully taken out the battery.
- No. 45, Royal Marines, led by Lieutenant Colonel Ries, would also head to the bridges to link up with the 6th Airborne Division

Lovat would march with No. 3 to relieve Major Howard. Millin, of course, would march with Brigadier Lovat. Each Commando consisted of 24 officers and 440 other ranks. The men were divided into troops each of three officers and sixty men. The plan was for No. 4 to split into two sections. One, the French section, was led by Commander Kieffer. The remainder of the unit would be led by Lieutenant Colonel Dawson. Kieffer's men would attack Ouistreham from the front and Dawson was to approach from the rear. The No. 4 Commandos headed down the main road from Lion-sur-Mer to Ouistreham.

"We said goodbye to the French troops who had landed with us as they branched off to attack the casino. They had a terrific battle but achieved their object, though not without loss. Some were captured, murdered, and buried in a front garden. These Frenchmen stayed with 4 Commando until VE Day. Magnificent men they were," said Private Bidmead.

Ouistreham had been heavily bombed by both the RAF and the Royal Navy. Dozens of civilians were killed or wounded, and many buildings had been flattened. Once the bombing stopped, the people set up a first-aid post in the town square, although 'Le pharmacie' had been leveled in the bombing.

"They're landing! They're landing," announced Charles Lefauconnier, the mayor of Ouistreham, as he ran into the town square. The residents of Ouistreham let out a great cheer and some of them started to weep.

Before reaching Ouistreham, the No. 4 commandos offloaded their rucksacks in front of the fashionable pre-war villas of Riva Bella. From the second floor of a war-damaged holiday home at the side of the road, a man stuck his head out of the window and waved the French flag. Carrying on down the road, the commandos overpowered Nazi defenses by throwing grenades into the blockhaus bunkers, using flamethrowers to disarm pillboxes and slaying snipers. The snipers were particularly pesky as the commandos headed south. Camouflaged in individual holes near the road, the snipers had to be stalked like the Highland deer of the Scottish Highlands.

Outside of Ouistreham, the commandos came upon a ten-foot anti-tank wall. The wall would delay the approach of the armoured vehicles, but it also gave the commandos good cover as they approached the town. The commandos pushed inland along Boulevard Aristide Briand.

Pierre Desoubeaux was walking through Ouistreham looking for wounded neighbours, when he ran into the commandos coming up from the beach. They were whistling the Marseillaise, badly. Desoubeaux broke down into tears. One of the commandos handed his pipe to the Frenchman. Desoubeaux would treasure the pipe for the rest of his life. When the team got to the first-aid post, the town people called out 'Tommy! Tommy!'. To their surprise, these Tommies were not British, they were French commandos.

In Ouistreham, the momentum of the commandos was slowed down for the first time. The Germans had turned the local casino into a fortress. Fortunately, the local gendarme passed on very precise German firing positions to the commandos, so they didn't lose any men approaching the casino. Another local elderly Frenchman, who was a veteran of World War I, approached the commandos and offered to join them. He was given a rifle and he joined the fight. He also pointed out where the communications cables lay, and the commandos severed the German's information flow.

As the battle for Ouistreham began, the Germans were quick to take cover in a defensive position. Holed up in the heavily fortified casino fortress, the German force maintained a strategic advantage. They were able to retain their position relatively easily as the casino had a clear view of the entire village. From there, the German snipers could pick off anyone that moves, limiting the ability to attack the casino. Lance Corporal Rollin was readying himself in an offensive position when a sniper hit him in the head, seriously wounding him. Captain Lion was the doctor in the unit, so he dashed out to attempt to tend to Rollin, but he was hit also, and killed. The unit had come to a standstill in its attempt to liberate the town.

The French commandos had landed in LCI 523 and LCI 527, but also had tanks on LCA[52] 13. Kieffer tried to radio for artillery, but there was no response. He ran back to the outskirts of town and managed to flag down one of the first Churchill tanks that managed to work its way around the anti-tank wall. The tank approached down the main road and continually blasted the casino until the walls started to cave in. The Germans who were in the casino were still firing from the crumbling building. The combat then became a particularly gory encounter as the fighting concluded with man to man combat using bayonets. Most of the Germans were killed but eleven were taken prisoner as the casino was finally captured.

---

[52] Landing Craft – Artillery

Once the battle for the small village was over, there was a visible satisfaction in handing the town back to the control of the French townsfolk, especially under the leadership of Kieffer and the French commandos. In a bloody battle where the Germans had some considerably heavy artillery, the British commandos and French commandos combined to take the casino in less than a half hour. The British were able to transport the Royal Army Medical Corps to the first-aid post to help the wounded commandos and help work on some of the civilian wounds that were inflicted by the British bombardment of the town.

Before leaving the beach, Lovat assessed the German artillery and surveyed a captured pillbox. He was impressed by the construction and its function. The poured concrete was reinforced so that it would withstand simple machinegun fire. The two-foot thick walls were six-feet high and had a further concrete ceiling. The placement of the pillbox provided an enfilade that was difficult to traverse. Some batteries had 75mm guns and fired mortars that made aim less important. While Lovat knew these defenses were twice as good as the British version, he also knew that his commandos were trained to move 'like a knife through enemy butter'.

Lovat's No. 3 Commando unit gathered the first of the German gunners that were captured and tried to assess the German defenses. Captured German prisoners would be immediately interrogated, then marched down the line to the beach. Over 10,000 prisoners would be transported back to the south of England during the next month. In Allied countries, the newsreel at the start of a movie would show this line of captured Nazis, with the narrator stating: 'Their days as Overlords are over'.

Some of the captured Germans at the beach were snipers. They were questioned by the commandos who, of course, had a German-speaking soldier trained in interrogation techniques. The Germans were questioned on troop sizes and positions in order to assess the success of the overall mission and the dangers in the next objective.

The snipers were also asked if they had killed any of the Allies on the beach. On seeing Millin, one nervous soldier confessed that he had the piper in his sights, but he didn't pull the trigger because he thought he better not kill "der verrückte Dudelsackpfeifer". The direct translation is "the crazy piper" but the connotation is that they thought he was "simple". The transcript from the interview would say "dummkopf" and some of the unit started to refer to Millin as "the mad piper".

"Well if I was mad, Lovat was even more mad than I was, I suppose," Millin declared later.

Ironically, Millin had landed on the beach with only a dagger and his pipes for weapons, and it was his pipes that had kept Millin alive. The bagpipes were the reason that he survived so far that day, without a scratch on him. The weight of his soaking wet wool kilt was pulling on Millin, so he changed into his denim trousers, before the commandos started to march inland.

Corporal Peter Masters, from No. 10 Commando X-Troop, was one of the German-speaking Jewish commandos. Masters had escaped the Nazi regime, and he had been trained specifically on interrogating German soldiers. He rode up on his bicycle to find Lovat being presented with two captives.

"Oh, you are the chap with the languages," said Lovat. "Ask them where their mortars and their howitzers are."

Masters questioned the two soldiers but got no response. He looked at Lovat who appeared to be getting impatient. Other commandos were vacating the beach and had started to gather around the two captures. After the carnage on the beach, some commandos thought that they should just execute the Germans and get on with it.

"Look at that arrogant German bastard," one commando said. "He doesn't even talk to our man when he's asking questions."

It was at that point when Masters' language skills probably saved the men's lives. He realized that the troops were probably Russian or Polish, and not German at all. Masters knew that French was on the curriculum in school, so master's switched the questioning to French. One of the prisoners responded. The man was Polish, and he had studied some French. Lovat listened and when the questioning turned to French he took over. Lovat spoke French better than Masters. As a Scottish Lord, he was well versed in the language of Bonnie Prince Charlie and Mary Queen of Scots.

Once the interrogation was complete and Lovat had what he needed, he turned to lead the march inland. No. 3 Unit was heading to the bridges by way of St. Aubin d'Arquenay. As they crossed through fields, Lovat seemed to have an inane ability to walk through the German minefields. He told the troops to 'play grandmother's footsteps' and the commandos stepped exactly where Lovat stepped as they marched across country fields.

"We were held up by a sign that said, 'Achtung! Minen!'. Then Lord Lovat comes along with his bloody piper and goes right through it, saying, 'Come on, follow me!'. We didn't know it was a dummy minefield," explained Lieutenant Wilson, who was leading a thirty-man section in the No. 3 Commando unit.

Every field was marked with a skull-and-crossbones and the words 'Achtung Minen', whether it was mined or not. Lovat quickly discerned that none of the ones that were surrounded by barbed wire contained mines. When they headed across a field without mines, they first had to cut their way through the barbed wire. A small controlled explosion, thanks to a Bangalore torpedo, and a gateway through the wire was open. A few of the mined fields had been recently visited by a herd of cows, so Lovat followed the cow path to pass through the mines.

The commandos reached the outskirts of Hermanville-sur-Mer, a small village of less than 50 homes. With a quick assessment, it was clear to Lovat that the Germans had taken up position and snipers were in several of the houses. He decided that they did not have the time to address this resistance.

"Don't worry about the opposition here," Lovat explained to his men, "the infantry will clear it up, because that's what they're here for. Our job is to meet up with the Airborne on the two bridges and we haven't got long to do it."

The commandos continued down a road that bypassed the small village. Lovat paused when he came to a body. It was a commando who had landed on one of the first LCIs and had been shot in the chest by one of the snipers. For the first time, a tear welled up and ran down his cheek as he bent over to remove the man's dog tags. He paused too long and one of the other commandos was feeling exposed.

"He's dead, sir," called out the commando impatiently.

"He's dead. Don't you understand? A bloody fine officer," Lovat responded.

Lovat continued to lead the troops across the fields, then across a road, then across a railway line. The commandos were still carrying their rucksacks and were wet from the waist down, but they still kept their march to a good pace. Lovat didn't even slow down to look at a map. He had never been to this area of France, but after all the planning, it was extremely familiar to him. Once they were across the train tracks, the smoke from the beaches started to lift and the commandos were entering open country. The din of the war on the beach was now starting to fade. They were three miles in and had breached the Atlantic Wall, the mixture of overlapping defenses that had been constructed such that there was no weak point. However, already that day, the commandos had proceeded through naval mines, beach defenses, land mines and snipers.

As they marched inland, the commandos passed the bodies of wounded, dying or dead men, most of which were British. Many were paratroopers that had the misfortune of landing in the wrong location. Others were men who had successfully fought their way in from the landing craft, only to be caught by a sniper on French soil. Millin saw one of the commandos from his boat take a bullet and fall to the roadside. It was the young boy with the cowboy paperback that the piper thought was too young to be going to war. A medic rushed up to the commando and Millin looked at the boy's face. There was a particular look that the wounded were wearing, and this hit looked serious as the shot caught the boy in the chest. The piper was aware that the next sniper fire could come from any direction and it could be aimed at any one of the men as they marched inland.

Lovat paused the troops and they set up an aid post in the concrete emplacement. This would become a clearing station for the wounded. Almost immediately, injured soldiers started to arrive. As soon as the radio was set up, Lovat (Sunshine) went to receive a status update. One of his officers, Lieutenant Colonel Mills-Roberts (Sunray), leading Number 6 Commando, had good news.

"Sunray calling Sunshine. First task accomplished. Report minor casualties. Now on start line regrouping for second bound. Moving left up fairway on Plan A for Apple. Still on time. Do you read me? Over," Mills-Roberts said.

"Loud and clear," responded Lovat acknowledging that the beach defenses had been cleared and Mills-Roberts' men were now marching to cross the bridges, where they would head to relieve the paratroopers at the Merville gun battery. The next contact was from No. 4, but it was not all good news. They had taken Ouistreham but Kieffer had been hit by mortar shrapnel during the landing and Colonel Dawson was injured in the leg and head. The bulk of the units were now heading towards the bridges.

Lovat checked his watch. Major Howard had seized the bridges and better yet, the bridges were still both intact. However, Howard was unsure how long they could hold the position and there was still five miles more to march. It was time to push on again.

The commandos pushed through the outskirts of the small seaside village Colleville-sur-Orne. The French townsfolk seemed to be aware that they were in the middle of an invasion, but they were not heading for cover. They were on the streets shouting 'Anglais! Anglais!', as the commandos marched passed. Perhaps, because they could get shelled by naval artillery if they were locked in the house, as well as if they were out on the streets, they decided they might as well be out on the streets. As the commandos passed quickly through the town, Millin played a march. The French gave him a round of applause as he marched past. Two nuns came out of the church and were handing out small glasses of wine. Millin unfortunately had his blowpipe in his mouth and he knew if he stopped playing, Lord Lovat would turn around. There was some firing, and the civilians ran the opposite direction to the rear of the commandos. The soldiers were running towards the gunfire and the civilians were running away.

No. 6 commandos were now linking up with Lovat's unit as they made their way to the bridges. In addition, a Churchill tank also caught up to the commandos and joined the procession. There was also a German officer in the parade, marching with a gun pointed into his back. While the tank could have gone first to provide protection and lead the men down the road, it was quite the opposite. The men went first to protect the tank as the armoured vehicle would be critical in holding the bridges. The commandos continued in two squads, one along the towpath of the canal and the other by road towards Bénouville. Lovat and Millin were again together in the group heading towards the canal road.

The commandos worked their way down the road. They passed by the 8th Brigade who were digging in for battle against any reinforcements that might be heading to the beach. Brigadier Lovat's commandos had no plans to wait for Germans, they were going to go find them. The commandos walked in single file on either side of the road, ready to jump into the ditch, fields or foliage if they encountered fire. Millin became very conscious of his lack of a rifle. Lovat looked over and nodded. Millin raised his pipes and started to play again. They continued to march and Millin continued to play. Lovat was a piping connoisseur and a bit of a critic, even in the midst of the invasion battle.

"You missed out three notes there piper!" Lovat called out to Millin at the end of one tune.

Lovat's critique actually helped Millin. Everyone else was armed, yet Millin didn't feel vulnerable as long as he had to concentrate on what he was playing. The commandos were walking in aircraft formation (single file on both sides of the road) and the road was raised, sloping to the canal on the left, with higher ground surrounding the canal on the right. They were very vulnerable and any Germans who were nearby would either take aim or flee as the sound of the pipes approached. About halfway to the Bénouville bridge, snipers fired from either side of the canal, as well as from the cornfields on the right side of the road.

Millin was piping *Highland Laddie* when he saw a sniper moving in a tree about one hundred yards ahead. There was a flash from the German's rifle as he squeezed off a round. Millin stopped playing and he looked behind him. All the other commandos had hit the dirt and were laying down on the road readying their rifles. Even Brigadier Lovat had taken to one knee. The sniper scrambled down the tree and dashed into the partially grown cornfield. The German's head was bobbing up and down as he escaped through the corn. Lovat stood up, watched the movement of the corn stalks, took aim with his rifle and fired one shot. The movement in the corn stopped. He sent two men into the field to see what happened. They came back with the sniper's body. For the second time that day, Millin had just witnessed Lovat kill a man the way he would shoot a stag running through the Highland fields.

With confirmation that Lovat's shot had been deadly accurate, he turned to Millin and said "Right, Piper, start the Pipes again."

Millin started playing *Lochan Side*, a well-known Scottish tune that had a good tempo for a quick march. Crossing through the fields, Lovat's commandos approached St. Aubin d'Arquenay. On first sight, there was a feeling of lament as the men viewed the town that had been two-thirds demolished from British shelling earlier that morning. The sidewalks were covered in wood, bricks and broken glass. Telephone wire was lying in twisted coils down the centre of the road. The commandos entered slowly, with their bayonets fixed. Eyes were constantly darting from window to window of each building, watching for the Mauser of a German sniper sneaking out. The commandos made it halfway through the small town without seeing any movement, from Germans or civilians. At the centre of town there was a crossroad. It was there that a man and woman were on their knees in a pile of rubble. They pointed to what used to be a house but was now a flattened heap of planks and bricks. The rest of the family were strewn among the ruins, clearly injured by the bombings. Lovat called for the medics to come forward and help the French family.

Suddenly there was a snap in the air. Behind Lovat's head stone chips flew into the air. The sniper had missed.

"He's over there," called out a commando and three men ran across the street towards the sniper's location.

The snipers usually only took one shot. It would be too easy to spot them if they came out for a second attempt. The commandos still approached with caution. When they reached the house where they saw the shot emanate, they tossed a grenade through the bottom window and then another through the top. Seconds later they kicked down the front door and entered the house. A few sprays of Tommy gun bullets and the commandos exited, holding a thumbs up.

Outside of St. Aubin d'Arquenay, the commando forces could see a German platoon coming down the road towards them. The commandos quickly dove into the ditches on either side of the road. The Germans were clearly not expecting to see the British this far inland. They were either not paying attention or the sun blocked their view, but they crossed a field in clear view of the commandos and Lovat's men were able to count thirty of them.

The commandos readied themselves for a fight. Lovat was relieved to take his 80-pound rucksack off. The commandos were in position and Germans proceeded oblivious to the upcoming danger. Two commandos manoeuvred to the back of wooden shed and quietly hoisted a Vickers K machinegun up to the roof.

"Pick the officers and NCOs and let them come right in," was the order that was whispered and quickly spread through the commandos.

On queue, the commandos let fire a barrage of bullets and the German patrol fell, bunched up in a bloodied heap. No commandos were hit. A few commandos approached and made sure all were dead. There was a thumbs up and the commandos marched out of Saint-

Aubin-d'Arquenay and continued towards the bridges. Millin started up his pipes and the commandos quick marched. They were now on the road that led straight into Bénouville from the west.

The sound of the pipes working their way down the road would seem anachronistic to many of the enemy soldiers; even more so when the sound emanated from an approaching elite commando force. However, at this point, it was actually serving a vital function. Radio equipment was still relatively short-range and unreliable. The pipes provided a simple and effective method of communication to the men at the bridge. Shortly before D-Day, Brigadier Lovat had met with Lieutenant Colonel Pine-Coffin and Brigadier Poett in England. The three men agreed that when the commandos approached the bridge, Brigadier Lovat would have his piper play. Then if it was all clear at the bridge, Pine-Coffin would have his bugler sound.

The war diary of the 6th Airborne Division for 12:00, reads as follows: 'Piper of 1 ss Bde heard at ST AUBIN'.

"At 1200 hours … the piper of 1 Special Service Brigade could be heard in St Aubin," Poett noted. "This was the pre-arranged recognition signal, but I did not give the answering bugle call as this would have meant that the way was clear for the Special Service Brigade to come through. Until the whole of Le Port had been cleared this was not the case."

Le Port was not clear and the area around the bridges was occupied by German forces. A steady sound of 'tonk' followed by a high-pitched descending squeal could be heard in the direction of the bridges. The mortar fire was a clear indication that the Germans were mounting counterattacks on the bridge positions.

"The Airborne sounded in trouble," Lovat recalled, "and it was our job to bail them out."

The commandos would have to pass through the town of Bénouville before reaching the bridge. From the intelligence reports, there could be as many as 50 German soldiers lying in wait in the village. Major Howard's men had cleared some of the houses towards the bridge, but most of the houses were still potential dangers. The village would need to be secured to complete the link up with Major Howard's Ox and Bucks.

When Lovat's men arrived at Bénouville they came under fire again. They couldn't march down the main street to the bridge. Millin stopped playing the pipes. The commandos took cover behind a low wall at the entrance to the village.

"A German half-track, upturned in a ditch, provided some protection for wounded men," recalled Brigadier Lovat, thankful for finding the armour that Sergeant Thornton disposed of at 2:00 a.m.

Lieutenant Colonel Mills-Roberts from No. 6 asked Millin to run into town playing the pipes on the way to draw fire. He was across the road as he called out to Millin.

"Right, piper, play us down the main street," Mills-Roberts ordered.

"No, I won't be running. I will just play them as usual," Millin said.

Mills-Roberts looked at the piper. He thought for a moment and then nodded.

Millin stood up and piped the commandos into the town. They followed behind him with their guns searching through the town's windows. The troops gradually slowed down and came to a stop. Millin was still piping *All the Blue Bonnets are Over the Border*, again. One of the commandos launched a shell at the church to the left. Two men ran into the church to see if the shell had taken out any of the snipers that would have probably been in the church tower. Other commandos then ran along throwing grenades into the windows of the buildings and houses. The main road was dust filled with the sounds of buildings caving in from the explosions. As the dust and smoke settled, Millin marched through playing his pipes once again. Millin reached the end of the main street. At this end of the street, the Ox and Bucks had cleared most of the buildings in the small hours of the morning, but Millin wasn't aware of that when he bravely marched through. Lovat came over to his piper and smiled.

"Well, we are almost at the bridges. About another half a mile. So, start your pipes here and continue along this road and then swing round to your left. Then it's a straight road down to the bridges," Lovat instructed.

Millin started his pipes up again and proceeded to march down the road, playing the now familiar tune.

> *"March! March! Ettrick and Teviot-dale,*
> *Why my lads dinna ye march forward in order?*
> *March! March! Eskdale and Liddesdale!*
> *All the blue bonnets are over the border ..."*[53]

Millin's eyes were now very focused on keeping a look out for snipers.   On his left ahead, he recognized a group of French commandos and beyond them he saw the Bénouville bridge. It was a relief to see some of the No. 4 Commandos, but there was still about 200 yards to go. The bridge was shrouded in a thicket of black and grey smoke. The black smoke was from exploded munitions and the grey was smoke screens that had been set to obscure the bridge from the snipers. The sound of mortars firing, rapid-fire machineguns and single shot sniper bullets, filled the air, so Millin tried to drown them out.

Ahead, Major Howard's men were facing increasing fire as Germans were arriving to try to make their way across the bridges to the beach. The counter attacks for control of the bridges were well underway. As the commandos approached the first bridge, they passed another grim reminder of war as both unburied airmen and dead Germans lay on the side of the road.

Millin piped Lovat to the bridge. The men at the bridges could all hear the skirl above the noise of machineguns and sniper fire. Howard's men, and the paratroopers who had arrived to provide early relief, all would remember the sight and sounds of the arrival of the commandos.

"We were at the bridge over the river where the gliders came in, Pegasus Bridge. Suddenly, out of a field, here's Lovat again, and his piper starts to play. Some men break into tears. Behind Lovat came a groan from a wounded Jerry," Lieutenant Wilson recalls.

Lieutenant Sweeney (Horsa 95) was lying on the east side of the bridges, exhausted. He was just wondering if he would ever see England again, when he suddenly heard the approaching sound. Sweeny nudged Lieutenant Fox next to him.

"Listen! You know, Dennis, I can hear pipes!" said Sweeney.

---

[53] All the Blue Bonnets are Over the Border – Traditional Jacobite Tune / Sir Walter Scott

"Don't be stupid, Todd, we're in the middle of France…", replied Fox.

"Bagpipes? What are you talking about? You must be bloody nuts," added Sergeant Thornton.

As the sound became louder and clearer, Sweeney smiled knowing that he was right. He was then overcome with both joy and relief when "out of the trees stepped commando piper Bill Millin followed by Lord Lovat, a tall man wearing a green beret and a white sweater and carrying a walking stick."

"We were moved around a bit to meet any German counter attacks as they developed, then shortly after noon we heard the sound of the pipes of the commandos led by Brigadier the Lord Lovat who marched through our lines as cool as a cucumber and led his men across the bridges to his own objectives," recalled paratrooper Private Brennan, who was 19-years old when he arrived at the bridges at 3 a.m.

"I think on reflection that was the sweetest music I ever heard," reflected Private Butler one of the paratroopers that had provided the first wave of relief in the middle of the night.

"It's them! It's the commandos!" yelled Private Edwards (Horsa 91) as the distant noise grew louder and he recognized it as the high-pitched, uneven wailing of war pipes!

Edwards and the rest of the bridge troops erupted into cheers. "Shouting and cheering, we all expressed our joy together," wrote Edwards in his diary, "yelling things like, 'Now you Jerry bastards, you've got a real fight on your hands.'"

"Word came through that the Commando Brigades leading elements were in the vicinity," remembered Private Clark (Horsa 92). "Within a few minutes the wail of bagpipes was heard, and Lord Lovat and his

piper crossed the canal bridge. It was shortly after 1300 hrs our spirits
rose … relief at last!"

"I can hear bloody bagpipes," said Private Allen (Horsa 95).

"Don't be silly, you silly bugger," laughed Private Wood (Horsa 95).

"Les, I can hear bagpipes," insisted Allen.

"You must be going out of your sweet mind, suffering from
shellshock," answered Wood. "Wait a minute, I can hear bloody
bagpipes too!"

In the first aid post, Lieutenant Smith lay there with his unusable
wrist and leg. Captain Vaughan had wanted to give him morphine, but
he refused. Someone asked Smith if he had seen the commandos
arrive.

"As a matter of fact, I heard them arrive," Smith smiled in retort,
"because, you know, this bagpipe business!"

"At about midday, we finally heard the skirl of bagpipes that
heralded the approach of the Commandos under Lord Lovat," recalled
Lieutenant Todd.

"The skirl of the bagpipes became louder," recalled Major Howard.
"We could see Lovat striding ahead of his men, clad in his trademark
Aran wool jumper with Millin beside him blowing away for all he was
worth."

Private Eric Woods was posted on the west side of the Bénouville
Bridge. He was stationed there with another soldier guarding the
bridge when he heard the sound of the pipes.

"Do the Germans play bagpipes?" Woods asked the other soldier.

"I don't think so," was the reply.

"I thought I could hear bagpipes," Woods stated. In a few minutes, the mysterious bagpipe sound was revealed.

"The pipes were an exceedingly welcome sound to all of us who were with Lieutenant Colonel Pine-Coffin, who could not give the call on the bugle to indicated that the route to the bridges was clear. It was indeed very far from clear," said Brigadier Poett.

Private Tough was clearing the area around the bridges shortly before the commandos arrived. Alone, he was caught by surprise when four German troopers fired on him. Ricochets, stones, dirt and pieces of shrapnel hit his right hand. He was no longer able to operate his Bren gun. Another bullet went through his front pocket and stopped in his army issue prayer book. A German approached and fired point-blank on Tough as he instinctively pulled up his knees. A third bullet hit him in the right leg, just below the knee. The German soldier left him for dead. Tough, living up to his name, crawled back to the bridge, staying below the sniper fire. The next thing he remembered was being patched up as the commandos were arriving.

"I have vague recollections of Lord Lovat's piper playing as he came across the bridge," Tough recounts. He was in no condition to watch the arrival of the commandos, but somehow remembers hearing the skirl of the pipes.

"Along the towpath coming towards us was one lone piper playing merrily away," Lieutenant Sweeney wrote in the Ox and Bucks regimental journal, in 1994. "Some 50-yards behind him stretched a long line of troops; the Commandos had arrived to help us. A bugler stood up nearby and sounded a call. Hollywood could not have contrived a more dramatic scene. Those who had landed from the sea had linked up with those who had landed from the air."

No one was happier to hear the sound of the pipes than the Horsa pilots and co-pilots. The link up meant that the airmen could now make their way down to the beach to catch a boat back to England. They were required to be back at base in case a second airborne invasion force was required. Of course, the success of the invasion made that backup plan unnecessary. Pilot Barkway, who Captain Vaughan had just placed on a morphine drip, would not be returning with his fellow pilots.

Lovat and his commandos arrived down the country road, the piper about three feet in front of the Brigadier, and the commandos marching, in single file, on either side of him. They marched through the smoke screen, towards the bridge, with Millin piping all the way. On understanding that the approaching skirl was bagpipes, a massive feeling of relief overcame the men. The paratroopers turned to watch the imminent arrival when they heard the pipes, as they knew the reinforcements had arrived. The link up to the thin red line was complete. The Allies had the territory from the bridges to the beaches. More reinforcements would be coming throughout the day and the brave paratroopers might actually survive the war. Even Howard had not been that confident just a few short hours ago.

On Lovat's signal, Millin stopped piping and they marched the final 100 yards. Millin recognised Quartier-Maître Chauvet from the No. 4 Commandos resting on the side of the road. Given that they had landed and taken Ouistreham, their timing was very impressive. All that training at Achnacarry had come in handy.

"Don't forget you promised to show me the sights of Paris," Millin called out to Chauvet.

"It's a bit early to talk about being a tourist," Chauvet mused in return. After four years away from France, he still had a thick French accent.

Lovat stopped marching when they reached the café, just to the right of the bridge. Café Gondrée is a two-story red brick building that was built at the end of the 19th century. Because the owners, Georges and Thérèse Gondrée, had provided so much of the intelligence, this meant that the first battle in the invasion had taken place just outside their front window. Many of the tired paratroopers hugged the commandos, with tears running down their cheeks. With this meeting of airborne and seaborne forces, the first major objective in the assault on Sword beach of Normandy was complete.

There were still sniper shots coming in, so the commandos had to watch where they were walking and stay low at particular points. There was a metal wall beside the bridge and each man would crouch down along the wall when they wanted to cross the road. Finally, one commando got tired of this exercise and he slipped down along the canal, up through the bushes to the trees just behind the German rifleman. He flipped a grenade down and the sniper was silenced. The commandos had been at the bridges no longer than five minutes, and now you could walk across the road standing upright.

Corporal Parr (Horsa 91) emerged from the café, just in time to see the unmistakable figure of Lovat, wearing a roll-neck white pullover, a green beret and a pack on his back. Parr stepped into the roadway and clipped a salute.

"We're very pleased to see you sir," said Parr nervously, looking at Lovat who had more of an air of an Elizabethan buccaneer than a British Army officer.

"Well done, well done," said Lovat, before asking for Major Howard.

Parr directed Lovat to Howard's temporary HQ in a pillbox. Now that he was no longer playing, the piper's mind was back in the war. He could hear the occasional sound of shrapnel and rifle-fire clanging off the metal of the bridge. He saw wounded men being carried on stretchers into the café, which was now the first-aid post. Georges Gondrée came out of his home, shouting, laughing and crying, all at the same time. He had a bottle of champagne and three glasses. He ran up to Lovat and giddily, in French, offered the Brigadier a glass of champagne. Millin and Parr both anticipated they would be drinking from the other two glasses.

"Pas maintenant, je travaille," Lovat said.

Lovat held up his hand and the Brigadier headed over to find Howard, leaving Millin standing in front of the café. Since his commanding officer had declined the champagne, Millin understood this to mean that there would be no champagne for him either. Private Gray (Horsa 91) and Corporal Gardner (Horsa 91) arrived at the café and saw the three glasses. Georges, holding the now opened bottle of bubbly, offered a drink to all the men outside his establishment. Gray,

Gardner and Parr all accepted a glass of champagne and they made a toast to the commandos. Fatigued and thirsty, Millin looked over his shoulder longingly as Corporal Parr relaxed for the first time that day.

"Bill Millin was a very hot, tired, thirsty, dusty Scotsman," Parr recalled with a grin.

Lovat arrived at the temporary Ox and Bucks HQ. Howard appeared seconds later holding out his hand and addressed Lovat with evident relief.

"Very pleased to see you, old boy," Howard said.

"Aye, and we're pleased to see you, old boy," Lovat responded. He looked at his watch and added "sorry, we are two minutes late."

The commandos had arrived two minutes and thirty seconds behind schedule. Howard smiled at Lovat's apology, after all he had held the bridges all night long and Lovat had only made him hang on for an extra 150 seconds.

"About bloody time!" Howard said, as he returned a wry smile.

"I was two minutes late," Lovat admitted to Howard at a D-Day reunion, "but I can tell you now, the Navy was two minutes late at getting us ashore! I kept my date."

Howard explained to Lovat that no Germans had made it across either of the bridges, but they were sniping constantly especially from the east side and the bridges were under constant fire. It was clear to Lovat that his troops needed to engage with the Germans and make them scatter if the bridge position was to be held.

"John, today, we are making history," Lovat said to Howard and he headed back to get his piper.

The Brigadier returned to his men that were gathering in front of the café. Lovat looked over at his commandos, wearing the most serious face he had put on that day. Then he looked at his piper and said, "Right, let's walk over the bridge. Millin?"

Millin stood to attention. He placed the bagpipes on his shoulder and was just about to inflate the bag.

"For Christ's sake, Piper," Lovat barked, "wait until we get to the other side!"

Millin was relieved and he kept the pipes on his shoulder.

"Right, we'll cross over. Now, don't play, wait until I tell you," Lovat instructed.

With that, Lovat and Millin quickly headed over the bridge. Debris and shrapnel could be heard crashing into the side of the bridge. Once they had made their way across Lovat signaled and his piper, now on the other side, started playing a march. The troops headed across the bridge in double-time. Not all the commandos made it over the bridge. Captain Vaughan was accompanying the commandos across the bridge and he witnessed one of Lovat's men drop with a bullet into his head through his green beret. Some commandos crossing the bridge after that would wear steel helmets. Lovat believed that going into war with a steel helmet was like 'having a piano on your head … you can't think, and you certainly can't move with speed'. The reality was the 'tin hat' of the infantry would not stop a sniper's bullet aimed at the head. Like the British, the German snipers had been trained to aim for the head as there are so many ways to survive a bullet to the chest. Once the troops had crossed, Lovat raised his hand and Millin stopped still with his bagpipes over his shoulder.

One of the sappers who died crossing the bridge was Lance Corporal Mullen. He was crossing the bridge, as a commando behind him was shot by a sniper. Mullen turned around to go back to help, and he was also gunned down. Lovat first met Mullen at the raid on the Lofoten Islands and he fought alongside him when the commandos participated in the Dieppe raid. However, Lovat had seen Mullen's paintings and knew he was truly an artist, not a soldier.

"Wounded and half-drowned in the landing, pulled over by a heavy rucksack, then picked out and dragged over the sand, Mullen the artist, like a broken doll, lay with both legs shattered, at the end of a bloody trail," Lovat recorded. "He was beyond speech but out of pain; a glance showed a hopeless case and death was busy with him. A gifted man, Mullen should have landed later with the reserves, but he would not hear of it. No volunteer in the whole brigade was prouder of his beret."

Legend would have it that Lovat and Millin marched across that first bridge, while the piper played his bagpipes in ambivalent bliss. Some would even say that he marched back and forth across the bridge, the way he had marched on the beach. However, if they had tried that performance, a German sniper would have shot both soldiers. By that time of the day, with the sun high in the sky, any German that was tasked with defending the bridges was able to take a position to fire pot-shots. When the event is captured by Hollywood, it would be a march over the bridge with the pipes blaring. However, the second bridge was to be where the real legend was formed.

"Another 200 yards along this road, Piper, there is another bridge but we won't have the protection that we have here because it's not a metal-sided bridge, it's railings, and when you get there, no matter what the situation, just continue over. Don't stop," Lovat instructed Millin.

With a nod, the piper started up his pipes and marched along the road. He played *March of the Cameron Men*, a fitting tune to match his father's kilt but not very fitting to parade with the Chief of the Clan Fraser. The commandos again followed him. When he got to the second bridge, the Ranville bridge, he repeated *All the Blue Bonnets are Over the Border* again. His piping was starting to wane as his embouchure muscles started to give way. He had been piping on and off for the past five hours and he could feel the weight of his rucksack, which now included his father's wet kilt.

As Millin piped the commandos to the bridge, two airborne officers on the other side were dug into a small pit and were frantically signaling. They were pointing down to the right side of the river, obviously trying to warn Millin about snipers. Under orders, he kept marching towards the bridge. Eventually, the two men started shouting.

"Go. Get off," they cried out.

Their thought was that either Millin should stop playing or stop crossing the bridge. To do both would surely be suicide. Millin could hear shooting all around the bridge and he now knew that snipers were ready to fire at anyone spotted trying to cross the bridge. Millin turned around and looked at Lovat who was right behind him.

"Carry on," instructed Lovat.

Millin continued piping and he continued to march. This time he felt extremely vulnerable. It felt like the longest bridge he had ever crossed. The commandos crouched down with their rifles out as they crossed the bridge, but Millin and Lovat remained upright. To his men, Lovat showed absolutely no fear and he seemed oddly at ease in the line of the enemy's attack. He almost acted contemptuously as the German's attempted to fire at him. Millin thought that Lovat looked like he as out for a walk on his ancestral lands in Beauly. This outward appearance did not display his inner awareness of how close to annihilation they both were. German bullets continued to ping off the bridge's steel fencing.

"When I got on to the centre of the bridge," recollects Millin, "The firing ceased, and it didn't start again until I had reached the other side."

Millin and Lovat continued marching as if they were in a parade, until they reached the other side of the bridge. Millin shook hands with the two astonished paratroopers as he jumped into their trench. Several commandos, tired from having just completed an eight-mile march carrying an 80-pound rucksack, were shot by snipers crossing this second bridge.

"Piper Millin struck into a march and played us across the water (I should mention that no piper played on the first occasion while crossing the canal)," recalled Lovat when asked to reflect on crossing the bridges. "Peter Wilson, an old friend from early days in B Troop, was shot through the head as No.4 Commando crossed later that afternoon. Derek (Mills-Roberts) had a man killed by a sniper, pierced, curiously, through the nostril. Several other ranks became casualties, but the good music drowned the shooting and we managed to strive over in step – almost with pomp and circumstance!"

The paratroopers that had landed in gliders were exposed not just in their position, but in their supplies.

"I had salvaged a few maps. I brought a few maps with me and we'd covered them with chalk and set those up, so we could mark them up. We really had very little equipment because most of it was still in the gliders and we hadn't been able to get it out … those gliders that had crashed," said one trooper.

That afternoon, more and more men and equipment arrived at the bridges. Lost paratroopers from the previous night's landings, were also making their way to the bridges. Hundreds of new gliders were landing in the fields surrounding Howard's men. More reinforcements and artillery worked their way up to the bridges from the beaches. Soon, jeeps came into town, towing antitank guns. As the fresh recruits arrived at the bridges, Corporal Parr, who had just finished his second glass of champagne, greeted the arrivals. He relieved the tension as he led the Ox and Buck in jeers aimed at the reinforcements.

"Where the hell you been?"

"War's over!"

"A bit late for parade, chaps."

Hidden in an elderberry bush all day, Private Roemer and Private Bonck have been sneaking over to drink canal water as they waited for German reinforcements.   When Roemer heard the sound of the bagpipes, he decided that the territory was now permanently under British control and he was behind enemy lines.

"Sometime after noon next day, we heard and saw some more troops with a piper at their head, moving from the direction of the beaches to cross the bridge," recalled Roemer. "I found out later they were Lord Lovat's Commando Brigade."

Thirsty and hungry, Roemer finally walked out from the bushes with his hands in the air and surrendered himself to the commandos. Bonck followed him.

"Thank goodness for us they didn't kill us. I'll always be grateful to them for that," Roemer said with a sad smile. "But I think we must have looked so pathetic, they quickly realised we were not much of a threat."

Roemer and a handful of other German prisoners were lined up in front of a Sherman tank. The photograph that was taken will appear on the front page of many newspapers around the globe; a picture of the cowardly German Army surrendering.

Some commandos stayed very briefly at the bridges while further reinforcements continued to work their way in from the beaches. Crossing the bridge was still hazardous as new crops of German snipers showed up. Several of the Commandos took to crossing underneath the bridge and wading their way across the water to avoid the sniper fire. The only challenge was getting up and down the slippery bank on either side of the river. Lieutenant Mercer-Wilson also went under the bridge and was shot. He was listed as having been shot by a sniper, but there were no snipers under the bridge. In reality, when climbing up the side of the river, he offered his rifle butt to another soldier to pull him up. The soldier grabbed the gun by the trigger, only to find the safety catch was off and the rifle fired straight at Mercer-Wilson.

"In the record book it says he was killed by sniper fire," Private Spearman recounted, "As far as the family is concerned, I suppose this is a nicer way to put it."

In a clump of trees across the bridge, Lovat met with Lieutenant Fox and Sweeney. They gave the Brigadier an update. The firing on this side of the bridge had started to intensify as elements of the infantry from 21st Panzer Division were now arriving. Some commandos would be assigned to stay at the bridges to assist in holding the position and the main force would come to the aid of Lieutenant Otway who had now taken up position in Amfreville. The element of surprise would no longer be on the side of the commandos.

On the east side of the Ranville bridge, almost immediately, the skirmishes to establish complete control of the bridge started. The commandos started firing at the Germans as they advanced and drove up through the middle to split the German infantry. Whether they knew it or not, they were completing a manoeuvre that used to be called the Highland Charge.

Driving down the road away from the bridges, Lovat led the commandos in single file, towards Hauger. There were more skirmishes along the way and the commandos found themselves on the front lines again. They turned down a narrow leafy lane. At the end of the lane, there was an opening and a cluster of French farmhouses. Outside one of the houses, French peasants had gathered to watch and listen to the approaching battle.

Unlike in the cities, there was no economy in existence at all anymore. Away from the urban centres, for four long years, these simple farmers had endured Germans coming to take food and supplies whenever they wanted to. This was not a rich community, but they were loyal French and they were hoping to see the Allies arriving. The commandos came through an opening in the hedges and started to cut through the properties. A small, poorly dressed, bare-footed French girl, Josette Lemanissier, came running towards Millin.

"Music, music, music," Josette called out excitedly with one of the few English words she knew.

"What do you think?" Millin asked looking at Lovat.

Lovat smiled and said, "Okay then, give her a tune."

Despite the gravity of the day, Millin started up his drones and for the first time since he landed, he didn't play a marching tune. The piper played a famous fun Scottish tune *The Nut Brown Maiden*. He only played a few bars before he heard some German mortars launch in his direction. The commandos and French country folk all lunged for cover.

"Music critics," thought Millin.

The mortars continued to blast away for a few minutes without hitting anyone. When it was over the commandos got up and quickly made their way back to the road. The red-headed Josette waved her goodbyes to Bill as he scurried away along the row of hedges. The commandos were unaware that they were heading directly toward von Luck's Panzers. They had left their only tank at the bridge and were only equipped with a few anti-tank guns.

It was early afternoon and Major von Luck's Panzers had finally been released to attack the British from the east. Heading towards the bridges, the skies were starting to fill with spitfires out on patrol. The aircraft spotted the tank movement, but von Luck was not concerned about the fighter planes, until they disappeared. The spitfires cleared the skies in what looked like a retreat; however, they were leaving because they had called the tank position into the Navy. The *HMS Warspite* was offshore ready to fire at 'targets of opportunity' and launched a massive munitions barrage with deadly accuracy.

"All hell broke lose," von Luck remembered. "The heavy naval guns plastered us without pause. We lost radio contact and the men of the reconnaissance battalion were forced to take cover."

Von Luck ordered his battalion to take a position near Escoville. Despite being aware for over 12 hours that there was a British assault, if not invasion, the German Major had been incapacitated by his standing orders not to advance.

"We failed," said German Leutnant Kortenhaus, "because of heavy resistance from the British navy. We lost thirteen tanks out of seventeen."

The delay provided enough time for the 6th Airborne and the 51st Highland division to follow up and lay minefields to keep the Panzers from cracking the line. As the day wore on, the skies filled with planes, similar to the way the sea had been filled with ships in the morning. The planes made the men on the beaches, the men on the bridges and the men marching inland, all feel safer. The commandos and the Panzers had been headed on a collision course, but the delayed assault by the German tanks allowed the RAF and Royal Navy to immobilize von Luck's counter-offensive.

As Lovat's commandos continued on their way, they did not know how close they had come to a confrontation with the Panzer tanks. Although Millin saw the explosions, it was just one of many assaults the Navy was launching behind enemy lines. However, if not for these particular explosions, he would have marched with his pipes and dagger, against a regiment of German Panzers.

Headed north, the commandos reached Le Plein, a small hamlet outside of Amfreville. A large German force had been ordered to hold their position there as it held a view over the Orne River Valley. As the commandos turned to head to Amfreville, a well-aimed mortar strike hit the troops. Chunks of shrapnel sprayed across the commandos, cutting into legs. It was clear that the Germans were now tracking their progress.

"The fire fight was thickening," recalled Lovat, "but men were being killed. The Germans had started to react fiercely. We had run into trouble. The enemy had to be dislodged without delay."

Millin watched as commandos were wounded fighting their way through Le Plein. The battle was tougher than had been expected. The German infantry now had orders to engage and to hold all positions. However, the commandos would need to take this small village to link up to Amfreville and complete a dotted line that would be the eastern flank. The only other relief that would be provided that day, were other commandos working their way across the bridges. Several commandos were killed in the fight, but Le Plein was captured.

The commandos headed out through more hedged fields to find the paratroopers. It was still afternoon when No. 3 Commando arrived in Amfreville and found a worn down, exasperated Lieutenant Otway in position at the Chateau. He sat waiting under a white stone statue of Jesus as if he was praying for help. Otway's answer came in the form of commandos that rapidly cleared and seized the town. The soldiers settled into a defensive position and prepared for an inevitable counterattack by the Germans. This was now the bridgehead.

A small force of commandos headed east of Amfreville and reached a spot where all the hedges were covered with white dust. They were beside a quarry. A number of paratroopers were laid up there wounded on stretchers. Lovat proceeded forward to understand how he would direct the attack on the next village if needed. Millin went into a barn where he saw that it was full of wounded. He looked back outside and saw Lovat sitting on the grass observing the combat position.

"I wouldn't like his job," the piper thought as he watched his commanding officer.

Brigadier Lovat was 32-years old and in the two years leading up to the invasion, he had been advanced to a very high position of authority and responsibility. Suddenly, Lovat stood up, returned to gather the troops and then they moved forward again. They approached along rows of hedges, keeping below the enemy sightline. As they moved from field to field, they were aware that Germans could be behind each hedge row, particularly snipers. They were in hedgerow country (bocage in French), which gave the Panzers a challenge navigating but also provided good cover for German infantry.

A barrage of mortars started bursting in the field on the other side of the hedges. One of the blasts came close to the commandos and everyone dove into a ditch. Some shrapnel burst towards Millin. It might have killed the piper, if it wasn't for his pipes. The shrapnel hit the bagpipes and not the piper. Millin tried playing them later, and although they were broken, he still managed to get a sound out of them. The drones were out of order, but he could make a noise that sounded similar to music.

"Lighter moments? I can't think of any," reflected Lovat when asked about the lighter side of war. "When the piper lost his pipes with a direct hit from a mortar shell, I suppose that was quite funny."

Millin looked up as he heard the constant sound of the RAF fighters, bombers and gliders. It was a wonder that they were not crashing into each other as the planes completely shrouded the skies. Hundreds of incoming gliders landed in the fields beside the Orne River containing troops, jeeps, artillery and equipment.

"That evening our hearts were gladdened by the arrival at dusk of hundreds of planes and gliders flying steadily through a very heavy anti-aircraft barrage," said John Airy. "They bore the remainder of the 6th Airborne Division and many landed among us. Sadly, many of the gliders crashed and the young paratroopers were killed instantly. But those that survived were later to take up our position at the bridgehead, and they were heartened to see us, as comrades."

"Right. We won't go into the village today. We will go up and occupy the farmhouses on the edge of the road," Lovat said.

"On some high ground overlooking the beachhead we were told to say, hold on, and fight, not yield an inch," Private Bidmead recalled.

The German troops had continued to mount increasing attacks on the paratroopers and reinforcements at the bridges. In order to continue to hold the bridges, more men had to safely arrive as reinforcements. The next round would be landing in gliders, not parachutes and should arrive closer to the bridges. This prompted Brigadier Lovat to diverge from the original plan and instead hold a tighter perimeter on the high ground to the east of the Orne River. Losing this position on the high ground would mean that the Germans would have a clear view of the incoming Airborne troops' landing ground. It was extremely fitting that Lovat had marched his piper in from the beach and decided to stop when the reached the 'highlands' of Normandy.

"The high ground up above, commanded a view of the beaches," recounted Lovat, "and if the enemy had held the high ground, I think the battle might have easily gone the wrong way because they could have shelled the beaches and nothing could have gone ashore."

Geography: East of the Orne River, the commandos now held the village of Amfreville and the two nearby hamlets. Le Plein (also spelled Le Plain) was held by No. 3 and Le Oger (also spelled Le Hauger and Le Hoger) was held by No. 4. Today, both hamlets are integrated into Amfreville. No. 6 Commando took up positions in Amfreville. No. 45 Commando headed to Merville, cleared a few Germans that had occupied the destroyed battery after Otway's men vacated it, and took up position there. Heading east to the next village, Lovat led commandos until they stopped in some fields with farm buildings surrounded by hedges. This would provide a degree of cover for the night. The commandos had reached the outskirts of the Bréville-les-Monts.

The commandos, whose primary skills were assault landings and raids, were now in a defensive position on the eastern perimeter of the entire invasion force, with no reserves coming in that night. Lovat's order to dig in for the night meant Brigade HQ would occupy one of the farm buildings and other men would assume defensive positions in the fields.

To dig in, the men used a new commando entrenching tool that included a miner's pick and long spade on a shortened handle. The shovel was carried on their belt. The advantage of the new tool was that the shovels were light. The disadvantage was they took three times as long to dig their trench, so the buddy system was in effect. Millin joined up with another Scotsman that he had just met. Corporal MacGill was a heavily armed soldier.

"Piper," MacGill said. "This is to knock out any fucking tanks that try to come along this road in front of us."

MacGill passed Millin a PIAT gun. The piper had landed on the beach with only a dagger and now he had an anti-tank gun. Millin and MacGill selected the spot to dig their slit trench. Before digging in, they surveyed the field around the area to make sure they were not picking a location that had some hidden danger. The two men dug a slit trench and agreed that they would share sleeping and watch duties.

The men 'brewed up' and for the first time since landing they ate. Most commandos had rations for the first 48 hours. The little 'Tommy' cooker in their kits was sufficient to boil the water for their tea and heat one can of tinned food. Millin patched up his bagpipes that had been damaged so he could make some more reasonable sounds the next day.

Some men smoked cigarettes, which also doubled to keep the mosquitoes away. Private Waddington had just climbed into his trench and lit a cigarette when he discovered that someone had stored some petrol in his pit. The fuel ignited, burning Waddington's face and severely disfiguring him.

Millin and MacGill took a quick final march around, when a mortar blast exploded near to them. The two men scurried back to their trench and decided to stay still for the night. Millin took the first shift sleeping. Other than the occasional high-pitched sound of mortar fire, the night was quiet, but that did not necessarily provide for a good sleep.

"It was menacingly quiet," Lieutenant McDougall recorded.

At Sword beach, the invading forces had achieved remarkable success. The gliders had successfully taken both bridges that were wired for demolition. The beach landing had been greeted with only moderate defenses and firepower. The commandos had achieved their primary objective by 1 p.m., linking up with the airborne troops and the sniper fire at the bridges had been minimalized by the commandos and paratroopers. The east side of Sword beach was secure, however the west flank of the British landing forces was unable to link up with the Canadian forces at Juno beach. This left the door open for the German 21st Panzer Division to mount a counterattack, but that would be stopped by the Allied antitank weapons, air strikes and the tanks that had landed on D-Day.

The mission was a huge success for the Ox and Bucks and the paratroopers. Once the commandos arrived 13 hours into D-Day, the 6th Airborne Division was supposed to pull out, but it was to be eight weeks before they were on the move again. Their time in Normandy had taken a heavy toll on the troops with many men killed in action, men wounded, and men taken prisoner.

"There were 28 of us on our glider," Corporal Evans (Horsa 93) said. "Only eight of us came back. It was the worst shock of my life going back to the barracks room and seeing all those empty beds."

The Allies had made a number of mistakes but would not need to take the lessons learned into a second invasion. The dropping of paratroopers at night was a considerable failure. The RAF pilots had not been adequately trained on the proper techniques for a regular drop, far less one at night. The night-drop was planned to give the paras the cover of darkness, but the result was soldiers being dropped behind enemy lines in the wrong location. An early dawn drop would have allowed greater accuracy with some degree of cover. The RAF also had failed miserably to soften up the beach landings as they were unsuccessful in bombing the German batteries. Despite these failings, the invasion was a masterful success.

"Well, being a young guy, I thought it was like the Fourth of July, to tell you the truth," Yogi Berra said. "I said, 'Boy, it looks pretty, all the planes coming over.' And I was looking out and my officer said, 'You better get your head down in here if you want it on.'"

Of the survivors that day, some wouldn't survive the ongoing combat over the coming year, but many went on to live a normal, and in some cases, extremely successful life.

- New York Yankees **Yogi Berra** had manned a naval support craft,
- Actor **Henry Fonda** was a quartermaster on the destroyer *USS Satterlee*,
- **J.D. Salinger** landed on Utah beach with six chapters of *The Catcher in the Rye* in his pocket,
- 20 years before he played Scotty on *Star Trek* **James Doohan** was with the Canadian Army on Juno beach,
- Golfer **Bobby Jones** landed in Normandy but refused to talk about it,
- Oscar-winning actor **David Niven** was one of the first officers to land on D-Day,
- Actor **Charles Durning** landed with one of the first waves on Omaha beach,
- Before becoming Obi-Wan Kenobi **Alec Guinness** was part of the British Navy helping to land aircraft on D-Day, and
- Actor **Richard Todd** parachuted into Normandy and marched to the bridges with Pine-Coffin. He would go on to star in a movie about the relief efforts at the bridges.

By the end of 'the longest day', the Allied command was looking at the reports of a very successful day. The Allied forces had sustained 4,000 casualties compared to the German forces of 9,000 dead. While the casualties were high, they had been prepared for something much worse. Gold, Juno, Omaha, Sword and Utah beaches were all secured and further troop landings could arrive as planned. The French Resistance had been fully engaged and the Free French were now fighting along side the Allied troops. And most importantly, Meteorologist Stagg was vindicated in his weather forecast.

The 1st Special Service Brigade had linked up with the 6th Airborne Division, and together they would hold the eastern flank of the evasion secure for over 80 days without relief. The strategic points on the Caen Canal, the Orne River and the Dives River, were all now in British control. At Sword beach, the salient from that sector extended five miles and the British had landed 29,000 troops with only 630 casualties. While any loss of life is horrendous, the landing on that particular beach was a great success. The Juno and Omaha losses were much higher. German casualties were also extremely high, and many more had been taken prisoner. Rommel's Atlantic Wall had been permanently pierced in a single day.

On paper, the Atlantic Wall had looked impenetrable. The German Army had spent millions and used thousands of labourers to pour tons of concrete using reinforced steel rods that could have been used to build tanks. Across the northern coast, bulldozers and backhoes had dug thousands of miles of trenches. In that water and on the land, they had planted more than a million mines. With the amount of money, material and manpower that was dedicated to the Wall, it would have to be considered a failure since a piper could sail and march right through it in a morning.

Meanwhile, Hitler, who was holding daily military meetings at his headquarters in the Bavarian Alps, remained in a cheerful mood. Despite the news of an invasion in Normandy, the German High Command was still convinced that Normandy was a diversionary tactic and the real invasion was now going to come at Calais. Besides, the weather reports looked like they would be on the German's side for the real invasion.

"The news couldn't be better. As long as they were in Britain, we couldn't get at them. Now we have them where we can destroy them," Hitler told his staff.

The failure of the Wehrmacht to defend the beaches, the failure of the organizational structure to deploy the Panzer Divisions and the failure of the Luftwaffe to even show up for the battle, would punctuate the turning point in World War II. Since the British had not reached their objective of Caen, the commandos did not fully appreciate the massive achievement of the first day. The significance of linking the beaches to the bridges, was better understood by the German defenders.

"I remember well Rommel told us, if there was a landing somewhere in France and we can't get the invaders back into the sea within the first 24 hours that would be the end. All the effort would be too late," von Luck said.

Field Marshal von Rundstedt had adamantly believed that the static Atlantic wall would be sufficient to slow down any Allied invasion on the Western front. The defenses would provide enough time for the German Army to launch a counterattack, especially as the invasion was going to come via Calais. Rommel, however, disagreed with von Rundstedt and believed that the invasion force must be defeated on the beaches. He would never get his chance to plead his case for the Seventh and Fifteenth Armies to change positions.

In the evening of June 6th, a long sleek black limousine[54] was speeding away from Germany towards Normandy. With its gleaming chrome and extra long bonnet, the obsidian coloured vehicle looked like the quintessential archvillain's automobile. Inside the car, Field Marshal Rommel was quietly assessing the failure of inaction. Once in Normandy, Rommel took control of the troop positions. He wrote a long letter to Hitler pleading for reinforcements. He knew that without more support from tanks and armoured divisions, they would not stop this invasion. The British now had air superiority and more infantry would continue to land on the beaches over the next week. Near Pas-de-Calais, the Germans continued to hold the bulk of their armoury.

"Him being very nice to us, by ordering this," explains Walter Tanner, who landed with the 7th Battalion Parachute Regiment and was speaking about Hitler's insistence on keeping tanks close to Pas-de-Calais, "saved the day for us, because let's make no mistake about it, if he had 've released those tanks, I really, in all honesty, don't think D-Day would have been successful."

Hitler and his staff would maintain for days that Normandy was a diversionary tactic and insisted on guarding the shortest distance between Britain and Europe. Normandy did not have the same harbour system that Calais could offer. Without a harbour, there could not be

---

[54] The car is a 1937 Horch 830 BL Cabriolet.

an effective use of the naval resources to land equipment and supplies. The Germans had not fathomed Britain's mammoth engineering achievement known as Mulberry harbours. On the afternoon of June 6th, 400 large harbour components were towed from England to Normandy. The 1.5 million tons were assembled in two weeks to create massive temporary harbours. While one harbour was destroyed in a storm, the other landed over two million men, 500,000 vehicles and four million tons of supplies. The Mulberry harbour was even more effective than what the port at Calais had to offer.

"It was a sound scheme to have experienced the heavy stick of Dieppe," said Lovat, " and then landing on an empty beach and getting the heavy stuff ashore, lorries and the heavy equipment, with Mulberry harbour. I think that was a brilliant stroke … you could almost call it genius. We'd have never landed at a defended port, which was considered essential at one stage of the planning."

It was Millin's turn for sentry duty. His sleep had been very restless, and he found himself just lying waiting for MacGill to wake him.

"Right, you get a rest, and I'll take a shift," Millin said.

He got no response from MacGill.

"Is there anything I need to know?" the piper asked.

Still no reply. Millin was sure that his sentry had fallen asleep on the job, so he gave him a shove. No motion, not even snoring. Millin gave the corporal a bigger shove, then he noticed his hands were covered in blood. Millin rolled MacGill over and discovered blood was dripping through the back of MacGill's jacket. He was dead. MacGill had been hurt by the shrapnel from the earlier mortar and was lying dead in the slit trench. Millin panicked and jumped out of the trench to get the medics.

There was nothing the medics could do, so the corporal's body was taken behind the farmhouse. Millin had the choice of digging another trench or sleeping where he discovered MacGill's body. Being by himself, he opted to spend the rest of the night in his original slit trench. For the rest of the night, he would be alone, without a sentry. The piper looked up at the dark skies with the occasional artillery fire flash and thought of all the men that he had witnessed die in one day. Morning couldn't come fast enough and Millin probably grabbed no more than two hours of restless sleep.

"Yesterday evening we were all sipping pints in the canteen in Southampton, talking about wives and girlfriends. Now they're lying dead in a ditch having soil thrown over them," thought Millin, watching the night skies.

On June 7th, the commandos set out again. As they marched forward, they passed fields and fields of empty gliders that had landed infantry during the night. The gliders showed the challenges of landing under cover of night as the empty vessels lay nose-down into the ground, tail in the air, on their side, and even split in half. The horrifying circumstances that had confronted the glider crews were evident. Marching past fields, occasionally the commandos would see the bodies of dead paratroopers who had been shot on the way down. Lovat warned his commandos to leave the bodies. The Germans had booby-trapped some of the bodies such that turning them over to retrieve dog tags would result in an explosion.

To most of the men, the second day felt very different than D-Day. The feeling of over confidence had dissipated, and they had time to face the realization that men who were alive yesterday morning, were dead today. Men they had known, trained with and fought alongside.

"We kept on going, kept on going, forward and forward," said French Commando Corporal Gautier as he compared June 6th to June 7th, "the next day of course, we realized what had been going on. On the first day we didn't realize it, it was too quick for us."

The French commandos had planned to be in combat for only four days before receiving their next orders. However, when Caen was not liberated as planned, they wound up fighting for three months. The commandos had to defend the bridgehead at all costs, and this included access to the bridges over the Orne River and the Caen Canal.

Inland ten miles, lay the heavily fortified city of Caen, the over-ambitious objective for D-Day. The reality of how uninformed that objective was, now faced the troops assigned to take the city. The German occupation of Caen had been a hard reality for the past four years. The Gestapo, the S.S. and the 21st Panzer Division all had headquarters here. It was understood by both the Nazis and the Allies, that Caen would be an important strategic location. The city would need to be taken before the Allies could head down the road to liberate Paris. This was not something that the Germans were going to give up readily and there was no longer an 'element of surprise'.

Surrounding Caen was 'hedgerow country', where fields were smaller than England and divided by tall bushes instead of stonewalls. The battles in hedgerow country were challenging for troops who had not gone through the commando training. Many had never seen hedgerows laid out in this manner and there were numerous skirmishes with Germans based in one set of hedgerows and the Allied forces in another. This type of terrain was ideal for snipers. Crossing through each row of hedges, the commandos would have to try to ensure that there wasn't a sniper, or two, positioned in the next set of hedges.

"You made your way along the hedges, from hedge to hedge. The worst part were the hedges where the Germans were likely to be, a long way away. I used to expose myself on the way out, at various places, so that if they were on the alert or they were in a position, they would let fire at me," Private Spearman said, describing his experience with hedgerow warfare. "In that way I felt at least I knew where they were. They were less likely to hit me then than they would be when I approached their position."

Fighting their way across hedged fields, with farmhouses and small thatched-roofed outbuildings that could house German troops, the commandos continued to establish their position. The Germans soon figured out the commando tactics and started placing booby-traps in the hedges, both to maim and to set off warning flares for patrols. It didn't take long for the commandos to learn how to disarm the traps.

In addition to defending the Orne bridgehead, the 1st Special Service Brigade and the 6th Airborne Division, also commenced their attack on Bréville-les-Monts the next day. In order to accomplish both objectives, the commandos adopted the tactic of offensive defense. Bréville was a crucial position on the way to liberating Caen. Germany's counterattacks would come from the 21st Panzer Division, as well as the 346th and 711th Infantry Divisions. This gave the Germans an artillery and manpower advantage.

German soldiers continually tried to breach the line. Trained snipers like Private Treacher sat in key positions and waited for German attempts. Men in forward positions had code words that changed each day. Yesterday, the request was 'Bacon' and the response was 'Eggs'. Today, the request word was 'Bread' and the response was 'Butter'.

One confusion happened when a five-man patrol went out in the daytime but ran into a large platoon of Germans. The patrol had to lay low and wait until 'the coast was clear', before returning to their positions. They arrived back at the Forward Defense Line after midnight, and the code had changed.

"Fire," a voice called out from the dark.

The patrol froze in their boots. All five men knew that sniper rifles were now aimed at them.

"Butter?" one of the patrol answered.

"Fire," the voice repeated, louder and with a bit of 'last warning' edge.

"Don't bloody fire, we're British you arsehole," another of the patrol yelled out.

This was as good as knowing the 'Smoke' response, but those five men never went out again, without knowing two days worth of codewords.

On another occasion, a Canadian came walking into the British position. The code word was called out, but the Canadian claimed to be lost and said that he hadn't been told the British codewords. In fact, this was an English-speaking German dressed in a Canadian uniform that had been picked up at Juno beach. The German soldier's orders were to infiltrate the British line and note where the key positions were being held. The ploy didn't work however as the same codewords were used across all Allied beaches. Instead of finding out the British positions, he was questioned by members of Troop X and the fake-Canadian gave up the German positions.

The first major German counterattack was against the position held by 1st Special Service Brigade on June 7th. While the German infantry charged in strength and almost broke the line, No. 3 Commando unit aggressively went on the attack and drove them back. The next attack was on June 9th, when again tactical manoeuvring allowed the British forces to surround the Germans and drive them back. Later that day, British bombers flew overhead and parachuted down supplies and rations.

On June 10th, a reconnaissance mission noted a large gathering of German infantry on the outskirts of Bréville. It appeared to be the start of a consolidated German offensive. The troops were readied. The attack commenced with massive artillery and mortar fire on the No. 4 commandos, followed by an onslaught of German troops. The commandos were able to overcome the attack after a gory hand-to-hand combat. Twice more the commandos came under a similar attack that day. The paratroopers and commandos were able to catch the Germans approaching for another attack, holding off firing from the trees until the Germans were within 50 yards. There were very few survivors on the German side.

"The Germans entered our defensive rectangle, two sides of which bristled with rifles and Brens. Not a shot was fired until the massed enemy was about sixty yards away. Then all weapons opened up. There was chaos in the orchard, killed and wounded lay still; the rest came on, but the attack had lost its impetus," Lieutenant Colonel Mills-Roberts reported.

The Allied coordinated support also attacked the Germans when the Forward Operating Base radioed the German positions to a naval battleship, which launched an attack using its 150mm guns. The troops were taken aback by the delay in the orders and the size of the blast. The FOB operator would be on the radio and then call out 'shot one'. Nothing happened for five seconds until the massive artillery came screaming overhead. This part of the exercises had not been rehearsed at Commando Castle.

The battle for Bréville would continue for two more days before a final retreat by the Germans and the village was in the Allied hands for good. Many German troops were killed or captured during the engagement; however, the commandos also took a fair number of casualties as well.

On June 12th, Brigadier Lovat sent for Millin. As the piper approached, he could see the Brigadier was in a heavy conversation with two other officers. They were observing an artillery bombardment by the 51st Highland Division. Millin stood beside his commander and waited instructions.

"Push off," Lieutenant Colonel Johnson said to Millin.

Millin decided that he had better back away and let the men continue their discussion. He had only just left when he heard a stray shell fall short of its target. The force of the blast threw Millin forward on his face. Millin looked down at his tunic and it was covered in blood. He had felt the heat of the blast and thought maybe he had been hit, but it was just a nosebleed caused by his fall. Millin got his breath back and turned around to see the three officers, all lying on the ground. There was no movement.

Lieutenant Colonel Johnson fell dead. The other officer, Brigadier Kindersley was seriously wounded and lay unconscious. Lovat had also been hit by the shrapnel.

"You had to throw yourself on the ground. If you didn't throw yourself quick enough, you could get hit by the shrapnel," Private Spearman said, describing how to take protection when you hear the sound of incoming shelling. "Lord Lovat was always extremely bold and brave. And it would take a lot for him to take cover, but in the end, he got wounded. And I think it was for this reason he did get wounded. If he had been a little bit more cowardly like we were, and gone down, I think he could have avoided his wounds that he got …"

Men grabbed a stretcher and they took Lovat into the farmhouse. The doctor attended to Brigadier Lovat and Brigadier Kindersley, or as they were known before the war: The 15th Lord Lovat and The Second Baron Kindersley of West Hoathly. Piper Millin looked down at Lovat and he saw 'that grey colour that the wounded get'. It wasn't clear that either of the two leaders were going to make it. The doctor rolled Lovat over and there was a hole, large enough to put a fist in, caused by the shrapnel. When Millin saw Lovat's back, he ran to find a priest. He knew Lovat was a devout Catholic and he would want a priest to give him the last rites.

Seeing how badly wounded the Brigadier was, other commandos also believed that Lovat was not going to make it. He was unconscious and hooked up to the crimson sack of a battle-field blood transfusion. Lieutenant Colonel Mills-Roberts assumed command of the commandos. When Lovat came to consciousness, he asked to speak to Mills-Roberts.

"Not a foot back, not a foot back" Lovat repeated.

Lovat was put on a jeep to be taken back to the beach. Millin was sure this would be the last time that he would see the Brigadier. Several commandos watched as the jeep was leaving.

"Gentlemen, I count on you to hold on at all costs," Brigadier Lovat implored the commandos softly in his parting words.

Lovat was a man of courage, competence, character and humility. He was an aristocratic leader that inspired men to rise to the circumstances. His men respected him and even held him in awe. That day, he was evacuated and although he survived, his injuries would be the end of his military career. He spent the next six months in hospital.

For his efforts and leadership, a grateful French Fourth Republic would award him with the Légion d'honneur and the Croix de Guerre.

Reflecting on his time in Normandy, Brigadier Lovat felt for the loss of his men and his orders to leave the bodies where they fell. With German snipers all around, retrieving one body could lead to another. The men would wait until the cover of night and then would make recovery missions. Lovat wrote:

> *There was no question of a truce when it came to bury the dead. If there were snipers about, we were too tired to notice as we made a round of the forward areas, nor can I remember the names of those who fell: the first elation after victory outweighed by a deeper sense of loss. The aftermath was desolation.*
>
> *The survivors as always rose magnificently to the dark hour: stretcher bearers moved along the front line; doctors and the walking wounded, helped by medical orderlies, came and went. Burial parties performed their appointed duties.*
>
> *The Band of Brothers was very close that day ... and so we dug the commandos' graves, lowering them into groundsheets in long straight rows; then set about making them wooden crosses to mark each spot. Later the men, after repairing the trenches, brewed up tea to start again. Funerals in the field, rough and ready though they be, seem less bleak than those performed with formal rites, as though the soldier whose calling deals with sudden death can find a way to stand easy in its shadow.*

Lovat was able to take his boots off for the first time since landing. Before leaving, he wrote the following proclamation:

"The commandos wish everyone a warm hello. The commander of the Green Berets greets his friends and wants to tell them that Hitler is already wetting his pants. Have courage. We are going to win. Vive La France!"

The message was pinned up at every crossroads as the commandos continued the march to Caen.

Some of the commandos returned to Amfreville for a ceremony to commemorate their arrival and the liberation of the town. All the local French civil leaders were there to unveil a plaque. Brigadier Mills-Roberts was there to take the salute. Before the presentation, the commandos were paraded into the town square. The event is filmed by the Allied Army and the film would be used in news reels seen in France, United States, Canada and Great Britain. Private Millin led the parade playing a new set of bagpipes. It was July 14, 1944, Millin's 22nd birthday.

The commandos remained in their combat position, on the front line of the bridge defense, for 78 days without relief. Three different major attacks on the German position in Caen were required to drive the Nazis out. The city wasn't taken until July 20th. During the combat, the RAF dropped 2,500 tons of bombs and Caen was completely decimated.

When August came, the commandos began to aggressively push forward in what was called 'a breakout'. On August 18th, they advanced three miles, unopposed, to the village of Bavent. Their reconnaissance had indicated that the Germans had taken up position there, so a fight was expected. The German infantry had evacuated that morning. The village was turned over to Captain Lofi, who had taken command of the French Commandos after Kieffer had been reluctantly evacuated. Lofi and his men were cheered on by the local village people.

Hungry for an engagement, the commandos marched on to Bricqueville. Again, the village was empty of Germans but there were signs that the retreat was recent. It was now apparent that the German Army was pulling out. The plan changed once again, and the troops rapidly deployed to liberate villages. Reacting quickly to German withdrawals, the paratroopers and the commandos leapfrogged one another infiltrating German strongpoints and taking towns. As speed was integral in keeping the enemy off guard, there was no time for reconnaissance.

The green berets were the first to go, marching all night to arrive and to take 43 surprised POWs in the hamlet of L'Epine. There was some fighting, but the lightening style march and arrival had its desired effect. The paratroopers, the red berets, were next to take the town of Grangues, with the commandos again following the paratroopers to take Beaumont-en-Auge. Utilizing near Highland tactics, they liberated the towns and villages along the Dives River. On August 22nd, they were able to stop for a well-deserved sleep. For the first time, the commandos had reached a part of France that did not display the scars of battle.

According to unit diary records: 'We entered a part of France which had not been a battlefield and for the first time were among undamaged houses and in a habitable area. The French people everywhere accorded us an enthusiastic welcome, complete with flowers and cries of 'Vive l'Angleterre' – and the odd bottle of wine – as we marched through.'

After that, the lack of engagement began to frustrate the commandos as they would arrive in a town only to find out that the mortars that had been fired from that town, were launched from a mobile position on the back of a jeep. The frustration continued until Beuzeville.

When the troops entered Beuzeville, the fervor to engage the enemy extinguished by the overwhelming reception the commandos received as they entered the town through the main street.

"People were cheering and waving and thrusting bottles into ready hands. Most of these folk were genuinely delighted to see us," recalled Lieutenant McDougall. "Particularly the older generation, many of whom stood with tears of joy coursing down their furrowed cheeks, saluting as we passed. They were saluting us not as men, but the return of their respect."

In contrast to the reception given to the commandos, the towns people who had been complicit with the German occupation, were now facing the punishments for their actions. Down a side street, as the commandos marched by, Sergeant-Major Dunning spotted some French men forcibly shearing and shaving the hair off a young woman. The price for collaborating with the Nazis.

The commandos remained in Beuzeville until September 6th, when they were told to pack up. This time, they headed back to Britain. Millin was in Normandy, in combat, for three months. Of the 2,500 commandos that landed on the beaches of Normandy, most of whom were volunteers, there were 978 casualties. More than fifty percent of the officers were killed in action. They remained 83 days straight, without relief.

Caen was the extremely over optimistic objective the British had set for the first day of the invasion. The German resistance and counterattack would take a full day to engage but it would engage. This led the Allies to struggle in their attempt to break out of Normandy. A centre for German Panzers, the German army was able to hold Caen for another six weeks. The fighting was fierce, and the town was demolished before it was over. The once quaint French city now lay in ruins. When Caen fell, the road through France became much easier. By August, French troops led the Allies into Paris, marking the end of the Normandy campaign.

In Paris, No. 4 Commando unit under the leadership of Lieutenant Colonel Dawson, were invited to be celebrated by the people of France as they marched down the Avenue des Champs-Élysées.

"We received perhaps the most gracious compliment the French nation could pay," recalled Dawson, "we marched as a unit and alone (apart from the French naval band which led us) from the Ministry in the Place de la Concorde to the Arc de Triomphe, where Philippe Kieffer and I laid a wreath on the Unknown Soldier's tomb and relit the flame. I doubt if any other British Regiment has ever been honoured in this way."

Millin's family learned about his involvement in the D-Day landing, when they read about the commandos in the newspapers. After a brief leave, Millin accompanied No. 4 Commando to Holland, then he finished the war in Lübeck, Germany.

In May 1945, the Allies formally accepted the unconditional surrender of Nazi Germany. Hitler had committed suicide a week earlier.

"This is your victory. It is the victory of the cause of freedom in every land. In all our long history we have never seen a greater day," Winston Churchill said on May 8, 1945.

Reflecting on his time in France, young Millin thought of it as an adventure. He knew that he was fortunate he hadn't been injured, but as a Private, he had been thrust into the spotlight by a Brigadier. He knew that he had contributed beyond his rank. Millin had been asked to perform and he performed as he was asked. He had marched across the French countryside and had celebrated with the French as their villages were liberated. Not bad for a Canadian-born Scot brought up in an industrial city then trained in the Highlands. He was reticent to admit it, and he would never want to take away from those that gave so much, but Millin had enjoyed his time in France.

Brigadier Lovat was awarded the Distinguished Service Order.

8.   Time to Pay the Piper

Amazing Grace! how sweet the sound
That saved a wretch like me.[55]

Lord Lovat had left his piper in front of the Gondrée café on June
6th, 1944. Georges Gondrée came out to greet the arrival of the
commandos, filled with joy and the understanding that the British
Army had landed on the beaches of Normandy. Bill and Georges spoke
while the Brigadier assessed the combat situation, and the two men
became instant friends.

That afternoon, the café became the first aid post, the mess hall and
the unofficial headquarters for the Allied forces in the area. Georges
dug up the 98 bottles of champagne that he had buried to hide them
from the Germans in 1940. He opened up the first bottle and started
handing out free drinks to any of the soldiers that would stop to take
one. There were 54 Germans stationed in Bénouville and fortunately
they never discovered Georges stash.   John Howard who led the
airborne glider assault, ordered his men to attend 'a medical check-up
at the café' so they could each get a drink.   Men like 18-year old
Private Mason from Liverpool had only drank beer before and was

---

[55] Amazing Grace – Traditional / Hermann Baer

trying champagne for the first time. Georges served free drinks to the troops all day, a tradition that would endure with free champagne served to veterans every June 6th thereafter.

The family continued to build their relationships with Bill Millin and all the veterans well after the war. When Sandy Smith visited the Gondrée's café, Thérèse showed him the headboard where his bullet shot into their bedroom. Georges and Bill wrote to each other throughout their lives. They got together whenever Millin returned to France for D-Day remembrance ceremonies. Georges passed away in 1969 and Thérèse in 1984. Piper Bill came from Dawlish at his own expense, to lead Georges and Thérèse to their final resting place. Bill also remained in contact with the Gondrée's daughters.

The café has been listed as a historical monument since 1987. Although Georges and Thérèse are no longer there, their daughter Arlette still runs the café. Arlette Gondrée, who was six years old at the time of the liberation, still upholds her promise to her mom not to let any Germans into the café.

One of the more unlikely relationships after the war, developed between Hans von Luck and John Howard. Von Luck was the German Major in charge of the Panzers that were closest to the bridges and Howard was the British Major who had taken the bridges. The two men met a various post-war Normandy functions and related to each other. Both men were regular army, and both understood the burden that came with leading men into battle. Von Luck had attended military school and selected his life path, long before the Nazis came to power in Germany.

"I thank Major John Howard, my British adversary on D-Day," von Luck said in the introduction to his book Panzer Commander, "who as the 'hero of Pegasus Bridge' has passed into war history and is today my friend."

Likewise, Howard held the professional soldier von Luck in high regard. The two men would discuss the events of June 6th, from a military strategy point of view. Von Luck was sure that if he had been let loose earlier, he could have taken the lightly guarded bridges to delay the Allied advance or even change the outcome of the war.

"If you want to know what it was like 'on the other side of the hill,' ask my friend Hans," John would tell anyone that wanted to understand what it was like to be a German soldier, not a Nazi, but a soldier, during the war.

Howard and von Luck attended one D-Day event in Bénouville, when Arlette Gondrée refused to let them into the café, because von Luck was German.

The bridge that crossed the Caen canal, near Bénouville, was a Scherzer swing bridge, originally built in 1935. On June 6, 1944 the bridge was called the Bénouville bridge. On June 7, 1944 Georges Gondrée fastened a crudely painted sign saying: 'PEGASUS BRIDGE'. He chose the name to honour the men who wore the shoulder emblem of the British Parachute Regiment. The patch depicts Bellerophon riding the flying horse Pegasus. It was one day after D-Day and the first commemoration for the invasion was erected. The original 110-ft long Pegasus Bridge was removed in 1993 to make way for the widening of the Caen Canal.

"My biggest thought walking across the bridge today is this is the last time," John Howard lamented in 1994, "but they need a new bridge and that's that. We can't stop progress."

In 2000, the old bridge was rescued from rusting into oblivion. It was moved to a canal-side position between Bénouville and Ranville, forming a key exhibit for the Pegasus Memorial Museum. If you look at the counterweight on the original bridge, you can see the large dent where the airplane dropped the bomb that bounced off the superstructure.

In recognition of the Horsas and the brave men who landed in the gliders to free the bridges, the Ranville bridge was renamed to the Horsa bridge. On June 6, 1989, the Mayor of Ranville unveiled a plaque to commemorate the capture of the bridge and officially renamed it to the Horsa bridge. The plaque recognizes the glider pilots and the platoons of Lieutenant Fox and Lieutenant Sweeney.

During the Normandy invasion, the German Army distributed pamphlets stating that the commandos would be treated as 'political prisoners'. This was their way of stating that the Commando Order was still in effect and commandos would be executed. After the war, Generaloberst von Falkenhorst was tried for violating the rules of war by passing the Führerbefehl (Commando Order), which required the execution of commandos. He was convicted and sentenced to death, but the sentence was later commuted to 20 years.

Ray Clapperton, who piloted the tug that cast off Horsa 94 over the wrong river, would make six more trips to France in a Halifax bomber in June 1944. In July, he stopped flying bombers. In Squadron 3 of the RAF, Ray piloted a fighter plane[56] and would earn an 'Ace' status, with 24 confirmed planes and rockets (V-1) downed. In September 1944, he was shot down by a round of flak over Kranenburg, Germany. He survived his plane crash and would spend the rest of the war in a POW camp.

The man who voluntarily led the attack on the bridges, Den Brotheridge, was cutdown by a machinegun. Years of training to provide two or three minutes of crucial assault and then his life was over. Appropriately, he was recommended for the Military Cross. The cross is awarded to soldiers who perform 'an act or acts of exemplary gallantry during active operations against the enemy on land'. Brotheridge displayed the highest qualities of leadership and bravery. His charge displayed an outstanding example which motivated his men to seize the bridge intact. In World War II, there were 10,386 Military Crosses awarded. However, the award cannot be given to someone who was killed while executing the action that was assigned to them, so Brotheridge was turned down. As a reward for running first on to the bridge, the bridge that was essential in establishing the eastern flank of the Normandy Invasion and thereby saving thousands of lives, Den Brotheridge was posthumously Mentioned in Despatches.

Most of the Allied troops that were killed in the Normandy Invasion, are buried in the Commonwealth War Graves. Brotheridge was buried in the Ranville churchyard, close to where he was buried when the fighting was over. This tiny cemetery has a line of 47 headstones along the churchyard wall, including the grave of an unknown German soldier.

---

[56] A Hawker Tempest V EJ504

Nobby Clark was in David Wood's platoon and he helped carry his commanding officer to the first-aid post. Nobby survived the fight at Pegasus bridge unharmed. He went on to fight with the Ox and Bucks in some of the key battles in Europe, including the 'Battle of the Bulge' in December 1944 and the 'Crossing of the Rhine' in March 1945. Posted in the Baltic in April 1945, he was hit four times and lost his right hand. Harry 'Nobby' Clark passed away in 2006.

After the war, Ted Owens did not talk about his war experiences, until it came out one day accidentally.

"I come from a generation which did not articulate the pain or the horror of the war years," Ted stated. "Like so many others, I had internalized my war time experiences. Alcohol or tears were my only solace, to be borne in private."

One of his friends who knew Ted had fought in the war, volunteered him to tell is story when a speaker failed to show up at an event. It was 64 years after the war. Ted recounted the story of being paralyzed by shrapnel then lying on the beach in Normandy as a commando said: 'This poor blighter's had it'. He told the mesmerized audience about being found conscious, shipped home, patched up, then sent back to get shot in the throat.

After sixty years, Ted's bravery became public knowledge and he attended many D-Day memorials. At one remembrance, he was at Omaha beach when Queen Elizabeth paused to speak to him.

"Did you fight in this area?" Her Majesty asked.

"I fought at Sword beach at the other end," Ted answered with great respect. "I got very badly injured on the beach at Walcheren and at the Battle of the Bulge."

"Oh, you went over the top once too often," the Queen replied.

"Yes Ma'am. I don't think they liked my face!" Ted responded.

In 2019, Owens published the story of his life: *Ted 'The Welsh Goat' Hero*. Later that year, while attending the 75th anniversary of D-Day in Pont-l'Évêque, Owens passed a poster in commemoration of the town's liberation. Underneath the title 'Hommage à nos Libérateurs' was a picture of a young Ted Owens on the poster. He smiled at the poster, knowing he still had 14 pieces of shrapnel in his shoulder, as a reminder of his time on Sword beach on June 6, 1944.

After clearing the enemy defenses on the east side of the Pegasus bridge, David Wood received injuries that would keep him out of action for the rest of the war. The enemy fire shattered his leg. He was evacuated to a divisional post in Ranville, then back to England. Due to the multiple fractures, when his left leg was reset it was one inch and a half inches shorter than his right. He would wear a built-up shoe for the rest of his life. David served 36 years with the army and passed away in 2009, survived by his wife Sarah Alice.

Geoff Barkway's memory of the mission to land a glider at the Pegasus Bridge is very vivid up to a point. The pilot of Horsa 93 remembered taking off, then the challenges of landing, and then running back into his Horsa to get someone a stretcher. After that, everything went fuzzy. He heard a gunshot, followed by a burn entering his wrist, and then he fell out of the glider into the pond beside the plane. However, Geoff doesn't know how long he was there for or who came to rescue him. He remembered briefly waking up at the first-aid post by the bridge but doesn't know if he was in the Gondrée café or another building. His arm was in a sling when he came to and he was very thirsty because of the loss of blood.

The next thing he remembered is being on a jeep. His co-pilot told him afterwards that they were still under fire from snipers when he was being driven down to the beach. Geoff came out of the effect of the morphine to find himself on Sword beach under a tarpaulin, then he was transported on a DUKW[57] to a tank landing ship, which transported him to Portsmouth. On Friday, June 9th, Geoff was admitted into the Royal Hospital Haslar. By Sunday, Geoff finally had clear function of his thoughts for the first time since being shot. A nun in the hospital came by his bed and held up the Sunday papers to show him that the invasion was going well. Geoff reached out for the paper

---

[57] Colloquially known as a Duck, the DUKW is a six-wheel-drive amphibious modification to the 2½-ton CCKW truck.

and realized his right arm had been amputated. It had been infected by gangrene. Geoff was right-handed.

"I'd thought that I'd still got my arm, you see," Geoff explains, "because you can always feel your fingers, your ghost limbs, because of the nerves."

Shortly afterwards, it was announced that the Horsa pilots would be awarded the Distinguished Flying Medal. When the unit received notice, Geoff Barkway's name was missing. Owing to an administrative error, Geoff's medal was mistakenly awarded to a pilot with a similar name. The other pilot did not speak up as he was killed in action. Since Geoff was no longer with the unit, he was unaware of the award. When he learned of the medals to the other pilots, Geoff made no comment. The other pilots were all upset however, and the error was rectified. Unfortunately, the correction was not processed in time for Geoff to attend the investiture at Buckingham Palace.

In 1945, Geoff married Eileen Underwood, who he met while she was serving with the Auxiliary Territorial Service. He went on to earn an Engineering degree and had a long career with London Transport. He and Eileen had two sons and two daughters. Geoff Barkway passed away in June 2006.

19-year old Helmut Roemer had run away from the attack on the bridges and spent the day hiding in an elderberry bush. When he heard the skirl of the bagpipes, he surrendered to the commandos and had his photograph taken in front of a Sherman tank. The picture captures Roemer as a scared young boy standing in the front row of the Nazi prisoners. The propaganda portrays the weakness and cowardness of the German Army, highlighting Roemer's actions. He had decided to run, hide, then surrender, rather than stand and fight. Roemer lived for years with his embarrassment as his photo was published on the front page of dozens of newspapers. Just as he had put the shame behind him, the photo resurfaced again, this time being published in numerous history texts. The history books stayed in circulation a lot longer than the newspapers.

"It did affect me," recalled Helmut, speaking of his poor military performance on the Pegasus bridge. "When I met my future wife, Luise, at a dance class in the late 40s, I warned her, 'Do you really want to marry me? After all, I'm a coward'."

Helmut's wife told him to be grateful for what he did, otherwise he might not be alive. The couple went on to have six sons with whom Roemer ran a family hotel in Hilden, near Dusseldorf, and a wholesale drinks company set up by Roemer's father.

"Now I realise that the Pegasus Bridge adventure was a defining moment in my life" reflected Roemer. "It was there that my second life began."

In the 1960s, like several of the German forces that were at Bénouville, Roemer befriended John Howard. The German troops would meet John in Normandy, where he attended every June 6th memorial until his death in 1999.

Staff Sergeant Lawrence, the pilot whose Horsa 94 landed at the wrong bridge, had managed to fight his way back to the Pegasus bridge, then to the beaches, then back to London. His next mission, Operation Market Garden, was to land a glider in the Netherlands. He was killed in action on September 18, 1944.

Wally Parr had a number of obligations after the war. Every Christmas he had to send chocolates to Georgette Gondrée to make up for scaring her as a little girl, and to replace the chocolate bar that her mother wouldn't allow her to have in the basement of the café. In return, Georgette would send him champagne.

For the anniversary of D-Day, Jack 'Bill' Bailey was interviewed by ITV. Of all the stories he chose to tell, he recounted the time that he was in the gun pit and Wally Parr ruined his tea by firing the German gun. Bill visited Wally at his home on several occasions and the same ritual took place.

"Do you want a beer Bailey?" Wally would ask.

"No, you know what I want Irene," Jack said to Wally's wife.

All the men that were on Horsa 91 knew Wally's wife's name. He had given the glider the name when he scribed 'Lady Irene' in chalk on the side of the aircraft as he boarded. Irene smiled, knowing that Jack had still never officially forgiven Wally … for the shell blast, in the gun pit, by the bridge, that spilt his tea. The two men would reminisce, then Irene would return with a big mug of 'Sergeant Major's': a tea with lots of milk and sugar.

Wally Parr read an American magazine that contained an article about the battle for the bridge. He was surprized when the author mentioned how, during the battle, 'the dastardly Germans', in their cruelty, had shelled the local maternity hospital. Wally felt slightly guilty.

"This was the first and last time I had shelled pregnant woman and newborn babies," Parr confessed.

Wally also felt bad for sitting back and enjoying a glass of champagne, while young Private Millin watched. Whenever Wally met Piper Bill at an event, usually commemorating the D-Day invasion or the capture of the Pegasus Bridge, Wally would apologize for not sharing a glass with the piper. In 1984, for the 40th anniversary of D-Day, Bill Millin had a photograph enlarged. He mailed a copy of the picture to Wally and signed it.

"To Wally Parr and the paras of Pegasus Bridge, I still regret that glass of champagne we never had when we met on the sixth of June, 1944. My kindest regards to your dear wife, Piper Bill Millin, Number One Special Services Brigade."

Wally cherished the poster and eventually donated it to the Indiana Military Museum in Vincennes, Indiana. Wally Parr died in 2005 at the age of 83.

Stan Evans never spoke about D-Day. If he thought about Normandy, he thought about 28 men leaving on his glider and the 20 empty beds back in his barracks. He was awarded the Croix de Guerre by Charles de Gaulle, but he didn't show up in Paris for the award. He didn't attend the 25th anniversary of the invasion, nor the 50th, nor the 60th. When the war ended and he returned home, Stan told his wife that he would never talk about what he saw, and he lived up to his promise.

Brigadier Lovat had spent six days in battle in Normandy. After the war, the story of the commandos had become the story of Brigadier Lovat and his piper. Lovat's exploits had earned him immediate notoriety and he was cast as one of the war's great heroes, a modern-day Rob Roy. For Piper Bill however, the knowledge of what he had done was limited to a few thousand men who had seen and heard him in Normandy, and very few knew his name. This did not concern Bill, however. He was a quiet, unassuming man who came to life when he played the pipes or talked about playing the pipes. He was happy to have fought for his country and to have survived the war. Bill was 19-years old when he joined the commandos and 23-years old at the conclusion of the war. What was at first exciting, soon became a grim reality as he had to step over bodies of people he knew. The bagpipes were the thing that helped him get through D-Day. When asked about his experience playing the pipes at the Normandy landing, Bill described the experience as 'enjoyable'.

"I enjoyed playing the pipes, but I didn't notice I was being shot at. When you're young you do things you wouldn't dream of doing when you're older. I was concentrating on my bagpipes and Lovat is a bit of a critic of bagpipers, so I had to watch what I was playing, so I had no time to think about anything else," he said.

When Bill Millin was granted leave after Normandy, instead of going home to his parents in Glasgow, he went straight to Fort William to see a girl that he had fallen in love with while training there. Bill was told that she had died of cancer while he was in Normandy.

Millin was 'demobbed' in 1946. He was offered employment at the Lovat estate, where he worked chopping down trees. Bill lasted just over a year, but then the quiet of the Highlands became too mundane compared to the excitement of the previous years. He quit and seeked a new life elsewhere, eventually joining a theatre company, where he played his pipes on stage in London, Stockton-on-Tess and Belfast. Eventually, Bill took advantage of the veteran's retraining program and trained as a mental health nurse. He worked in three different hospitals in Glasgow where he met and married Margaret Mary Dowdalls in 1954. Their son John was born in 1954 and Bill eventually taught him the chanter but didn't push him into the bagpipes. In order to make ends meet, Bill, Margaret and John moved in with Margaret's parents.

When Margaret's parents took ill and both died of cancer within weeks of each other, Bill and Margaret needed to find a new place to stay. Bill remembered fondly his Army training in Devon and the family moved to Dawlish in the 1962. The piper was living just over 100 miles from where he set sail on D-Day. Bill became senior nursing officer at the Langdon Hospital and Margaret took a position as a sister tutor. In the hospital ward, Bill continued to play his bagpipes to amuse patients.

Bill always maintained great respect for Lord Lovat and was greatly appreciative of the opportunities that had been afforded him.

"People thought that I was mad, that I was of the type of Lovat," Bill said, "but I was only the type of Lovat because I'd been in his presence all the time. He stood about while other people were grovelling about trying to dig in on the beach. He was just standing there and if he stood there, I stood there."

Shimi Lovat didn't speak often about his own personal role in the Normandy invasion. However, he was always pleased to speak about his men and the great respect that he had for the commandos. He was particularly proud of the Brigade's accomplishments on D-Day.

"I personally remember them as vividly as though they happened yesterday," Lord Lovat said, speaking about the events of World War II. "Certain things were tragic, certain things were triumphant, but the great thing is the spirit of comradeship that exists between soldiers. You never forget a face if you are along side him in action. It makes you straighten your back."

In 1945, Winston Churchill asked Lovat to accept the position as the Captain of the Honourable Corps of Gentlemen-at-Arms in the House of Lords, but Lord Lovat declined the offer. Instead, he accepted a position in London as the Parliamentary Under Secretary of State for Foreign Affairs in Churchill's government.

For the decade before the end of the war, a Conservative Prime Minister had been the head of state in Great Britain without an election. The Labour party had agreed on a coalition that would negate the necessity of an election during the war. However, once the war was over, the election of 1945 showed that the British public no longer needed a wartime Prime Minister. In an unexpected landslide victory, Clement Attlee's Labour Party defeated Winston Churchill's Conservatives. It was the first time that the Conservatives had lost an election since 1906. Churchill was now the leader of the opposition, a role that he was not well suited for. Lovat left London and went back to Inverness.

Shimi Lovat survived his injuries and the war. His injuries however, limited Shimi's options and prevented him from pursuing a full-time military career. In 1946 he was made a Commander of the Venerable

Order of Saint John. In 1949, he gave up the regular army and transferred to the reserves where he stayed active until 1962.

"It is one thing to go on the warpath, quite another to stay put and take what's coming to you," Shimi wrote.

Shimi was deeply involved in local politics in Inverness. In 1942, Shimi Lovat had been appointed as Deputy Lieutenant of the Inverness-shire county, and two years later as Justice of the Peace. He also sat on the Inverness County Council, believing public service to be his duty. Lord Lovat would serve for more than 40 years in politics. With the commercialization of air travel, Shimi travelled widely on clan business. He also went big-game hunting and would speak on Highland affairs in the House of Lords. Through the peerage of being The Lord Lovat, Shimi represented the Scottish Highlands in the House of Lords.

Shimi Lovat was also the chieftain of the Lovat Shinty Club. Shinty is a form of field hockey largely played in the Scottish Highlands. Shimi became a breeder and judge of shorthorn cattle. There was also a considerable effort required in running the Lovat ancestral lands and Beaufort Castle. In the 1960s he signed over Beaufort Castle and most of his estates to his eldest son, Simon, Master of Lovat, as a hedge against inheritance tax.

When the Royal family came to visit Scotland, The Lord Lovat and Rosamond often hosted them. The Lovats accompanied the Queen Mother to unveil a statue to the Commandos at Spean Bridge near Fort William. Later, a young Queen Elizabeth visited another memorial statue in France. In preparation, Lovat talked with her about the war, but never specifically about his role. Whenever Lovat described the role of the commandos in newspapers and television interviews, he always downplayed his own part. He was not secretive about what had happened, he just didn't want to celebrate it. He was not a rough man; he was just doing his duty and had the natural stature of a leader.

"After the war he simply came home to the place and the family he loved – and he picked up his other life," said his daughter Tessa.

Shimi and his wife had six children, leaving Rosamond either pregnant or with a newborn for most of the war. Their first son Simon was born one month before the war in 1939, followed by Fiona in 1941, Annabel (Tessa) in 1942, Kim in 1946, Hugh in 1947 and finally Andrew in 1952. Rosamond also lived through an upheaval and confusing time on her side of the family. In the span of two years ending in 1942, her father had remarried someone Rosamond's age, he moved to Kenya, his wife took a lover, the lover was shot, her father was charged with murder, her father was acquitted, then finally he returned to Britain where he committed suicide. The family never spoke about Rosamond's father's tragic end to his life, even among themselves, except to proport his innocence.

As for Lovat's siblings, Magdalen married the Earl of Eldon before the war. Veronica joined a mobile ambulance unit in France where she met and married Lt. Alan Phipps. Phipps served with distinction but was killed in the Battle of Leros in 1943. Hugh Fraser was commissioned to the Lovat Scouts, served through World War II and went on to become a Conservative Member of Parliament and a government minister.

At the age of 21, a young man from Dublin landed a job as a war correspondent and was assigned to cover the Allied Forces during World War II. He reported on the air war in Europe and then he was embedded with Patton's Third Army. After the war he emigrated to the U.S. and in 1951 became a U.S. Citizen. He married a novelist and soon after started his career as an author. The young author became fascinated with the Normandy invasion, so he started researching the events around D-Day. He spoke with thousands of participants from all different factions of the war. When he uncovered events that interested him, events that added a degree of humanity or heroism, he delved deeper into the background of the individual stories. Eventually he heard the story of the glider units landing at Pegasus Bridge, of Lord Lovat and his piper. He realized that he had stumbled on a story of individual bravery that was historic in nature.

The former war correspondent knew the material would be perfect for a book, a collection of sometimes related stories that would tell the events of D-Day though the eyes of individuals. He continued his interviews, speaking to over 3,000 people, including those involved with the bridges and Sword beach.

General Gale suggested that the author speak to John Howard to get the details on the taking of the bridges. John related the story of the Ox and Bucks at the Pegasus bridge and he brought Billy Gray along with him. Gray was selected because he witnessed the events firsthand as a Private in the Ox and Bucks. A young stocky Englishman, the Army decided Grey would best represent the fitness and fighting spirit of the military. At the end of the interview, Gray was asked if he had any final thoughts. Thinking about that day where the fighting began at sixteen minutes after midnight, and continued until midnight the next night, Grey said 'Yes, it was the longest day'. In fact, because it was actually 11:16 p.m. French time when the fighting began, the Ox and Bucks were in combat for 25 hours on D-Day.

The former war correspondent, Cornelius Ryan, now had the title of his book. *June 6, 1944: The Longest Day* was divided into three sections: The Wait, The Night and The Day. The book was an instant success and it wasn't long before there was talk of a movie. Bill Millin's name was about to become universally associated with the events of D-Day.

9.   **The Longest Day**

Many men won't see the sunset
When it ends the longest day.[58]

In 1962, the D-Day invasion was portrayed in the movie *The Longest Day*. The film was based on Cornelius Ryan's 1959 book and won two Academy Awards. In writing the book, Ryan and his team interviewed more than 3,000 people, including Billy Gray, Ted Tappenden, Richard Todd, Terrance Otway, Philippe Kieffer, Lord Lovat and Bill Millin. The book presents the history of D-Day by following the involvement of a cross-section of officers, troops and civilians. The movie parallels the book and presents the landing from multiple viewpoints including US, Canadian, British, French and even German officers and troops, as well as civilians.

Darryl F. Zanuck paid Ryan $175,000 for the film rights (one of the most expensive book rights' deals at the time) and also used him as a screenplay writer. Four other screenwriters were also used, including James Jones (who wrote *From Here to Eternity*).

Producer Zanuck presented different views by using different directors to create a contrast in style. Veteran English director Ken

---

[58] The Longest Day – Paul Anka

Annakin worked on the British and French scenes. Fresh off of the success of *Ben Hur*, Hungarian-born American Jewish director Andrew Marton was used to film the U.S. troops sequences. Finally, Austrian Bernhard Wicki directed the German scenes.

The Longest Day was billed as a blockbuster and it was very successful when it was released, partly due to the large international ensemble cast. The cast included:

Robert Mitchum,
Richard Burton,
Henry Fonda,
Red Buttons,
Peter Lawford,
Eddie Albert,
George Segal,
Robert Wagner,
Rod Steiger,
Sean Connery,
Curd Jürgens (who was imprisoned in real-life by the Nazis),
Roddy McDowall,
Edmond O'Brien,
Paul Anka (who sang the theme song, which was adopted by the Canadian Airborne Regiment),
Don Adams,
Sal Mineo,
Fabian,
Richard Dawson
… and John Wayne.

Name actors all received $25,000 each for their part, all except John Wayne. Zanuck had been critical of Wayne's actor/production company in the press and the two men were feuding. Zanuck said that Wayne's production company would lose money making films. To work with Zanuck, Wayne insisted on getting $250,000 for four days of work. Zanuck considered using Charlton Heston, but the studio wanted Wayne. Even though Wayne despised Zanuck, he had to take the role because, ironically, his production company had lost a lot of money making *The Alamo*. In addition, Wayne insisted that his name was separated in the opening credits, to which Zanuck agreed. Wayne assumed the film would start with 'Starring John Wayne, also starring … everyone else'. However, Zanuck fulfilled the contractual obligation by putting 'Starring ... everyone else, also starring John Wayne' in the opening credits.

Several of the cast members had seen action as servicemen during the war, including Eddy Albert, Henry Fonda, Leo Genn, Kenneth More, Donald Houston, Rod Steiger and Hans Cristian Blech (who's scars on his face were acquired fighting for the Nazis on the Eastern Front. Also, John Robinson, Richard Todd and Joseph Lowe who fought in Normandy on June 6th. Lowe landed on Omaha beach with the Second Ranger Battalion and scaled the one hundred-foot cliffs at Pointe-du-Hoc. He scaled the same cliffs again for the movie, 17 years later.

Zanuck was adamant that the film present scenes that were historically accurate. For the vehicles and artillery, Zanuck wanted to use the authentic equipment whenever possible. He tracked down two Messerschmidt trainers that were still in use in Spain and two Spitfires that were still being used by the Belgium Air Force. A tank was also found under the sand when the film crew was getting the beach ready for filming at Ponte du Hoc. For the naval scenes, Zanuck worked a deal with the U.S. Navy to film their fleet when they were on manoeuvres near Corsica. 23,000 U.S. troops were used in the filming. The Horsa gliders were more of a challenge because of their single-use construction. Britain didn't over produce Horsas and most crash landed to deliver soldiers in 1944. To solve this, Zanuck contacted the company that produced the original planes, and had them restart the production line. Because only one Horsa was manufactured, the same glider is shown landing at the Pegasus bridge, three times.

The German troops shown in the movie appeared as Nazi soldiers aged 20 to 30 years old. In reality, the division posted at Normandy had teenaged boys from the Hitler Youth (which was more like the Boy Scouts) and older men from the reserve regiments. The more experienced troops had been posted in Calais as the Nazis believed the misinformation that had been strategically fed to them. Many of the Allied veterans that had faced these German troops were haunted by the faces of the young boys that they killed. In prior Hollywood releases, German troops were typically presented as goose stepping, insane, evil madmen. Zanuck avoided this type of negative propaganda and instead the Germans are presented as soldiers fighting a war. To this end, Adolph Hitler is never shown in the movie.

Ryan's book makes a very readable history text, because of the anecdotal style. The historical facts are presented through stories about actual participants, with several themes tied together across a timeline. Shot in black and white as a docudrama, *The Longest Day* replicates the book's flow, portraying both sides of the conflict through several vignettes describing the events of D-Day. By shooting in black and white Zanuck could splice in actual footage from D-Day. It was the most expensive black and white movie ever filmed, until *Schindler's List* (1993). When the filming went over budget, Zanuck used his own money to finish shooting. The movie had a $10 million budget, partly because the scenes with non-English actors were shot both in their native tongue and in English. Zanuck shot the scenes using English, just in case the studio didn't approve his use of foreign languages, however the full English version was never released to theatres.

The Allied army's success is featured however the film also captures the repugnancy of war and the loss of lives. While the battles scenes are tame compared to the more accurate and graphic scenes in *Saving Private Ryan*, they work quite shocking for their day.

"Only two kinds of people are going to stay on this beach, those that are already dead and those that are going to die. Now get off your butts," barked Brigadier General Norman Cota (Mitchum) after the troops landed on the beach at Normandy.

Robert Mitchum was not impressed by the real US Army troops that participated in the landing craft scene. The extras didn't want to jump into the cold water when they were shooting the scene. Mitchum was so disgusted that he jumped in first to embarrass the soldiers into acting like it was D-Day and they had to get to shore.

In one of Mitchum's scenes, Cota (Mitchum) instructs a soldier on how to wear his lifejacket. The instruction was exactly the wrong procedure. It is also exactly how many of the 946 U.S. troops died in Exercise Tiger (the exercise kept secret for over 30 years until Ken Small uncovered it). If a soldier put his life preserver around his waist, then carried his equipment strapped around his chest, he would likely flip over, head under water and feet in the air, and he would drown. The scene would have been particularly upsetting for Brigadier General Cota, who was living with the secret of Exercise Tiger and had recommended the changes to lifejacket use after the disaster.

Lieutenant Colonel Benjamin Vandervoort was disappointed when he found out that John Wayne was playing him in the movie. At the time, John Wayne, was 54-years old playing Vandervoort who was 27-years old on D-Day. He had hoped that the part would go to Charlton Heston, who was younger and lighter (a critical factor in playing a paratrooper). Richard Burton also felt that he was too old for the part he was playing. He was playing an RAF pilot and Burton stated that he didn't remember seeing any pilot over 30-years old.

In order to maintain as many realistic scenes as possible, the movie used both Allied and Axis advisors, who were participants on D-Day. Dwight D. Eisenhower was used as an advisor but he walked out on the first day stating that he was too frustrated with inaccuracies. The French commando leader, Phillipe Kieffer, and one of his commandos, Maurice Chauvet, were also used as advisors. However, Chauvet walked off the set, in protest, stating that the movie was glamourizing D-Day for the sake of box office sales, rather than presenting the grim reality that the troops on ground lived and died through.

Richard Todd, who was a young officer in the 7th paratroopers, was also used as an advisor for the parachute scenes. After the war, Todd became an actor of considerable notoriety. He was asked if he wanted to play himself in the movie, to which he responded that he could never take such a small role. In the end, Todd was cast to play the part of Major John Howard. As Howard, Todd gets one of the most notable lines in the movie when, after landing in the Horsas, Howard (Todd) shouts out "Up the Ox and Bucks. Up the Ox and Bucks." He then proceeds to lead the men in the storming of the bridge.

Helmut Roemer, who has had to live with a photo capturing his embarrassment of surrendering at Pegasus bridge, is also portrayed in the film. This time he is depicted as a skinny and bewildered young soldier throwing his flare into the sky and running away. Roemer hated to see how he was characterized, especially as it was largely based in truth.

For the landing at Sword Beach, Lord Lovat was used as an advisor. Of course, Lovat, who was very detailed, included the role his piper played in the landing. When the film was released, many believed that Bill had played himself in the movie. However, the part of Bill Millin was played by Pipe-Major Leslie de Laspee of the London Scottish Territorial Army (the Queen Mother's official piper). Bill (Laspee) is featured piping on the beach, piping as the commandos march inland, and piping again as he crosses the Pegasus bridge.

During the press tour for the film, an interview was set up with Lord Lovat, Peter Lawford and Daryl Zanuck at the Pegasus Bridge. Lovat was asked why Bill Millin, who would have been 40-years old during the filming, didn't play himself.

"My old piper works in a bar in Glasgow now, I believe, and is too fat to play the part," Lovat responded. Lovat had obviously fallen out of touch with his piper.

Working on the film, Lord Lovat fell asleep in a cab heading into Caen. He woke up to see the car driving towards a group of German soldiers. Instinctively, he jumped out of the moving car and landed in a ditch. Emerging from the ditch and his sleep, he realised the soldiers were just film extras.

For the action at Sword Beach and the arrival of the commandos, the scenes were filmed in Normandy. While Lovat and Bill's role in the film display courage, their bravery is not out of place with other characters in the movie. Lovat (Lawford) disembarks the landing craft wearing a white, knitted turtleneck and carrying a WWI rifle, while Millin (Laspee) stands facing the disembarking soldiers as the pipe music plays. This scene is particularly inaccurate as Millin followed Lovat off the craft. The movie piper is also shown still inflating his bag, not moving his fingers on his chanter, as pipe music is blaring throughout the scene. For the number of scenes that the piper and his music were featured in the movie, the film should have used a piper as a consultant, especially as they had the Queen Mother's Piper on the set.

After the Horsa gliders land and Major Howard's men take the bridge, the film shows the concern on the faces of the Ox and Bucks who are ordered to hold the bridges. Richard Todd's performance as Howard was universally praised.

"It's only a matter of time before the counterattack," Howard (Todd) says.

"What about the paratroopers?" a soldier asks.

"The 7th paras might not get here for hours," Howard (Todd) responds. "Lovat and his commandos, it could be midday before they get here. The question is, how long can we hold?"

"Hold until relieved. Hold until relieved," a voice echoes in the background as Howard (Todd) remembers his orders. This would become one of the iconic lines from the movie.

When Howard (Todd) states 'The 7th paras might not get here for hours', it is a bit of an inside joke, as Todd was a member of the 7th paratroopers that came to relieve Howard. This joke is continued again in a later scene when Howard (Todd) addresses a young paratrooper as he arrives. The young man is an actor who is playing the 1944 version of 25-year old Todd. For this scene, the real-life Todd provided the actor Todd with the actual beret that he wore on D-Day.

Todd barely survived D-Day. On the day of the invasion, his commanding officer moved him to a different plane. The plane he was originally scheduled to jump from, was shot down, killing everyone on board.

The success of the book *The Longest Day*, lay in the stories of several individuals that were highlighted. The movie gave those stories mass reach. In 1957, John Steele received a letter from Cornelius Ryan. The letter was a standard questionnaire for each contact to provide biographic information to tell their story. Steele returned the short questionnaire with one short answer:

Where were you on June 5, 1944 at midnight?	Suspended ON the belltower, under the cornice of the church of Sainte-Mère-EGLISE.

As soon as Ryan received this answer, he circled it with a red felt pen and he knew this story would make his book, especially as the response came from someone who was still alive and in the United States. Ryan called Steele and made copious notes during the call: 'the Germans took him down', 'taken down from the church at three in the morning, put in a truck', etc. The story is 20 lines long in the book, but it provided some interesting reading in the middle of a gory war. Steele's name became known internationally. He was invited to attend prestigious events including one in Washington with five generals and an admiral. Comedian Red Buttons played Steele in the movie, adding to the light-hearted reflections of the scene, but Buttons played the scene seriously which maintained the gravity of Steele's situation. The scene was two minutes long, and Buttons perfectly captured the gravity of the situation through Steele's terrified face.

The scene worked, even if it did take some artistic license. While the film had major stars and showed the actions of the greatest generals, millions of movie goers would talk about two people: John Steele and Bill Millin, both ordinary men who performed their duty with bravery.

The film often attempts to mix realism with humour, a strange combination for the subject matter. As in John Steele's story, most of the scenes with the bagpipe already provided a certain natural comic relief. The piper's march seems to really sit in juxtaposition with the surrounding events. However, many of the smaller roles depicted were written to instill an almost slapstick level of humour. Most of the out-of-place humour is provided by the two Irish fictional characters, Private Clough played by comedian Norman Rossington and Private Flannigan played by a young Sean Connery.

"Come out, you dirty slobs! Flannigan's back!" Flannigan (Connery) calls out to the Germans. Then Flannigan (Connery) jumps off the boat, falls and lands with his face down in the water … all to the tune of the bagpipe music.

The taking of the village of Ouistreham is prominently featured in the movie. Only French and Germans are used in this scene as the film concentrates on Kieffer's commandos. The battle scene is well detailed lasting for over eight minutes, although the casino shown in no way resembles the actual German stronghold. The key moments shown are a failed initial charge by the French commandos, the destruction of a foot bridge, the taking out of the German guns by an arriving tank and the second advancement by the commandos entering the casino with fixed bayonets.

In another scene, the paratroopers that have landed at the Pegasus Bridge are looking concerned as they are pinned down by 'the Jerrys'. The Captain radios in that they are expecting another counterattack, a heavy one. Two English soldiers on guard are drinking tea, when one elbows the other and says "Listen, I thought I 'eard bagpipes."

"Don't be daft," responds the other soldier.

They look down the road as the bagpipes become louder and they see a platoon of men marching down the centre of the road, with bombs exploding on either side, being paraded by a piper wearing a kilt.

"I told you I heard bagpipes. It's the reinforcements," says the first soldier gleefully.

Major Howard (Todd) also hears the sound of the pipes and exclaims, "It's Lovat!"

The camera switches to a close-up of Millin (Laspee) leading the commandos along with Lord Lovat (Lawford). The Brigadier is striding up the road in his non-standard uniform, wearing a white jumper under his battledress with 'Lovat' inscribed in the collar and carrying a historic sporting rifle.

When he arrives, Lovat (Lawford) shakes his hand and says, "Sorry I'm late, old boy."

"Better late than never sir," Howard (Todd) replies.

As the scene continues, Lord Lovat is referred to as 'Shimi'. He discusses the situation with the paratroopers who are at the bridge. He is told that there is rifle and mortar fire on the other side of the bridge.

"I guess we won't wait. We better get moving. Alright, we're going across. Millin…" Lovat (Lawford) calls out.

From his position on one knee, Millin (Laspee) snaps to attention and says "Sir. Black Bear Sir."

"Come on, everybody up. On your feet," Lovat (Lawford) commands.

With that, Millin (Laspee) starts to play, he and Lovat (Lawford) lead the commandos over the bridge. The music dubbed in for the pipes is *Black Bear*, a duty tune (a regimental quick march used by most military pipe bands) in 2/4 time that is associated with the Cameron Highlanders. Known as a sailor's hornpipe, the lively tempo makes it the fastest regimental march used in the British Army. Lord Lovat's impact on dialogue can be seen in scenes like this and adds to the realism of the movie.

However, the tune *Black Bear* is dubbed in to almost every time the bagpipes are heard, which of course was not the case. It is even used for the audio in one scene when Lovat calls out for *Blue Bonnets*, yet the piper plays *Black Bear*. It would appear that *Black Bear* was the only tune that the piper knew as it is the only one played in the film. As the pipe-led commandos march across the bridge, the camera switches to two soldiers in a foxhole, complaining about the noise of the pipes.

Zanuck and Annakin must have found the use of the pipes in war a humourous backdrop, as every scene with the piper and the commandos, includes the two Irish infantry who appear out of nowhere to make a feeble joke.

"There 'e goes. 'E's at it again … Did you ever 'ear such a bleedin' racket in all your life?" asks Clough (Rossington).

"Yeah, it takes an Irishman to play the pipes!" responds Flannigan (Connery).

There is a touch of casting irony, as the part of the Irishman Flannigan complaining about the bagpipes, is played by devout Scotsman Sean Connery. He puts on a terrible Irish accent and his Scottish brogue can still be heard. At the same time Lawford, who plays a Scottish aristocrat, makes no attempt to sound like a Highland lord. Connery would have been better cast in the role as Lovat, however he wasn't well-known yet. Later that year, Connery would become an international star with the release of his very next film *Dr. No*. Connery's role in the first James Bond movie was based on the book by Ian Fleming. Two of the German commanders in *The Longest Day* would play Bond villains in future movies.

Ian Fleming used Casino Barrière in Normandy as the model for his first book Casino Royale in 1953. Fleming had spent much of his time during World War II trying to come up with a deception to obtain an Enigma machine so Bletchley Park could decode the Nazi naval messages. This was where his fascination with the spy world began. None of Fleming's theatrical attempts to obtain the encryption machine were carried out, however the machine was recovered during Lovat's first mission with the No. 4 Commando unit.

The Longest Day premiered in London on Thursday, October 11, 1962, at the Royal Charity. Princess Margaret attended the showing, at the Leicester Square Theatre, for the aid of the Army Benevolent Fund. The movie was one of the biggest hits of the year, passing 20th Century Fox's other blockbuster that year, *Cleopatra*, and saving the studio from bankruptcy. Both Richard Burton and Roddy McDowell were filming Cleopatra in Italy at the same time as *The Longest Day*, but the film schedule was so slow for the other movie that they could easily fit their battle scenes into the schedule.

In addition to a financial success, *The Longest Day* was also a theatrical success. It received several Academy Award nominations, mostly in technical categories, and won Best Cinematography and Best Special Effects. The film has subsequently received criticism as there are no African Americans cast as soldiers. The movie eventually became the box office hit Fox needed, with $30 million in worldwide sales on a $10 million budget. When the movie was released on VHS, in 1994 on the 50th anniversary of the invasion, a colourized version was used. *The Longest Day* was included on the American Film Institute's 1998 list of the Top 100 Greatest American Movies.

As a seven-year old boy in France, Serge Athenour saw the movie *The Longest Day*. Watching the story of the D-Day piper, Serge wanted to be a future Bill Millin. He took up the pipes and dreamed of one day meeting Piper Bill. He became the chairman of the Mary Queen of Scots Pipe Band of France.

10. Son of a Piper

It was pride it was real and no tale from the past,
They were there to be legends to set marks that would last.
Soldiers may stand and soldiers may fall,
And this is about one who did stand tall.
A Scotsman was fighting in world war number one,
In the same kilt as our piper like father like son.[59]

After *The Longest Day*, Bill Millin's story transformed into Bill Millin's legend. Someone would tell the tale of 'The Mad Piper of D-Day' and a friend would reply 'that didn't really happen', followed by 'it did, I saw it in a movie'! Bill's pipes had catapulted him into folklore. Before the film, the piper's name was mostly only known amongst his commando comrades, while The Lord Lovat was known universally. The movie told the story of the piper and also accentuated the name of the piper. In every scene that depicts the character of Brigadier Lovat, he shouts out the name 'Millin' and the piper character promptly plays the bagpipes as he stands at attention or leads the platoon in a march.

---

[59] The Mad Piper – Civil War

Neither man knew it at the time, but thanks to Hollywood, Lovat's greatest gift to the civilian public was 'the mad piper'. The piper on the beaches and the piper on the bridges became a military icon, a symbol of youth, bravery and triumph. As the legend of the D-Day piper grew, Bill continued to attend memorials and celebrations. He would often be asked to march with his pipes. At Ouistreham, each June 6th, he would lead a larger and larger contingent of pipers that came specifically to join him.

The French particularly felt a real debt to Bill. They regularly invited him over to France for national memorial services. They made sure he could attend, and would have a place to stay, for every event in remembrance of the Normandy Invasion. They brought him over to Paris to attend a large World War II ceremony. He attended several Army-organized events and hikes, taking part as the piper. Piper Bill also visited America, where he lectured on his D-Day experiences.

In 1984, President Ronald Reagan attended the 40th anniversary of D-Day in Normandy. He spoke of the heroism of individuals and highlighted Bill's actions. He recounted a story that resembled the arrival of the Cavalry in one of Reagan's cowboy movies, even if all the facts weren't quite accurate.

"Do you remember the story of Bill Millin of the 51st Highlanders?" President Reagan asked. "40 years ago today, British troops were pinned down near a bridge, waiting desperately for help. Suddenly they heard the sound of bagpipes, and some thought they were dreaming. Well, they weren't. They looked up and saw Bill Millin, with his bagpipes, leading the reinforcements and ignoring the smack of bullets hitting the ground around him."

When Lord Lovat published his autobiography, *March Past*, most of the book concerns his life in the commandos. He concluded that the "causes of war are falsely represented: its purpose dishonest and the glory meretricious. Yet we remember a challenge to spiritual endurance and the awareness of a common peril endured for a common end."

In the early chapters of the text, Shimi speaks of his mother's European tastes, classic looks, slim figure and long tapering hands. Many of these features were passed on to her son. He also stated that she learned to endure tragedy as she lost two brothers in the First World War, lost a daughter at the age of 14, lost her husband who died young and lost a son-in-law in the Second World War. Shimi would also have to learn to endure. These same events to him were the loss of two uncles in the First World War, the loss of a sister at age 14, the loss of his father who died young and the loss of a bother-in-law in the Second World War. Shimi had also lost his father-in-law when Rosamond's father committed suicide. In addition, Brigadier Lovat had witnessed firsthand the loss of hundreds of young men who died in service of their country, under his command.

In 1994, Lord Lovat and Rosamond suffered utterly undeserved tragedy again. Their son Hugh was killed by a charging buffalo while on safari in Tanzania, then two weeks later, their son and heir, Simon, died of a heart attack while hunting on the estate at Beaufort Castle. Master Lovat had several business investments including a stake in vineyards in Australia, oil in North Africa, along with salmon fisheries in New Hampshire, Maine and Scotland. However, when he died, he was in debt £7,000,000.

Grief-stricken, Shimi Lovat did not attend Normandy for the fiftieth anniversary of D-Day later that year. However, he was interviewed at his home in Scotland. He explained just how precarious and important the first day was.

"If we hadn't gotten a footing that first day," said Lovat, "the war would have been delayed for a very long time."

In May 1994, Bill attended a 50th Anniversary D-Day event. The commemoration was held in Abilene, Kansas, beside the grave of Dwight D. Eisenhower, the Supreme Allied Commander and U.S. President. Abilene was Eisenhower's boyhood home. At the start of the service, tears welled as Hans von Luck pushed the wheelchair of John Howard. The opening procession included top U.S. Army generals, Navy admirals and D-Day survivors, and was led by Piper Bill playing his bagpipes. During the two-day event, Bill spoke to the large audience to retell the tale of his D-Day experiences.

"Mr. Millin generated waves of laughter through a packed hall with his droll recollections of feeling insane as he piped his commando brigade on Sword beach and was obliged to continue playing under direct order from his commander, Lord Lovat, as they moved forward. Later he discovered that German snipers had held their fire because they thought he was mad too," reported Ian Brodie.

In June of that year, for D-Day, like many before and after, Bill Millin went to Bénouville to play his pipes in memory of his fallen comrades. An American film crew that was familiar with Millin from

The Longest Day, saw him with his pipes. They asked if they could set up a scene in the morning with Millin marching across the Pegasus bridge, just like he did in 1944. Bill agreed and the next day the crew were setup at the new Pegasus bridge waiting, but Bill wasn't there. The crew heard the pipes in the distance and realized that Bill was piping on the bridge at the Pegasus Memorial Museum. They ran over to confront him.

"You have the wrong bridge," the crew member yelled a Bill, frustrated that they had lost the light of the sunrise.

"No, you do," replied Bill, knowing that he was piping on the bridge that he had piped on, just like 1944.

In March 1995, the 15th Lord Lovat, passed away.

One published obituary described the Lord Lovat as 'Gay, debonair, inspirational, and yes, lovable – arrogant, ruthless, at times terrifying, his personality is too complex to explain. Perhaps we should not try to, and simply remember that he was a Lovat'.

At the time of his death, Shimi would have been aware that part of the Lovat estate would need to be sold, most likely including the castle. Rosamond lost her husband and two sons within a year and would have no way to pay off the mounting debts. To pay the family's tax bill, Beaufort Castle was sold to Ann Gloag (owner of Stagecoach, Britain's larges bus line) for £2,000,000. Gloag's life had been the polar opposite of Lord Lovat's, starting the bus line up from her council house in Perth.

The pipes are not thought of as a versatile instrument, but Bill would tell you otherwise. He would highlight that they were used not just in battle, but also in parades, and at weddings and at funerals. At Shimi's funeral in St. Mary's Catholic Church in Eskdale, a grief-stricken Bill Millin played a lament of Lovat's favourite Highland songs, a fitting goodbye to the proud Scotsman.

With the death of Shimi's son the year before, the title of Lord Lovat now skipped a generation and passed to Shimi's grandson, Simon. The 16th Lord Lovat, Simon Fraser, assumed the title that was destined for his father only a year earlier. The Clan Fraser was now composed of tens of thousands of descendants around the world, with the largest contingency being in Canada. In 1997, during the Gathering of the Clans, 40,000 Frasers from 21 different countries came to Castle Fraser over a period of four days.

Ted Tappenden would forever be known as 'Ham and Jam'. His comrades from the Ox and Bucks had already given him this nickname, but *The Longest Day* solidified it. He returned to Normandy many times after the war, often taking his family with him. Ted passed away in April 1999. His ashes were scattered by his son, Barry, on the original bridge.

John Howard had retired from public service in 1974. He returned to Normandy every year to lay a wreath at the location where the gliders landed. He thought of all the men that died during the war, but always had a particular observance for the loss of Den Brotheridge. John lectured cadets in several NATO countries and lived out his days in Surrey. He passed away in 1999.

Bill Millin went to the Dawlish Museum in Devon and asked if they would like his bagpipes. He had marched through the streets of Dawlish as a commando training for D-Day. The chairman, Peggy Frobert, decided that they couldn't take them because the insurance value was too much for the small museum.

In 2001, Bill donated his World War II bagpipes, his father's Cameron kilt, his commando beret and his highland sgian-dubh, to the National War Museum of Scotland in Edinburgh. The display was titled 'The Mad Piper'. Bill's wife Margaret, who passed away in 2000, came from Edinburgh. She had asked Bill to donate the pipes to the city. In 2002, Alan Carswell, the museum's curator, contacted Bill to say that it had 'convincing evidence' that these were not the pipes that he played on the beach and that in fact the real pipes were on display in Normandy. Reluctantly, Bill took the pipes back.

Bill had played two sets of pipes during the war. He donated a set of pipes to the Pegasus Memorial Museum, but these were not the pipes that he used on the beach. They were the replacement set of pipes that he played elsewhere in Normandy, later in the campaign after shrapnel damaged his first set.

"Mr. Carswell may be the expert, but he has got it wrong on this occasion. He is entitled to his opinion, but he has lost out on a piece of history. The pipes I gave to the museum in Scotland are the D-Day pipes and the ones I gave to the museum in France are what I have called the Normandy pipes," Bill explained.

When questioned by the press, Carswell said that he was contacted by the Normandy museum who assured him that they had the set of pipes that was played on June 6, 1944. Rather than go on the word of another curator, all he had to do was look at the shrapnel damage on the pipes that were donated to the Edinburgh museum.

In 2003, while living in a nursing home in Dawlish, Bill had a stroke. The next year, he offered the beach pipes to the local museum in Dawlish and this time they accepted them. Bill's notoriety grew even greater when the Isle of Man issued a commemorative stamp to honor Scotland's role in the invasion. It featured an image depicting Millin playing his bagpipes during the battle at Pegasus bridge. Bill would still go to Normandy to lead parades, but he was now in a wheelchair and no longer played the pipes.

In 2005 the Dawlish Museum sent the pipes to the Conservation Department of the Royal Albert Museum in Exeter, where the pipes and kilt were preserved. Even though he had limited mobility, Bill regularly visited the Museum. He would give formal and impromptu talks on what part he played in the commandos. Also on display in the museum, are Bill's kilt, commando beret, and dirk. The exhibit includes photographic archives and a looped video telling of Bill's exploits. When he passed by the display with his uniform and bagpipes, in jest he would always salute. The museum noted that the people that were most interested in Bill's talks and the display, other than the French, were the Germans. They greeted Bill with great affection and treated him like a clan hero.

Bill continued to attend D-Day celebrations. Every year, more and more pipers would be there to greet him. From his scooter, he would lead the pipers along the boardwalk, through the memorial foot paths and across the original Pegasus bridge. The French people would hug and kiss him as the led the procession.

In 2009, on June 6th, Bill attended the D-Day observances at Sword beach, where France awarded him with the Légion d'honneur for gallantry.

In 2010, on June 6th, Bill was the guest of honour in Normandy for the anniversary of D-Day. From his wheelchair, he led a procession of pipers, veterans and civilians along the sidewalks of the Normandy shoreline. In Normandy, everyone knew him by name and understood what he had done. To his enjoyment, pipe bands played for him. However, when they played *Hieland Laddie*, he was sadly taken back to 1944.

"Whenever I hear that song, I remember walking through the surf," Bill reflected.

In August 2010, Piper Bill Millin, passed away peacefully in hospital in Torbay.

"He has been coming back to Colleville-Montgomery for many years to pay respects to his fallen comrades. We knew him well and everyone in this town has a sentimental attachment to him," said Guy Legrand, Mayor of Colleville-Montgomery. "He was undoubtedly a very brave man. But he was also kind, understanding and a great diplomat."

To his son John, Bill played two different roles. He was John's dad and he was the D-Day piper. As a father, John saw Bill as a fairly quiet, modest, even self-effacing man. However, when John saw his father play the pipes, he saw a more animated man, the type that would be capable of performing great acts of bravery.

"My father was 21 when he landed in June 1944. He was frightened, but he had a job to do," John said.

Since Bill had played his pipes at Lord Lovat's funeral, it was very fitting when John cited the Brigadier at his father's funeral. He quoted the words that Lord Lovat had told the commandos on D-Day:

"In 100-years time your children's children will look back and say they must have been giants in those day," John said, "My dad is our giant."

Winston Churchill once said, "A nation that forgets its past, has no future."

In *March Past*, Lord Lovat stated that the survivors of the battle in Normandy held a sacred duty to "enshrine the memory of those brave men who did not return."

Across Great Britain, there are many commemorations in honour of the commandos. In Westminster Abbey there is a statue of a Commando soldier in the cloisters. The statue was unveiled by Winston Churchill in 1948. In Scotland, at Spean Bridge near Fort William, is the Commando Memorial. The unveiling of the Memorial was attended by the Queen Mother and a kilted Lord Lovat in 1952. In the Spean Bridge Hotel, there is a permanent Commando exhibition, which includes an illustrated history of No. 4. Despite these tributes, Normandy will always remain the heart of D-Day remembrances.

A visit to Normandy, is a visit to France's lush northern corner, French architecture, and of course French cuisine. There is a strange mix of old-world charm and 20th century utilitarian buildings. Some villages survived the war unscathed and their farmhouses date back to the times of Napoleon. Others, were bombarded by battleships, strafed by planes or withstood bitter infantry battles. Caen in particular, was completely decimated during the war and had to be completely rebuilt. Ouistreham, still maintains a mixture of post-war rebuilding, along with 17th century half-timbered buildings and stone churches.

Across the Normandy coast, nestled among the landscape, towns and beaches, there are several reminders of the war and sadly the price that so many young men paid. Farmlands are still marked out by hedgerow, the same high hedges that once hid soldiers and snipers. There is hardly a town you can visit in Normandy that doesn't have a statue, a monument or a cemetery. These reminders commemorate D-Day and the soldiers who fought in the many battles to liberate France. Of course, every June 6th, there are remembrances to pay tribute to the suffering and sacrifices of the heroes of the beach landings and liberation efforts.

The Pegasus Memorial Museum is on the strip of land between the Caen canal and the Orne River, between Bénouville and Ranville. It is dedicated to the men of the British 6th Airborne Division, the first of Allied troops to arrive in Normandy on the night of June 5, 1944. Here, the story of the capture of the bridge is told, including the glider flight, the taking of the bridge and the challenge to hold the bridge.

There is a Horsa glider at the museum where the public can enter and fully appreciate the precariousness of the midnight flight. The replica Horsa was unveiled in 2004 by the Prince of Wales. Jim Wallwork was there to show the Prince how the cockpit controls worked. The night before, at 12:16 a.m., Jim enjoyed a glass of champagne with some of the men from the commandos and the Ox and Bucks, at the Gondrée café.

The Merville Battery Museum is housed inside the original concrete casemates. The museum covers the batteries role in the German Atlantic Wall Defences and the lives of the soldiers who were stationed there as well as the story of the Allied soldiers who captured it. The site contains an ammunition bunker, dormitory, cookhouse, HQ bunker, ammunition bunker and other buildings. Every 20 minutes inside the casemate there is a powerful sound and light show which recreates the events of June 6, 1944.

Inside the Merville Battery Museum, there is a copy of a letter that the paratrooper Stan Eckert wrote to his mother:

> *Somewhere in France.*
>
> *Dear Mum,*
>
> *I am writing this letter at the bottom of a ditch very near the front line and I hope to get it posted pretty soon as my pal and I have a good idea that tomorrow we will be prisoners of war. I am writing this short note here so as if it is ever found by anyone, they can forward it for me.*
>
> *Do you know mum dear, I have never realised how much you meant to me, until now? If I can get home again, you will see a very different Stan, just wait and see. The same goes for dad, too, and the rest of the Eckerts. There is one thing that worries me, and that is what happened to Cyril. I hope and pray that he is safe and well.*
>
> *Well, mum, just sit and wait for the end of the war when I will be 'home' once again, for good. Don't worry at all, will you.*
>
> *With love to everyone at home, especially you.*
>
> *Your ever-loving son.*
> *Stan XXXXX*

The commando that found Stan's body, also found the letter that Stan's commanding officer had asked him to write. The letter eventually made it home to his 'mum', who he had anticipated seeing when he was granted his next leave.

In Ouistreham, France, there is the 'Musée du Commando No. 4', the only museum devoted entirely to one Commando unit. It contains weapons, pictures, models and other memorabilia of the British and French Commando unit. There is a tribute to Commander Kieffer, who landed on Sword Beach with 177 freshly-trained Free French commandos. Of course, the museum contains many exhibits on the taking of the casino to free Ouistreham, plus it also has a tribute to the commando training at Commando Castle in Achnacarry, Scotland.

Also in Ouistreham, is The Grand Bunker, Atlantic Wall Museum, a tribute to the breaking of Rommel's integrated defense structure. Inside the 52-foot concrete tower is a fully restored bunker recreating how the structure looked on June 6, 1944. The museum holds many documents and photographs, depicting the Wall's construction, the use of beach defenses and the location of nearby gun batteries. Another interesting aspect of the museum is the portrayal of everyday life in the tower for the German soldiers that lived there.

In Sainte-Mère-Église, for many years they would hang a parachute from the church tower on each anniversary of D-Day. Finally, the town erected a statue of John Steele. The dummy paratrooper is erected on the towers of the Notre-Dame-de-l'Assomption, hanging from his parachute. The walls around the statue are still covered in the pockmarks from the fight to liberate the town.

In addition to museums, there are several monuments throughout Normandy, including the Kieffer Monument on Sword beach, which was unveiled by French President Francois Mitterrand in 1984. The memorial 'La Flamme' is a large metal flame built on top of a German bunker. Close to the Pegasus bridge is a bronze bust of John Howard, in memorial of his dedication in capturing the bridges and liberating France. It marks the exact spot where the nose of Horsa 91 glider came to a stop in the barbed wire (30 feet short of the road and even closer to the bank of the canal).

Across Normandy are thousands of graves filled with British, Canadian and American troops. On entering one of these graveyards, you are immediately struck with the enormity of battle and the enormity of the loss. Each grave has a story, some are readily available, while others are lost in time.

In the Ranville War Cemetery, Stan Eckert could not be laid to rest next to his brother Cyril, because the space was not set aside in hope that Stan would be found alive. His grave lies in the same row as Cyril's, next to his best friend, George White, who was killed on the same day. There are headstones for 2,500 soldiers in the Ranville cemetery, and there is also one dog. When Emile Corteil was killed, his commanding officer decided that since the two were so devoted to each other, the Private and his dog should be buried together.

Among the many graves of the fallen soldiers in Normandy are:

- Robert Edward Johns, the youngest paratrooper (maybe the youngest soldier) killed in the Second World War.
- Fred Greenhalgh, the first soldier to die on D-Day when he was thrown out of Horsa 93.
- Denholm Herbert Brotheridge, who died leading the charge to capture the Pegasus bridge.

- Phillip Anthony Wellesley-Colley, who led a landing craft of disembarking commandos as he ran directly into the line of fire on Sword beach.
- Joseph Pasquale Jr., who died on Sword beach hoping to reunite with his brother who was in a prisoner of war camp.

In 1991, Henry 'Todd' Sweeney accompanied Hans von Luck as they visited the Ranville War Cemetery. Both Sweeney and von Luck were there to remember and honour their fallen comrades.

"He went to one corner of the cemetery to mourn his dead, and I went to the other to mourn my dead," Colonel Sweeney said. "It made me think what war is all about. At the time it was the only way out. But is it necessary? Isn't it a futile way of settling business?"

"Tell your young people," Jim Wallwork once pled, "that sometimes you have to fight and stand firm, World War Two was such a test. Take great care with your freedom as one day you may have to fight to preserve what you have."

Shimi Lovat sought no recognition or statues for himself during his lifetime. However, he would always try to participate in events that paid tribute for the fallen soldiers of the Commandos.

In 2014, British and French dignitaries gathered in Ouistreham, along with 100 members of the Clan Fraser, to unveil a memorial in honour of Brigadier Lovat. The bronze statue is a tall, slender likeness of Lovat the soldier, standing at ease. The effigy stands near 'La Flame' on Sword beach. The Lovat family contributed £100,000 themselves to fund the statue. That year, La Flame and the Lovat statue formed the backdrop for the D-Day services hosted by the Queen and U.S. President Barack Obama.

"The act of commemoration is a world event but the statue serves as a reminder that D-Day was all about individuals and individual sacrifice – not just my father and our family but every soldier and every family," said Lovat's daughter, Tessa Keswick (nee Fraser).

As Bill Millin's legend grew, eventually it spilled over to popular culture. The piper's story was featured in paintings, in literature and in song. Devon folk singer Sheelagh Allen started the musical accolades when she wrote the song *The Highland Piper* in 2006. Six years later, The Real McKenzies, a Canadian Celtic-punk band recorded *My Head*

Is Filled with Music[60]. Police Dog Hogan, a British folk band, released *Fraserburgh Train*[61]. In 2015, Civil War, a Swedish power-metal band, recorded The Mad Piper[62].

That's   British-Canadian-Swedish   folk-Celtic-punk-power-metal music, all inspired to sing about the same legend.

"He was what we would nowadays call a celebrity," Ken Sturdy mused, knowing that this status was not something that the unassuming piper strived for. "But he wouldn't like that as he was very modest. He used to joke that when the enemy heard him coming, they panicked at the sound of the pipes."

In 2009, Serge Athenour, the young French boy who was drawn to the pipes after seeing *The Longest Day*, was part of a group of French pipers (the Mary Queen of Scots Pipe Band) who travelled to Devon to meet with the legendary Bill Millin. The pipers spoke with Bill about the idea of erecting a statue in his honour in France. The mayor of Colleville-Montgomery had already donated a site, opposite of the place where Bill had landed on D-Day.

Bill didn't want a statue. However, the pipers of France were insistent that they would raise the funds to erect a memorial and they convinced the humble piper to let them use his likeness. Bill's only two conditions were that the memorial be dedicated to all who fought on the beaches, not just him, and that the design of his likeness be accurate, especially the kilt.

"As long as the detail is right. As long as the statue is dressed the same way that I was, in the right kilt, in the right fittings, then that's fine," Bill said reluctantly.

The goal was to raise £80,000 that year, commission the statue and unveil it at a D-Day memorial celebration in Normandy in 2010. Serge created the 'D-Day Piper Bill Millin Association' and a fundraising drive was organized. A year later, the funds remained far short of the goal. While the Dawlish Museum and branch of the Royal British Legion were great supporters of Bill, there was very little money raised from British donors. Most of the money that had been donated, came from French contributions.

---

[60] 'My name is Billy Millin, I braved the Norman Shore, Mortal shells, machineguns, D-Day 1944'

[61] 'And Lord Lovat stands and calls for a tune, From the Piper'

[62] 'Play for me brother like never before, Scottish Piper Bill, *Play Hielan Laddie* and *The Road to the Isles*, On your pipe of peace'

In 2010, when Bill's son John visited his dad, he could see the sadness in his father's eyes. Bill knew that he was not going to be around to see the unveiling of the statue. John told his dad not to worry, the statue would get funded and there would be a grand unveiling, in France at Sword beach.

"Will there be pipers there?" Bill asked his son, with a touch of melancholy.

"Of course, there will be pipers, there will be hundreds of pipers," John answered.

"There won't be a Millin piper though, will there?" Bill asked wistfully. Bill had taught his son how to play the chanter, but John never did take up the pipes.

"I will learn at least one tune, one of your favourites," John promised his father. "I will learn that for the day."

Bill thought back to his pipe training and the discipline imbued on him by Charlie Moir back in Shettleston. The pipes require a disciplined practice routine. It was often said that practice makes perfect, but with the bagpipes it is said that perfect practice makes perfect. That means daily playing. It is better to play 15 minutes per day than playing longer two times a week. Unsure if his son was prepared for the physical, mental and emotional challenge that comes with the pipes, Bill laughed.

"Well, good luck with that son," Bill mused back.

John realized that he had foolishly promised to learn the bagpipes, not an easy task for a man of his age. But, at 55-years old, he set out with the burden of learning an instrument that required years of training. The effort was to learn the instrument but also to develop the fitness and lung capacity required to keep the bag inflated.

"Dad was a very carefree father, he encouraged me to do what I was interested in and though he would have liked me to follow him with the pipes he did not force it on me," John recalled.

One month after Bill passed away, a memorial service was held in France in his honour. Pipe bands played Amazing Grace and members of Colleville-Montgomery town council threw flowers into the water at Sword beach. The pipes ended the remembrance by playing *Scotland the Brave* as they marched away. Serge Athenour attended the service, still trying to raise funds for the memorial.

"It was a great honour to meet him several times. He is an iconic figure that represents all the soldiers, so people who want to pay tribute to all those men can contribute," Serge said. "We hope the statue will become a central tribute for people in the future as the soldiers will not be here soon."

In 2013, three years after Bill passed away, pipers gathered once again at Sword beach. They piped and they marched, just as they did every year. This time the parade held more than 500 pipers from 21 different countries.

"They're playing for him, in remembrance of my dad," John reflected.

This year was special for the pipers in many ways. This would be the year the Piper Bill Millin statue, by French sculptor Gaetan Ader, would be unveiled in Colleville-Montgomery. It was also special because for the first time in a decade, there would be a Millin marching as a piper in the parade. John had learned the pipes well enough to join the parade.

"Dad played the pipes in remembrance of those who died in Normandy, and would play at commando events and often travel to Normandy for the commemoration," John reflected. "I play the pipes in memory of Dad and the Normandy veterans."

John attended the event with his wife Dorrie and their children Jessica and Jacob. He donned some of his father's belongings and joined in the parade. In the village next to Sword beach, where the commandos came ashore, there was a Millin piper piping once again.

"I've tried to wear and carry as much of my father's possessions as I possibly can today," John said, "... so in some way, he's here."

John put his newfound piping skills to use as he joined the march along the boardwalk, piping *Amazing Grace*, one of his father's personal favourites. He had fulfilled his promise to his father. A Millin piper attended the unveiling.

Guy Legrand, Mayor of Colleville-Montgomery, paid tribute to the piper whose bravery has touched the hearts of many generations of townsfolk. In the standing-room only ceremony that followed, John thanked the people who had helped make the tribute possible.

"Thank you to everyone here today. For your hard work and dedication over the last four years ..." said an emotional John Millin, "to realize my father's wishes, a place of remembrance for his lost friends … We are gathered here today to say thank you, to those who served in person, who fought here 69 years ago. Finally, my father loved France and he loved the French people … je vous remercier por cette homage de mon pere. Merci, merci beaucoup."

Overlooking the beach where the commandos disembarked to a mortar fire greeting and piper Bill gave the deadliest performance of his life, Bill Millin's likeness stands in tribute. The statue was erected in commemoration of a single act of bravery that symbolizes thousands of acts of bravery.

There are three plaques on the statue:

Plaque 1:

> THANKS TO OUR LIBERATORS
> MERCI A NOS LIBERATEURS

Plaque 2:

> ON D DAY, JUNE 6TH 1944, ON THIS SECTOR OF "SWORD BEACH", AS THE SCOTS HAVE DONE FOR GENERATIONS, THE BRIGADIER LORD LOVAT, CHIEF OF THE 1ST SPECIAL SERVICE BRIGADE, ALSO A HIGHLANDS CHIEF, ORDERED HIS PERSONAL PIPER, BILL MILLIN TO PIPE HIS COMMANDOS ASHORE.
> ABOVE THE ROAR OF BATTLE CAME THE SKIRL OF LIBERATION WITH THE PIPER LEADING THE WAY.
> THEY BOTH ENTERED LEGEND

Plaque 3:

> "IF THEY REMEMBER THE BAGPIPER, THEN THEY WON'T FORGET THOSE WHO SERVED AND FELL ON THE BEACHES"
>
> - - PIPER WILLIAM "BILL" MILLIN
>
> MEMORIAL ERECTED BY THE GENEROSITY OF THOSE WHO REMEMBER

As John Millin unveiled the tribute to the lone piper of D-Day, a lone Spitfire flew above the beach. The statue is a memorial to the

Piper Bill Millin's fearlessness and bravery, but just as Bill wished, it serves to remind us of all the courageous young men who fought on that day. After the ceremony, John was asked what his father would have thought if he had been there to see him lead the pipers in a tune.

"He would have been proud that I finally learnt to play," John said, displaying his father's same modesty, "though I'm sure he would have had something to say about my skill level."

On June 7, 2013, John Millin went to look at the metallic brown likeness of the piper, the day after its unveiling. This visit was without all the ceremonial pomp, just a son and a statue of his father. As he left the beaches of Normandy, John felt like he was leaving his father behind.

"I'm very proud of what my father achieved," John Millin said. "He was pleased at becoming a sort of iconic figure of D-Day, because it means that people would remember … it would focus people's attention on the lives that were given to free Europe at that time."

How many lives were affected, on that sixth day of June in 1944, by the sounds of the piper and his display of bravery? How many wounded and dying men were comforted by the melody of the pipes? The traditional music helped to lend familiarity to the unfamiliar. The sound of the pipes gave the enemy gunners a second thought before they pulled the trigger. The blare of the drones encouraged men to bravely run ashore. The music helped to guide confused soldiers, through the black and grey smoke, towards the safety of the seawall. The sheer display of courage, parading along the shoreline letting everyone know that they didn't need to fear enemy fire, emboldened others to soar. The skirl helped to signal forward troops who were nervously waiting for relief. How many lives were spared by an unarmed soldier, the lone piper, in the greatest battle of World War II?

They shall grow not old, as we that are left grow old:
Age shall not weary them, nor the years condemn.
At the going down of the sun and in the morning
We will remember them.[63]

[63] For the Fallen – Laurence Binyon

Headstones

Here are some of the many commemorations captured by the headstones of Normandy:

Ranville War Cemetery (Ranville, France): Stanley George Thomas Eckbert was killed on D-Day, after he wrote his letter to home. His headstone reads 'IN LOVING MEMORY OF DEAR STAN, A MUCH LOVED SON AND BROTHER, SO GREATLY MISSED BY ALL THE FAMILY'.

Ranville War Cemetery (Ranville, France): Cyril Albert Eckbert was killed in Normandy two months after his brother. His headstone reads 'IN LOVING MEMORY OF DEAR CYRIL, A MUCH-LOVED SON AND BROTHER, SO GREATLY MISSED BY ALL THE FAMILY'.

Ranville War Cemetery (Ranville, France): Emile Servais Corteil was killed by friendly fire, along with the dog that he landed with. His headstone reads 'HAD YOU KNOWN OUR BOY YOU WOULD HAVE LOVED HIM TOO. "GLEN" HIS PARATROOP DOG WAS KILLED WITH HIM'.

Ranville War Cemetery (Ranville, France): Robert Edward Johns was the youngest paratrooper (maybe the youngest soldier) killed in the Second World War. His headstone reads 'HE DIED AS HE LIVED, FEARLESSLY'.

Bayeux War Cemetery (Bayeux, France): Phillip Anthony Wellesley-Colley led a landing craft of disembarking commandos as he ran directly into the line of fire on Sword beach. His headstone reads 'ON WHOSE SOUL, SWEET JESUS, HAVE MERCY'.

La Delivrande War Cemetery (Douvres, France): Fred Greenhalgh was the first soldier to die on D-Day when he was thrown from Horsa 93. His gravestone reads 'NOTHING IN MY HAND I BRING SIMPLY TO THY CROSS I CLING'.

Bayeux War Cemetery (Bayeux, France): Thomas David Yates drowned as his comrade Anthony Rubenstein passed him, following the orders not to stop for anyone. His headstone reads 'BELOVED IS THY NAME BELOVED THOU SHALT ALWAYS BE'.

Ranville Churchyard (Ranville, France): Denholm Herbert Brotheridge died leading the charge to capture the Pegasus bridge. His headstone reads 'OUT OF THE BITTERNESS OF WAR HE FOUND THE PERFECT PEACE'.

Hermanville War Cemetery (Hermanville, France): Brian Joseph Mullen, who landed with the commandos at the Lofoten Islands, Dieppe and Sword beach, was killed returning to help a fallen commando on Pegasus bridge. His headstone reads 'ARTIST. HUSBAND OF JANET MULLEN. W.R.N.S.'.

Hermanville War Cemetery (Hermanville, France): Joseph Pasquale Jr. died before he could clear Sword beach. His brother couldn't visit the gravesite until 1945, when he was freed from a prisoner of war camp. His headstone reads 'SWEET AND TREASURED MEMORY OF MY DARLING HUSBAND WHO GAVE HIS LIFE ON "D" DAY'.

Normandy Command Structure

3rd Infantry Division:
Commander: Major-General Tom G. Rennie

> **1st Special Service Brigade**: Brigadier General Lord Lovat
>
> > No.3 Commando: Lieutenant Colonel Peter Young
> > No.4 Commando: Lieutenant Colonel R. W. P. Dawson
> > 1er Bataillon Fusiliers Marins Commando: Capitaine de Corvette Philippe Kieffer
> > No.6 Commando: Lieutenant Colonel Derek Mills-Roberts
> > No.45 Royal Marine Commando: Captain R.M N. C. Ries
>
> **2nd Battalion East Yorkshire Regiment**: Lieutenant Colonel G.F. Hutchinson
>
> > A Company: Major C.K. King
> > D Company: Major Barber

6th Airborne Division:
Commander: Major-General Richard N. Gale

> **5th Para Brigade**: Brigadier Nigel Poett, Deputy: Major Ted Lough
>
> > 7th Battalion Parachute Regiment: Lieutenant Colonel Geoffrey Pine-Coffin
> >
> > > HQ Company: Major Tullis
> > > A Company: Major Nigel Taylor
> > > B Company: Major Roger Neale
> > > C Company: Major R. Bartlett
>
> **6th Airlanding Brigade**: Brigadier Hugh Kindersley, Deputy: Colonel Reggie Parker
>
> > 2nd Battalion Oxfordshire and Buckinghamshire Light Infantry: Lieutenant Colonel Michael W. Roberts
> >
> > > A Company: Major Gilbert Rahr
> > > B Company: Major J. S. R. Edmunds
> > > C Company: Major Johnny Granville
> > > D Company: Major John Howard

256

Ian Moran

British Troop References

Name	Rank (on D-Day)	Service Number	Posting, Recognition and Notes
Ainsworth, John Alfred (Johnny)	Staff Sergeant	81376	Horsa 91 (co-pilot) - C Squadron, Glider Pilot Regiment
Airy, John	Private		No. 5 Troop, No.3 Commando, 1st Special Service Brigade
Allen, Douglas V. (Doug)	Private	5391953	Horsa 95 - No. 23 Platoon, D Company, 2nd Battalion Oxfordshire and Buckinghamshire Light Infantry, 6th Airlanding Brigade, 6th Airborne Division
Baacke, Fredrick William	Staff Sergeant	2120531	Horsa 96 (co-pilot) - B Squadron, No.1 Wing, Glider Pilot Regiment - *Croix de Guerre*
Bailey, Jack (Bill)	Corporal		Horsa 91 - No. 25 Platoon, D Company, 2nd Battalion Oxfordshire and Buckinghamshire Light Infantry, 6th Airlanding Brigade, 6th Airborne Division
Barkway, Geoffrey Sydney	Staff Sergeant	2582663	Horsa 93 (pilot) - B Squadron, No.1 Wing, Glider Pilot Regiment - *Distinguished Flying Medal*
Barwick, Christopher Cyril (Pete)	Sergeant	5383457	Horsa 94 - No. 22 Platoon, D Company, 2nd Battalion Oxfordshire and Buckinghamshire Light Infantry, 6th Airlanding Brigade, 6th Airborne Division - Killed in action or died of wounds (Herouvillette New Communal Cemetery)
Bellows, James	Sergeant	5497329	1st Battalion, Royal Hampshire Regiment
Bidmead, William (Bill)	Private		No. 4 Commando, 1st Special Service Brigade - King's Royal Rifle Corps
Boland, Oliver Frederic	Staff Sergeant	1449953	Horsa 92 (pilot) - E Squadron, No.2 Wing, Glider Pilot Regiment - *Croix de Guerre, Distinguished Flying Medal*
Boyle, Peter	Staff Sergeant	4983193	Horsa 93 (co-pilot) - B Squadron - Glider Pilot Regiment
Brennan, Gordon	Private		Motor Transport Section, Battalion Headquarters, 7th (Light Infantry) Parachute Battalion, 6th Airborne Division
Brotheridge, Denholm Herbert (Denny)	Lieutenant	237676	Horsa 91 - No. 25 Platoon, D Company, 2nd Battalion Oxfordshire and Buckinghamshire Light Infantry, 6th Airlanding Brigade, 6th Airborne Division - Killed in action or died of wounds (Ranville Churchyard) - *Mentioned in Despatches*

Butler, H. John	Private		No. 9 Platoon, Company C, 7th (Light Infantry) Parachute Battalion, 6th Airborne Division
Cadman, Roy	Private		No.3 Commando, 1st Special Service Brigade - Royal East Kent Regiment
Chatterton, George James Stewart	Colonel	91149	Battalion Headquarters, 1st Battalion The Glider Pilot Regiment, Army Air Corps - *Distinguished Service Order, Officer of the British Empire*
Chitty, John Albert	Lance Sergeant	6850530	No. 4 Commando, 1st Special Service Brigade - King's Royal Rifle Corps - Died on war service (Brookwood Memorial)
Churchill, John Malcolm Thorpe Fleming (Mad Jack)	Major	34657	No.3 Commando, 1st Special Service Brigade - Manchester Regiment - *Distinguished Service Order, Bar to the Distinguished Service Order, Military Cross*
Clapperton, Raymond Hedley (Clap)	Flying Officer	151700	Horsa 94 (tug pilot) - No. 3 Squadron, Royal Air Force - *Distinguished Flying* Cross
Clare, Thomas (Tommy)	Private	5385732	Horsa 96 - No. 17 Platoon, D Company, 2nd Battalion Oxfordshire and Buckinghamshire Light Infantry, 6th Airlanding Brigade, 6th Airborne Division
Clark, G. L. C.	Private	2059936	Horsa 95 - No.23 Platoon, D Company, 2nd Oxfordshire and Buckinghamshire Light Infantry, 6th Airlanding Brigade, 6th Airborne Division
Clark, Henry William (Nobby)	Private	6853548	Horsa 92 - No.24 Platoon, D Company, 2nd Battalion Oxfordshire and Buckinghamshire Light Infantry, 6th Airlanding Brigade, 6th Airborne Division
Clive, F	Private	6467039	Horsa 94 - No. 22 Platoon, D Company, 2nd Battalion Oxfordshire and Buckinghamshire Light Infantry, 6th Airlanding Brigade, 6th Airborne Division
Corteil, Emile Servais	Private	14410713	9th (Eastern and Home Counties) Parachute Battalion, 3rd Parachute Brigade, 6th Airborne Division - *Croix d'Honneur*
Curtis, Leonard Rupert	Lieutenant		Commander, 200th LCI(S) Flotilla, Assault Group J4 - Royal Naval Volunteer Reserve - *Distinguished Service Cross, Atlantic Star, France and Germany Star*
Cuthbertson, Leslie	Private		Royal Army Dental Corps, Army Medical Services
Dawson, Robert William Palliser	Lieutenant Colonel	130068	No. 4 Commando, 1st Special Service Brigade - The Loyal Regiment (North Lancashire) - *Commander of the Order of the British Empire, Distinguished Service Order, Mentioned in Despatches*
Day, John Edward (Eddy)	Lieutenant		E Troop, No. 45 Royal Marine Commando, 1st Special Service Brigade - Royal Marines - *Mention in Despatches*
Dean, Ellis (Dixie)	Lieutenant	288761	13th (Lancashire) Parachute Battalion, 3rd Parachute Brigade, 6th Airborne Division

Drew (Nomburg), Harry	Private		Troop 3, No. 10 Commando, 1st Special Service Brigade
Duder, Derek Harvey	Winged Commander	431102	Horsa 91 (tug-pilot) – 298 Squadron, Royal Air Force - *Distinguished Service Order*
Duncan, Tom	Private	2880451	No. 3 Commando, 1st Special Service Brigade - Gordon Highlanders
Dunkeld, Russell	Acting Able Seaman		HM Landing Ship (tank) 304, Royal Navy - *Legion d'Honneur*
Dunning, James Edwin	Sergeant-Major	7893672	No. 4 Commando, 1st Special Service Brigade - Royal Armoured Corps
Eckert, Cyril Albert	Corporal	6103133	13th (Lancashire) Parachute Battalion, 3rd Parachute Brigade, 6th Airborne Division - Ranville War Cemetery
Eckert, Stanley George Thomas	Lance Corporal	14404989	9th (Eastern and Home Counties) Parachute Battalion, 3rd Parachute Brigade, 6th Airborne Division - Ranville War Cemetery
Edwards, Denis (Eddie)	Private	5391739	Horsa 91 - No. 25 Platoon, D Company, 2nd Battalion Oxfordshire and Buckinghamshire Light Infantry, 6th Airlanding Brigade, 6th Airborne Division
Evans, J. L.	Captain		War Office official photographer, Army Film and Photo Section, Army Film and Photographic Unit
Evans, Stanley	Corporal	5391885	Horsa 93 - No.14 Platoon, B Company, 2nd Oxfordshire and Buckinghamshire Light Infantry - *Croix de Guerre*
Everett, Eric Jack	Private	6031906	Horsa 94 - No. 22 Platoon, D Company, 2nd Battalion Oxfordshire and Buckinghamshire Light Infantry, 6th Airlanding Brigade, 6th Airborne Division - Killed in action or died of wounds (Ranville War Cemetery)
Fox, Dennis	Lieutenant	184578	Horsa 96 - No. 17 Platoon, D Company, 2nd Battalion Oxfordshire and Buckinghamshire Light Infantry, 6th Airlanding Brigade, 6th Airborne Division
Fraser, Simon Christopher Joseph (Lord Lovat)	Brigadier General	44718	No. 4 Commando, 1st Special Service Brigade - The Lovat Scouts - *Distinguished Service Order, Military Cross, Deputy Lieutenant, Justice of the Peace*
Fussell, Peter Lincoln	Private	214506 & 461895	No. 4 Commando, 1st Special Service Brigade - Royal Army Service Corps - *British Empire Member, Member of the Order of the British Empire*
Gardner, Charles Henry (Charlie)	Private	5385497	Horsa 91 - No. 25 Platoon, D Company, 2nd Battalion Oxfordshire and Buckinghamshire Light Infantry, 6th Airlanding Brigade, 6th Airborne Division
Gillen, Patrick D.	Corporal	14430185	No. 6 Commando, 1st Special Service Brigade - Royal Norfolk Regiment - *Chevalier de la Legion d'Honneur*

Glass, Donald Cecil	Lieutenant	268120	No. 4 Commando, 1st Special Service Brigade - The Parachute Regiment, Territorial Army - *Member of the British Empire*
Godbold, Charles Henry (Claude)	Corporal	2033311	Horsa 92 - No. 24 Platoon, D Company, 2nd Battalion Oxfordshire and Buckinghamshire Light Infantry, 6th Airlanding Brigade, 6th Airborne Division
Gray, William (Billy)	Private	5392852	Horsa 91 - No. 25 Platoon, D Company, 2nd Battalion Oxfordshire and Buckinghamshire Light Infantry, 6th Airlanding Brigade, 6th Airborne Division
Greenhalgh, Fred	Lance Corporal	3449663	Horsa 93 - No. 14 Platoon, D Company, 2nd Battalion Oxfordshire and Buckinghamshire Light Infantry, 6th Airlanding Brigade, 6th Airborne Division - Killed in action or died of wounds (La Delivrande War Cemetery, Douvres)
Gregory, Albert	Lance Corporal	7380190	Horsa 93 - 195th Airlanding Field Ambulance - No.14 Platoon, B Company, 2nd Oxfordshire and Buckinghamshire Light Infantry
Guthrie, Leonard	Staff Sergeant	4749793	Horsa 95 (Co-pilot) - F Squadron, No. 1 Wing, Glider Pilot Regiment - *Croix de Guerre*
Harper-Gow, Leonard Maxwell (LMHG)	Captain	130210	Brigade HQ, 1st Special Service Brigade - The Parachute Regiment, Territorial Army - *Member of the British Empire*
Hedges, William Patrick	Private	5381332	Horsa 94 - No. 22 Platoon, D Company, 2nd Battalion Oxfordshire and Buckinghamshire Light Infantry, 6th Airlanding Brigade, 6th Airborne Division - Killed in action or died of wounds (Periers-en-Auge Churchyard)
Hellyer, Kenneth George	Private	6296547	No. 4 Commando, 1st Special Service Brigade - Royal East Kent Regiment - Died on war service (Carshalton All Saints Churchyard, Surrey)
Higbee, Jasper	Private		B Company, 45 Commando, 1st Special Service Brigade - Royal Marines
Hilton-Jones, Bryan	Captain	134763	Troop 3, No. 10 Commando, 1st Special Service Brigade - East Yeomanry - *Military Cross*
Hobart, Percy Cleghorn Stanley (Hobo)	Major General	23838	79th Armoured Division - *Mentioned in Despatches, Military Cross, Distinguished Service Order, Officer of the Order of the British Empire, Knights/Dames Commanders of the Order of the British Empire*
Hobbs, Phillip Allan	Staff Sergeant	6897785	Horsa 92 (co-pilot) - E Squadron, Glider Pilot Regiment - *Distinguished Flying Medal*
Hoodless, Donald Samuel	Lance Corporal	6478881	No. 4 Commando, 1st Special Service Brigade - Royal Fusiliers (City of London Regiment) - Died on war service (Brookwood Memorial)

Hooper, Charles Anthony (Tony)	Lieutenant	271237	Horsa 94 - No. 22 Platoon, D Company, 2nd Battalion Oxfordshire and Buckinghamshire Light Infantry, 6th Airlanding Brigade, 6th Airborne Division - *Military Cross*
Howard, John	Major	155710	Horsa 91 - Headquarters, D Company, 2nd Battalion Oxfordshire and Buckinghamshire Light Infantry, 6th Airlanding Brigade, 6th Airborne Division - *Distinguished Service Order, Croix de Guerre with Bronze Palm*
Howard, Roy Allen	Staff Sergeant	14200103	Horsa 96 (pilot) - No.15 Platoon, F Squadron, No.2 Wing, Glider Pilot Regiment - *Distinguished Flying Medal*
Howard, William (Smokey)	Corporal		Horsa 95 - No.23 Platoon, D Company, 2nd Oxfordshire and Buckinghamshire Light Infantry, 6th Airlanding Brigade, 6th Airborne Division
Ives, Frank Albert	Private	6014683	No. 4 Commando, 1st Special Service Brigade - The Queen's Royal Regiment (West Surrey) - Killed in action or died of wounds (Falmouth Cemetery, Cornwall)
Jennings	Corporal		Horsa 95 - No.23 Platoon, D Company, 2nd Oxfordshire and Buckinghamshire Light Infantry
Johns, Robert Edward	Private	14434704	13th (Lancashire) Parachute Battalion, Parachute Regiment, AAC
Johnson, Anthony Percival	Lieutenant Colonel	52653	Battalion HQ, 12th Parachute Battalion - *Distinguished Service Order*
Kelly, Jim	Corporal		41 Commando, 1st Special Service Brigade - Royal Marine, Royal Navy - *Legion d'Honneur*
Killeen, T	Corporal	4546144	B Company, 7th (Light Infantry) Parachute Battalion, 5th Parachute Brigade, 6th Airborne Division
Kindersley, Hugh Kenyon Molesworth	Brigadier	61108	Headquarters, 6th Airlanding Brigade - *Commander of the Most Excellent Order of the British Empire, Military Cross*
King, C. K.	Major	32009	A Company, 2nd Battalion East Yorkshire Regiment, 8th Infantry Brigade, 3rd Infantry Division - *Distinguished Service Order*
King, Peter Frederick	Sergeant-Major	328163 & 7536394	No. 4 Commando, 1st Special Service Brigade - Duke of Cornwall Light Infantry - *Distinguished Service Order*
Kirby, George Henry	Able Seaman, Coxswain		HMS Princess Astrid, 500th Flotilla, Royal Navy
Larkin, Claude H.	Sapper	2158201	Horsa 96 - 249th Field Company (Airborne)
Larkin, Cyril W.	Sapper	2003100	Horsa 96 - 249th Field Company (Airborne)

Lawrence, Arthur Cyril	Staff Sergeant	7584739	Horsa 4 (pilot) - No.15 Platoon, F Squadron, No.2 Wing, Glider Pilot Regiment - Killed in action or died of wounds (Arnhem Oosterbeek War Cemetery) - *Distinguished Flying Medal*
Laycock, Robert Edward	Brigadier	37258	B Squadron (Reconnaissance), 6th Airborne Division - *Order of St Michael and St George, Order of the Bath, Distinguished Service Order, Order of Saint John*
Leather	Sergeant		Horsa 92 - No. 24 Platoon, D Company, 2nd Battalion Oxfordshire and Buckinghamshire Light Infantry, 6th Airlanding Brigade, 6th Airborne Division
Leigh-Mallory, Sir Trafford	Air Chief Marshal		Commander I Chief, Allied Expeditionary Air Force - *Mentioned in Despatches, Order of the Bath, Distinguished Service Order, Companion of The Most Honourable Order of the Bath*
Lilley, L.J. (Les)	Corporal	6291391	No. 4 Commando, 1st Special Service Brigade - Royal East Kent Regiment (The Buffs)
Madge, D. W.	Lance Corporal	5510847	Horsa 93 - No. 14 Platoon, D Company, 2nd Battalion Oxfordshire and Buckinghamshire Light Infantry, 6th Airlanding Brigade, 6th Airborne Division - *Distinguished Service Order, Croix de Guerre with Bronze Palm*
Mason, Thomas John	Private		No. 4 Commando, 1st Special Service Brigade
Masters (Arany), Peter	Corporal		Troop 3, No. 10 Commando, 1st Special Service Brigade
Maxwell, Roy (Maxie)	Private		No. 4 Commando, 1st Special Service Brigade
McDougall, Murdoch C. (Mac)	Lieutenant		No. 4 Commando, 1st Special Service Brigade
Mears, Fred	Corporal	2828214	No. 3 Commando, 1st Special Service Brigade - Seaforth Highlanders
Mercer-Wilson, Peter Maziere	Lieutenant	118467	No. 10 Inter-Allied Commandos, Belgian Unit 1A - Killed in action or died of wounds
Mills-Roberts, Derek	Lieutenant Colonel	69334	No. 6 Commando, 1st Special Service Brigade - Irish Guards - *Commander of the Order of the British Empire, Distinguished Service Order, Bar to the Distinguished Service Order, Military Cross, Mentioned in Despatches*
Montgomery, Bernard Law	Field Marshal	8742	21st Army Group - *Order of the Garter, Order of the Bath, Distinguished Service Order*
Mullen, Brian Joseph	Lance Corporal	2075499	No. 4 Commando, 1st Special Service Brigade - Royal Engineers - Killed in action or died of wounds (Hermanville War Cemetery)
Neilson, J. M.	Captain	71518	Horsa 92 - 6th Airborne - 249th (Airborne) Field Company

Nelson-Smith, Harold David	Lieutenant-Colonel		1st Battalion Hampshire Regiment, 50th (Northumbrian) Infantry Division - *Military Cross, Croix de Guerre, France and Germany Star*
Newall, Aubrey John (Nobby)	Marine		No. 45 Royal Marine Commando, 1st Special Service Brigade - Royal Marines
Nield-Siddall, Warwick	Corporal		41 Commando, 1st Special Service Brigade - Royal Marine, Royal Navy
Orchin, Stanley Frederick	Lance Corporal	6145620	No. 4 Commando, 1st Special Service Brigade - East Surrey Regiment - Died on war service (Troon Cemetery, Ayrshire)
Otway, Terence Brandram Hastings	Lieutenant-Colonel	63633	Battalion Headquarters, 9th (Home Counties) Parachute Battalion, 3rd Parachute Brigade, 6th Airborne Division - *Distinguished Service Order, Legion d'Honneur*
Owens, George Edward (Ted)	Private	PLY/X 111420	41 Commando, 1st Special Service Brigade - Royal Marine, Royal Navy
Parr, Walter Robert (Wally)	Corporal	5184807	Horsa 91 - No. 25 Platoon, D Company, 2nd Battalion Oxfordshire and Buckinghamshire Light Infantry, 6th Airlanding Brigade, 6th Airborne Division
Pasquale, Domenic (Jim)	Private	7262386	No. 4 Commando - Royal Army Medical Corps - Prisoner of War (Stalag VIII-B, Lamsdorf)
Pasquale, Joseph (Joe), Jr.	Lance Corporal	7359503	No. 4 Commando, 1st Special Service Brigade - Royal Army Medical Corps - Killed in action or died of wounds (Hermanville War Cemetery)
Patterson, J. H. (Joe)	Captain		No. 4 Commando, 1st Special Service Brigade - Royal Army Medical Corps - H.M.S. Amarapoora, Royal Navy Reserve
Pearson, S.	Staff Sergeant	7897536	Horsa 94 (Pilot) - F Squadron, Glider Pilot Regiment - *Distinguished Flying Medal*
Pickersgill, Harold	Private		3rd Reconnaissance Regiment
Pine-Coffin, Geoffrey	Lieutenant-Colonel	40705	Battalion Headquarters, 7th (Light Infantry) Parachute Battalion, 5th Parachute Brigade, 6th Airborne Division - *Distinguished Service Order and Bar, Military Cross*
Poett, Joseph Howard Nigel Poett	Brigadier	38346	Brigade Headquarters and Defence Platoon, 7th (Light Infantry) Parachute Battalion, 5th Parachute Brigade, 6th Airborne Division - *Distinguished Service Order and Bar*
Porteous, Patrick Anthony	Major	73033	D Troop, No. 4 Commando, 1st Special Service Brigade - Royal Artillery - *Victoria Cross*
Priday, Brian C. E.	Captain	180636	Horsa 94 - Headquarters, D Company, 2nd Battalion Oxfordshire and Buckinghamshire Light Infantry, 6th Airlanding Brigade, 6th Airborne Division
Rayner, Raymond H. (Tich)	Lance Sergeant	5382222	Horsa 94 - No. 22 Platoon, D Company, 2nd Battalion Oxfordshire and Buckinghamshire Light Infantry, 6th Airlanding Brigade, 6th Airborne Division

Ries, Norman Charles	Lieutenant Colonel		No. 45 Royal Marine Commando, 1st Special Service Brigade - Royal Marines - *Commander of the Order of the British Empire, Officer of the Order of the British Empire, Mentioned in Despatches*
Rubinstein, Anthony	Second Lieutenant		48 Royal Marine Commando
Saunders (Salschin), George Victor	Sergeant		Troop 3, No. 10 Commando, 1st Special Service Brigade
Saunders, Hilary Aidan St. George	Lieutenant		Welsh Guards. Guards Division
Shorter, H. M. J. S.	Staff Sergeant	1876535	Horsa 94 (co-pilot) - B Squadron, Glider Pilot Regiment
Smith, Anthony D.C. (Tony)	Captain	130201	No. 4 Commando, 1st Special Service Brigade - Intelligence Corps
Smith, Richard Arthur Amyas (Sandy)	Lieutenant	228638	Horsa 93 - No.14 Platoon, "B" Company, 2nd Oxfordshire and Buckinghamshire Light Infantry - *Military Cross*
Spearman, William James	Corporal	2616669	No. 4 Commando, 1st Special Service Brigade - Grenadier Guards
Stagg, James M.	Captain		Meteorological Branch
Sturdy, Kenneth Gordon	Petty Officer (Signals)		41 Commando, 1st Special Service Brigade - Royal Marine, Royal Navy
Sturdy, Norman Kelvin	Private	2207337	Royal Air Force
Sweeney, Henry John (Todd)	Lieutenant	204283	Horsa 95 - No.23 Platoon, D Company, 2nd Oxfordshire and Buckinghamshire Light Infantry - *Military Cross*
Tanner, Walter William (Bob)	Private		No. 6 Platoon, B Company, 7th (Light Infantry) Parachute Battalion, 5th Parachute Brigade, 6th Airborne Division
Tappenden, Edward Mark (Ted)	Lance Corporal		Horsa 91 - Headquarters, D Company, 2nd Battalion Oxfordshire and Buckinghamshire Light Infantry, 6th Airlanding Brigade, 6th Airborne Division
Thornton, Charles (Wagger)	Sergeant	14209889	Horsa 96 - No.17 Platoon, B Company, 2nd Oxfordshire and Buckinghamshire Light Infantry - *Military Medal*
Tillett, John Maurice Arthur	Second Lieutenant	145422	Headquarters, D Company, 2nd Battalion Oxfordshire and Buckinghamshire Light Infantry, 6th Airlanding Brigade, 6th Airborne Division
Todd, Richard Andrew Palethorpe	Lieutenant		Battalion Headquarters, 7th (Light Infantry) Parachute Battalion, 5th Parachute Brigade, 6th Airborne Division - *Order of the British Empire*
Tough, George	Private	14330981	7th (Light Infantry) Parachute Battalion, 5th Parachute Brigade, 6th Airborne Division

Treacher, Edward Charles (Eddie/Tommy)	Private	POX 111881	B Company, 45 Commando, 1st Special Service Brigade - Royal Marines
Vaughan, Charles Edward	Lieutenant Colonel	142142	Commando Depot Training Centre, Achnacarry - East Kent - *Member of the Order of the British Empire, Officer of the Order of the British Empire*
Vaughan, John Jacob	Captain		Horsa 93 - Royal Army Medical Corps
Verrier, Sidney R.	Private	5836503	A Company, 2nd Oxfordshire and Buckinghamshire Light Infantry
Waddington, C.	Private	6291393	No. 4 Commando, 1st Special Service Brigade - Royal East Kent Regiment (The Buffs)
Wallwork, James Harley	Staff Sergeant	903986	Horsa 91 (pilot) - B Squadron, No.2 Wing, Glider Pilot Regiment - *Distinguished Flying Medal*
Wellesley- Colley, Phillip Antony	Lieutenant	72223	No. 4 Commando, 1st Special Service Brigade - South Nottinghamshire Hussars, Royal Artillery - Killed in action or died of wounds (Bayeux War Cemetery, France)
White, George Vincent	Private	6216556	9th (Eastern and Home Counties) Parachute Battalion, 3rd Parachute Brigade, 6th Airborne Division - Ranville War Cemetery
Williams, Charles (Charlie)	Sergeant Major	6009739	No. 4 Commando, 1st Special Service Brigade - 1st Battalion, The Essex Regiment
Wilson, Geoffrey	Lieutenant		No. 3 Commando, 1st Special Service Brigade
Wilson, Joseph (Joe)	Corporal		Battalion Headquarters, 9th (Home Counties) Parachute Battalion, 3rd Parachute Brigade, 6th Airborne Division
Wood, David James	Lieutenant	228639	Horsa 92 - No.24 Platoon, D Company, 2nd Oxfordshire and Buckinghamshire Light Infantry - *Legion d' honneur, Member of the British Empire*
Wood, Les	Private		Horsa 95 - No.23 Platoon, D Company, 2nd Oxfordshire and Buckinghamshire Light Infantry
Woodgate, John Thornicraft	Captain	156618	3rd Parachute Brigade, 6th Airborne Division,
Woods, Eric	Private		Horsa 96 - No.17 Platoon, B Company, 2nd Oxfordshire and Buckinghamshire Light Infantry
Yates, Thomas David	Lieutenant		48 Royal Marine Commando, Royal Navy - Killed in action or died of wounds (Bayeux War Cemetery, France)
Young, Peter	Lieutenant Colonel	77254	No. 3 Commando, 1st Special Service Brigade - Bedfordshire and Hertfordshire Regiment - *Distinguished Service Order, Military Cross, Bar to the Military Cross, 2nd Bar to the Military Cross*

Horsa Glider Landings

OPERATION "TONGA - COUP DE MAIN - LZs X and Y"

LZ 'X'	**Glider No**	**Landing**
903986 S/Sgt. Wallwork J.H. (1st pilot) C Sqn	)	(
81376 S/Sgt Ainsworth J. (MM) (2nd pilot) C Sqn	) 91	(
1449953 S/Sgt Boland O.F. (1st pilot) E Sqn	)	(All three Successful
6897785 S/Sgt Hobbs P. (2nd pilot) E Sqn	) 92	(according to plan
2582563 S/Sgt Barkway G. (1st pilot) B Sqn	)	(
4983193 Sgt Boyle P. (2nd pilot) B Sqn	) 93	(
LZ 'Y'		
7584739 S/Sgt Lawrence A. (1st pilot) B Sqn	)	(
1876535 S/Sgt Shorter H. (2nd pilot) B Sqn	) 94	(at wrong point
7897536 S/Sgt Pearson S. (1st pilot) F Sqn	)	(
4749793 S/Sgt Guthrie L. (2nd pilot) F Sqn	) 95	(according to plan
14200103 S/Sgt Howard R. (1st pilot) B Sqn	)	(
2120521 S/Sgt Baacke F. (2nd pilot) B Sqn	) 96	(400 yards from Bridge

1 SS Bde, War Diary, June 6th, 1944

1 SS Bde. 4 Cdo with Adv Bde HQ landed at LA BRECHE at H+30. They were 500 strong and their objective was the coastal bty at OUISTREHAM. 4 Cdo had suffered 40 casualties while landing including the CO. C Tp of the Cdo engaged the defences and gained the main coast rd, followed by the rest of the Cdo. Fighting French Tps led the Cdo towards OUISTREHAM, coming under hy fire. They overran the casino area and the assault on the bty commenced. After severe fighting the posn was taken. Casualties on both sides were heavy.

Meanwhile Adv Bde HQ contacted the CO 2 Bn E. Yorks. R/T contact by Bde HQ was made with 6 Airborne Div and it was learnt that the brs which the Bde intended to use were intact.

Bde HQ and 6 Cdo landed at 0840 hrs under hy gun and mortar fire. 6 Cdo took the lead when the rd was gained and the adv to the hrs commenced. Progress was slow because of the marshy ground and enemy mortar fire. The forming up pt was reached in 1 hr, by which time 3 and 45 RM Cdos had landed and they caught up with 6 Cdo. They had suffered few casualties. The brs were reached at 1230 hrs and contact nmde with 6 Airborne Div.

6 Cdo crossed the bra and sent their cycle Tp fwd to capture LE PLEIN. Bde HQ halted E of the river br. 45 RM Cdo passed over the brs towards thier objectives at MERVILLE and FRANCEVILLE PLAGE. 3 Cdo who had been held up, crossed the brs at 1530 and were diverted to protect Div HQ. Thus the original plan was abandoned and the Bde Comd decided to hold the high ground from MERVILLE for the night. Bde HQ moved to ECARDE and 6 Cdo consolidated in LE PLEIN.

4 Cdo rejoined the Bde at 2000 hrs, and dug in st HAUGER they had suffered hy casualties in fighting during the day. At the end of the day, 3 Cdo were still detached.

Bibliography

In researching this book, thousands of newspaper articles, one-on-one interviews and online websites/posts were reviewed.   In addition, the following works were relied on and the presented facts were multi-sourced for verification where possible:

Astor, Gerald, *June 6, 1944: The Voices of D-Day*, A Dell Book, 2002.

Ambrose, Stephen. *Band of Brothers*, Simon and Schuster, 1985.

Ambrose, Stephen. *D-Day June 6, 1944: The Climatic Battle of World War II*, Simon & Schuster, 2014.

Ambrose, Stephen. *From D-Day to Victory*, Simon and Schuster, 1985.

Ambrose, Stephen. *Pegasus Bridge*, Simon and Schuster, 1985.

Arthur, Max, *The Silent Day: A Landmark Oral History of D-Day on the Home Front*, Hodder & Stoughton, 2014.

Barber Neil, *The Pegasus and Orne Bridges: Their Capture, Defence and Relief on D-Day,* Pen & Sword Military, 2009.

Bowman, Martin W., *Air War D-Day. Volume 5: Gold Juno Sword*, Pen & Sword, 2013.

Bull, Stephen, *Commando Tactics*, Pen & Sword Military, 2011.

Cantwell, John D., *The Second World War: A Guide to Documents in the Public Record Office*, Public Records Office, 1998

Craggs, Tracy, *An 'Unspectacular' War? Reconstructing the history of the 2nd Battalion East Yorkshire Regiment during the Second World War*, A thesis submitted for the degree of Doctor of Philosophy, Department of History, University of Sheffield, 2007.

Dear, Ian, *Ten Commando 1942–45*, Leo Cooper, 1987.

Dopson, Laurence, "Senior Nursing Officer and Veteran of D-Day", *Nursing Standard*, pp. 33, Volume 25, Issue 5, October 2010.

Dunning, James, *The Fighting Fourth: No. 4 Commando Unit at War, 1940-45,* The History Press, 2013.

Dunning, James, *It Had To Be Tough,* Pentland Press, 2000.

Dunning, James, *Commando Trail*, Lochaber Tourism, 1996.

Dunning, James, *When Shall Their Glory Fade? The Stories of the Thirty-Eight Battle Honours of the Army Commandos*, Frontline Books, 2011.

Durnford-Slater, John, *Commando: Memoirs of a Fighting Commando in World War Two*, William Kimber & Co., 1987.

Edwards, Denis, *Devil's Own Luck: Pegasus Bridge to the Baltic 1944-45*, Pen & Sword Military, 1999.

Eisenhower Center, "Center holds two-day D-Day event", *World War II Dispatch*, pp.6 Vol. III, No. 2, Department of Defense, USA, Summer 1994.

Fowler, Will, *The Commandos at Dieppe – Rehearsal for D-Day,* HarperCollins, 2002.

Fowler, Will, *Pegasus Bridge: Bénouville D-Day 1944*, Osprey Publishing, 2010.

Foxall, Raymond, *The Amateur Commandos*, Robert Hale, 1980.

Gilchrist, Donald, *Don't Cry For Me*, Robert Hale, 1982.

Grehan, John (Editor), *75th Anniversary Special: D-Day*, pp. 68, Key Publishing Ltd., 2019.

Hastings, Max. *Overlord*, Simon and Schuster, 1984.

Holland, James, *Sand & Steel: A New History of D-Day*, Oxford University Press, 2019

Horwath, David, *D. Day The Sixth of June, 1944*, McGraw-Hill Book Company, Inc. 1959.

Howard, John, *The Pegasus Diaries*, Pen & Sword Military, 2006.

John, Evan, *Lofoten Letter*, William Heinemann, 1941.

Kershaw, Alex, *The First Wave, The D-Day Warriors Who Led the Way to Victory in World War II*, Penguin Random House, 2019.

King-Clark, Rex, *Jack Churchill 'Unlimited Boldness'*, Fleur-de-Lys Publishing, 1997.

Leasor, James, *X Troop*, Corgi Books, 1982.

Lovat, Lord, *March Past*, Weidenfeld and Nicolson, 1978.

Macrea, Alison, "An Eagla An Dearmaid", *Celtic Guide*, pp. 21, Volume 3, Issue 11, November 2014.

Masters, Peter, *Striking Back: A Jewish Commando's War against the Nazis*, Presideo Press, 1997.

Mayo, Jonathan, *D-Day – Minute by Minute*, Marble Arch Press, 2014

McDougall, Murdoch, *Swiftly They Struck*, Grafton Books, 1989.

Messenger, Charles, *The Commandos 1940–1946*, William Kimber & Co., 1985.

Millin, John, *Correspondence with Author*, 2019.

Millin, Piper Bill, *Invasion*, The Book Guild Limited, 1991.

Miller, Russell, *Nothing Less Than Victory*, Michael Joseph, 1993.

Mills-Roberts, Derek, *Clash By Night*, William Kimber & Co., 1956.

Miskimon, Christopher, "Glider Assault on Pegasus Bridge", *World War II Airborne Battles*, pp. 78, Sovereign Media Company, Inc., 2014

Owens, Ted, Ted, *The 'Welsh Goat' Hero: Memories of a Proud Welshman and WWII Veteran*, 2019.

Parker, John, *Commandos – The Inside Story of Britain's Most Elite Fighting Force*, Headline Book Publishing, 2000.

Poett, Sir Nigel, *Pure Poett: The memoirs of General Sir Nigel Poett*, Leo Cooper, 1991.

Ramsey, G. G., *D-Day Then and Now: Vol 2*, After the Battle, 1995.

Reed, Paul, *Walking D-Day*, Pen & Sword Military, 2012.

Ryan, Cornelius. *The Longest Day*, Simon and Schuster, 1959.

Sadler, John, *D-Day: The British Beach Landings*, Amberly Publishing, 2019.

Saunders, Hilary St. George, *The Green Beret*, Michael Joseph, 1949.

Saunders, Major Tim, *Commandos and Rangers: D-Day Operations*, Pen & Sword Military, 2012.

Shores, Christopher, *Aces High, Volume 2*, Grub Street, 1999.

Slaughter, John, *Omaha Beach and Beyond: The Long March of Sergeant Bob Slaughter*, Zenith Press, 2009.

Small, Ken, *The Forgotten Dead: Why 946 American Servicemen Died Off The Coast Of Devon In 1944 – And The Man Who Discovered Their True Story*, Bloomsbury Pub Ltd., 1999

Snelling, Stephen, *Commando Medic: Doc Harden VC*, The History Press, 2012.

Verrier, S. R., *Private Papers*, Imperial War Museums, 1944.

Von Luck, Hans, *Panzer Commander: The Memoirs of Colonel Hans Von Luck*, A Dell Book, 1989

Winter, Paul, *D-Day Documents*, Bloomsbury Academic, 2014.

Young, Peter, *Storm From The Sea*, Greenhill Books, 1989.

and

British Army, *2nd Oxfordshire and Buckinghamshire Commando War Diaries*, The Public Records Office, Kew, Richmond, Surry, 1944.

British Army, *3, 4, 6 Commando & 45 RM Commando War Diaries*, The Public Records Office, Kew, Richmond, Surry, 1944.

British Army, *6th Airborne Division War Diaries: WO171/425, WO171/595, WO171/591 and WO171/4320*, The Public Records Office, Kew, Richmond, Surry, 1944.

British Museum, The, *The whole Execution and Behaviour of Simon, Lord Lovat*, Registration number 1997,0223.1, 1747

Nomandie Tourisime, *D-Day Liberty: Land of Normandy*, pp. 36, 2019.

Key Websites:

https://backtonormandy.org/

http://britishfriendsofnormandy.org.uk/

http://gallery.commandoveterans.org/

http://spiritofnormandy.org.uk/

https://ww2talk.com/

http://www.1939-45.co.uk/

http://www.6juin1944.com/

https://www.bbc.co.uk/

http://www.britisharmedforces.org/

https://www.combinedops.com

http://www.commandoveterans.org/

https://www.cwgc.org/

https://www.dday-overlord.com/

https://erenow.net/

http://www.fallenheroesofnormandy.org/

https://www.findagrave.com/

https://www.forces-war-records.co.uk/

https://www.historic-newspapers.co.uk/

https://www.iwm.org.uk/

https://www.nationalarchives.gov.uk/

https://www.naval-history.net/

http://www.normandy1944.info/

https://www.paradata.org.uk/

http://www.pegasusarchive.org/

https://www.thegazette.co.uk/

https://www.tracesofwar.com/

https://www.wartimememoriesproject.com/

Oral Recollections:

Doug Allen

Geoffrey Sydney Barkway

Helen Bora

John Hildred Carlill

Henry William Clark

Matthew Culvert

Rupert Curtis

John Edward Day

Simon Christopher Joseph Fraser (Lord Lovat)

Peter Lincoln Fussell

Léon Gautier

Roy A. Howard

Bill Millin

John Millin

Warwick Nield-Siddall

Harold David Nelson-Smith

Aubrey John Newall

Walter Robert Parr

George Victor Saunders (Salschin)

Fred Smith

Richard Arthur Amyas Smith

James William Spearman

Walter William Tanner

Edward Mark Tappenden

Richard Andrew Palethorpe Todd

Edward Charles Treacher

Hans von Luck

Ernest Ronald Walker

John Thornicraft Woodgate

Index

Made in United States
North Haven, CT
13 June 2024

53538560R00168